Hawaiian Grammar

Hawaiian Grammar

Samuel H. Elbert
and
Mary Kawena Pukui

University of Hawaii Press
HONOLULU

8th printing, 2022

Library of Congress Cataloging-in-Publication Data

Elbert, Samuel H., 1907–1997
  Hawaiian grammar.

  Bibliography: p.
  Includes index.
  1. Hawaiian language—Grammar. 1. Pukui,
Mary Wiggin, 1895–1986 joint author. II. Title.
PL6443.E37   499'.4   78-21692
ISBN 0-8248-0494-5
ISBN-13: 978-0-8248-2489-1 (pbk)
ISBN-10: 0-8248-2489-X (pbk)

University of Hawai'i Press books are printed on acid-
free paper and meet the guidelines for permanence and
durability of the Council on Library Resources.

Ka hohonu i hiki ʻole ke ana ʻia, akā,
ua ʻike ʻia nō kahi mau papa.

The depths have not all been fathomed,
but a few reefs have been seen.

Contents

Tables   xi

Preface   xiii

Abbreviations and Explanations   xvii

1 Previous Studies of Hawaiian Grammar   1
   1.1 Chamisso   1
   1.2 Humboldt and Buschmann   3
   1.3 Hale   4
   1.4 Andrews and Alexander   4
   1.5 Primitives and Evolution   6
   1.6 The Last Hundred Years   8

2 The Sound System   10
   2.1 Consonants (p, k, ‘, h, l, m, n, w)   10
   2.2 Vowels (i, ī, e, ē, a, ā, u, ū, o, ō)   14
   2.3 Word Stress   16
   2.4 Junctures   18
   2.5 Stress in Phrases and Sentences   18
   2.6 Pitch Levels   21
   2.7 Natural Fast Speech   22
   2.8 Dialect Variations   23
      2.8.1 Ni‘ihau Dialect   23
      2.8.2 n for l and Glottal Stop for l and k   25
   2.9 Loan Words   27
      2.9.1 English as a Source   27
      2.9.2 The Word for Horse   30
      2.9.3 Biblical Terms   31
      2.9.4 Other Sources   33
   2.10 Relative Frequencies of Sounds   34
   2.11 Drift   35
   2.12 Notes on Orthography   36

3 From Sentence to Affix   39
   3.1 Sentences   39
   3.2 Phrases   41
   3.3 Words   43
   3.4 Particles   44
   3.5 Affixes   44

4 Classification of Verbs; Verblike Idioms   46
   4.1 Basis of the Classification   46
   4.2 Intransitive Verbs (vi)   48
   4.3 Transitive Verbs (vt)   48
   4.4 Stative Verbs (vs)   49
   4.5 Multiple-class Verbs   51
   4.6 Verblike Idioms   54

5 Verb Markers   57
   5.1 Classification of Verb Markers   57
   5.2 Aspect Markers   57
   5.3 Tense Marker   60
   5.4 Mood Markers   61

6 Verb Affixes and Thematic Consonants   64
   6.1 Prefixes and Reduplications   64
   6.2 Reduplications   64
      6.2.1 Types of Reduplication   65
      6.2.2 Meanings of Reduplications   66
   6.3 Prefixes to Verbs: Middle Layer   68
      6.3.1 Prefixes with Causative/Simulative
          Meanings   68
      6.3.2 Prefixes with Qualitative/Stative Meanings   71
      6.3.3 Other Prefixes   74
   6.4 The Causative/Simulative ho'o- and Its Alternants   76
   6.5 Rare Suffixes   78
   6.6 Thematic Consonants and the Suffixes and Particles
      They Introduce   79
      6.6.1 Inventory   79
      6.6.2 Nominalizers   79
      6.6.3 Passive/Imperatives   83
      6.6.4 Transitivizers   86
      6.6.5 Possible Analyses   88

7 Postposed Phrasal Elements   90
   7.1 Some Postposed Particles   90
   7.2 Directionals   91

7.3 *ai*   96

7.4 *ø*-Demonstratives *ala, lā/-la, ana*   99

7.5 Particles Following the *ø*-Demonstratives   100

8 Nouns and Substitutes, Locative Nouns, Compounds, Qualifiers   105

8.1 Nouns   105

8.2 Pronouns   107

8.3 Demonstratives   110

    8.3.1 *kē*-Demonstratives   110

    8.3.2 *ø*-Demonstratives *nei* and *nā*   111

    8.3.3 *ia*   112

    8.3.4 *ua*   113

    8.3.5 *neia*   114

    8.3.6 *pē*-Demonstratives   114

8.4 Possessives   115

    8.4.1 *k*-Possessives   116

    8.4.2 *ø*- and *n*-Possessives   118

8.5 Interrogatives   119

8.6 Locative Nouns   120

8.7 Compounds and Qualifiers   123

    8.7.1 Noun Compounds   123

    8.7.2 Verb and Noun-Verb Compounds   124

    8.7.3 Compound Proper Names   126

    8.7.4 Other Compounds   126

    8.7.5 Noun + Qualifier Sequences   127

9 Prepositions   131

9.1 Inventory of Prepositions   131

9.2 Subject Marker: *'o/ø*   131

9.3 Multifunctional *i/iā* and *iō*   133

    9.3.1 *i/iā*   133

    9.3.2 *i/iā/iō*: Definite Locative   134

9.4 Locative/Instrumental/Manner: *ma*   135

9.5 *ā*: Place to (Emphatic)   136

9.6 Possessives   136

    9.6.1 *a*- and *o*-Possessives   136

    9.6.2 Verbs with *a* and *o*   140

    9.6.3 *ø*-Possessives   142

    9.6.4 Fronted Possessives   143

9.7 Comitative/Instrumental/Similitude: *me*   145

9.8 Ablative: *mai*   145

9.9 Agentive: *e*   146

CONTENTS

9.10 Vocative: $\bar{e}/\phi$ 146
9.11 *na* and *no*   147
9.12 Simulative: *p$\bar{e}$*   150
9.13 Appositional Prepositions   150
9.14 Prepositional Phrases in Verbless Sentences   152

10 Determiners, Numerals, and Plurals   153
10.1 *k*-Words   153
10.2 Articles   154
10.3 Numerals   158
10.4 Other Plural Markers   162

11 Conjunctions and Complex Sentences   164
11.1 Conjunctions   164
11.2 Combining Phrases: Order   168
11.3 Combining Sentences   169
11.4 A Complex Sentence Analyzed   171
11.5 The Role of Fronting: A Summary   172

12 Interjections   174

Glossary   179

References   185

Index   191

Tables

 1 The Vexing Hawaiian *w*   13
 2 Sound Changes in Fast Speech   23
 3 Hawaiian Substitutions for English Consonants   28
 4 Hawaiian Substitutions for English Vowels   29
 5 Spellings of Hawaiian Words for Animals   31
 6 Hawaiian Drift   36
 7 Hawaiian Phrases   41
 8 Classification of Verbs   47
 9 Classification of Verb Markers   58
10 Hawaiian Prefixes   65
11 Thematic Consonants, Suffixes, and Particles   80
12 Spatio-Temporal Proximity Chart   93
13 Hawaiian Pronouns   107
14 *k*-Possessives   117
15 Locative Nouns without and with Articles   122

Preface

The "Notes on Hawaiian Grammar" included in the first three editions of the *Hawaiian-English Dictionary* have in this volume been revised and expanded. The original notes were written during the early 1950s, and since that time the number of students of Polynesian languages has increased considerably, with resulting increase in knowledge of these languages.

This new Grammar, therefore, presents an approach rather different from the previous one; however, it is not couched in the most recent linguistic terminology, partly because the authors belong to a different generation, and partly because it is hoped that this volume will be of value to all students and teachers of the Hawaiian language, whether or not they are trained in contemporary linguistics. The approach is data-oriented and structural, and most attention is devoted to the sound system and to the structure of words and phrases, with less concentration on complex sentences. Nevertheless, an attempt is made to cover the major features of the language; the result is probably the most comprehensive treatment ever made of Hawaiian grammar.

The analysis is based on the Hawaiian language as found in texts, in ordinary conversation, and in Kawena Pukui's memories. Only in discussion of certain particles and affixes has the structure of other Polynesian languages been considered, as in the hypothesis advanced in section 6.6.4 for the island name, Kaua'i.

The principal texts used in this study were Elbert's *Selections from Fornander's Hawaiian Antiquities and Folk-lore*; Moses Nakuina's polished retelling in the early 1900s of the legend of Pāka'a and his son, Kū-a-Pāka'a; and a collection of essays by Kahekina Kelekona (John G. M. Sheldon) lamenting the passing of old Hawaiʻi, together with a tearful recounting of the story of Koʻolau the leper. Kelekona's writing is Victorian, almost Dickensian, with a vocabulary of astonishing richness and complexity.

Texts, and particularly chants, are often hard to read. Many of them contain words no longer used and dialectal expressions and poetic sayings completely unintelligible without explanation. Further, glottal stops and macrons indicative of long vowels are not shown, word division is often erratic, and misprints frequent. In quotations from these sources errors have been corrected, glottal stops and macrons added, and capitalization and word division have been altered to accord with the recommendations in this Grammar.

The English translations of illustrative sentences may in some instances seem awkward, but close translations are helpful to students. Not every possible translation of an illustrative sentence is given. For example, *ia*, meaning both 'he' and 'she', is usually translated 'he' to avoid the awkward 'he/she' and 'him/her'. Since Hawaiian is mainly tenseless and English is decidedly not, translations perforce included tense, but the alternative tenses are not given for every Hawaiian perfective aspect.

Reading of the Grammar will be aided if the Hawaiian Dictionary is at hand, but intelligibility does not depend on access to that volume. However, the Grammar is by no means a substitute for the Dictionary. Meanings in the examples in the Grammar are in some instances *ad hoc* glosses; usually many more meanings and examples are given in the Dictionary.

Early Hawaiian grammars by Adelbert von Chamisso and W. D. Alexander, student papers, and the writings of Bruce Biggs, Patrick Hohepa, and Andrew Pawley concerning other Polynesian languages have been helpful in the years of preparation of this volume. Emily A. Hawkins' doctoral dissertation and William H. Wilson's masters' thesis, both at the University of Hawaiʻi, have aided materially in the present analysis; their work provided numerous examples of grammatical points, for example, Wilson's classification of verbs and his repeated caveats about *w*-glides. Term papers by Hawkins' students, especially Haunani Apoliona, John Dupont, Kehau Lee, and Makanani Lee, provided information incorporated into the Grammar. Alfons Korn read an early version and commented helpfully on the quality of the English. Albert J. Schütz read much of the manuscript and gave all-important advice, especially concerning the treatment of stress, loan words, and possessives. The versatile Edgar C. Knowlton, Jr., listed loan words in Chinese, Spanish, Portuguese, French, Greek, Latin, and Hebrew. The Reverend Kenneth L. Smith with great care prepared the lists for the section on loan words in the Hawaiian Bible. Robert L. Cheng provided information on loans from Chinese. Andrew Pawley patiently endured questioning on numerous matters, especially the difficult-to-recognize derivations containing the thematic consonants (section 6.6). Robert Hsu prepared a computerized count of sound frequencies. Niklaus R. Schweizer added information about Chamisso, the first Hawaiian grammarian. Four persons read the entire manuscript: Elizabeth K. Bushnell, John Charlot, Dorothy M. Kahananui, and William H. Wilson. They deserve medals for endurance. In addition, the authors thank Holcombe M. Austin for sharp-eyed proofreading, and the generous contributors, who remain anonymous, who insured publication of the book.

Most of all, Samuel Elbert wishes to thank his mother, Mrs. Ethelind Swire Beer, for her years of patience while he was far away and absorbed in Pacific studies, and for her encouragement for so many decades.

The Hawaiian language is anything but easy. The more one works on it, the more complicated it seems to get—new quirks, idioms, constructions, and vocabulary items turn up, as well as apparent exceptions to laboriously drafted rules. The authors know that this Grammar is but a beginning. They are confident that future students will continue exploration.

May a short personal note be injected here? The Grammar is a result of two longish spans of years dedicated to Oceanic languages. Kawena Pukui, at her birth in 1895, was given by her *haole* father to his own Hawaiian mother-in-law. Kawena's mother, Pa'ahana, mildly protested.

"But *haoles* don't give their children to others!"

"Your mother has only a few more years. Let her have this child!" was the rejoinder.

The grandmother knew no English and was wise in her ancestors' lore; though a devout Christian, she made silent little prayers to her ancestors' gods. Kawena had the opportunity to master Hawaiian and to learn something of the old culture, and

she has been ever thankful for her father's generosity and toler-
ance. Elbert was born in Iowa in 1907, but has been in the
Pacific area since 1934. His share of the book has been accumu-
lating forty years—Kawena's, eighty!

SAMUEL H. ELBERT

ABBREVIATIONS AND EXPLANATIONS
(for complete citations, see References)

app.	appositional case
C	consonant
caus.	causative
Dictionary	Pukui and Elbert 1971
FS	Elbert 1971
int.	intentive
Kep.	Beckwith 1932
lit.	literally
φ	zero, nothing, absence of a form
obj.	object
pas/imp.	passive/imperative
PCP	Proto Central Polynesian
PEP	Proto Eastern Polynesian
perf.	perfective
PPN	Proto Polynesian
pl.	plural
sg.	singular
sim.	simulative
subj.	subject
V	vowel, verb
vi	intransitive verb
vsadj	adjectival stative verb
vsl	*loa'a*-stative verb
vtd	deliberate transitive verb
vtsp	spontaneous transitive verb
*	reconstructed or ungrammatical form

Forms separated by slashes are alternants *(ē/φ, i/iā)*.

In translations, words supplied by the present authors are within brackets, except that forms of 'to be', nonexistent in Hawaiian, are not bracketed.

1   Previous Studies of Hawaiian Grammar

CHAMISSO

1.1   The first scholar to characterize the structure of the Hawaiian language was Adelbert von Chamisso (1781–1838), best known as a German poet and writer, less well known as a botanist and naturalist, and still less, as a grammarian. Chamisso spent twenty-nine days in Hawaiʻi in 1816 and 1817, four years before the arrival of the missionaries and a decade before the establishment of an orthography. He was the botanist aboard the Russian ship *Rurick* during its voyage around the world under the command of Otto von Kotzebue. The common tree fern, *hāpuʻu ʻiʻi*, is named *Cibotium chamissoi* in his honor, and a native violet, *ʻolopū*, is *Viola chamissoniana*.

    Although Chamisso was influenced by Rousseau and greatly admired what was then called "natural man," he believed, like most people of the times, in a regular evolution of languages from a primitive state to what was believed to be more advanced forms, such as the languages of Europe. Chamisso wrote of Tongan in a supplement dated 1819 to Kotzebue's *Voyage of Discovery* (English translation, 1967, vol. 2, p. 389): "We recognize in it [Tongan] the Malay system of language in the greatest simplicity, and, according to our opinion, in a state of undeveloped infancy. It is a pleasing, childish lisping, which can scarcely be called a language."

    But Hawaiian, he went on to say, does not even measure up to Tongan (Kotzebue 1967, vol. 2, pp. 390–391):

> The language of the Sandwich islands really appeared to us still more childish than the dialect of Tonga does in its grammar. We found in it only two pronouns, *Wau* for the first person, *Hoe* for the second, and only two adverbs to determine the time of the action, *Mamure* for the future, *Mamoa* for the past time. . . . The words formed, after the manner of children, by the repetition of one sound,

1

in which the root has sometimes one meaning, sometimes another, and sometimes none at all, which are much more frequent in the common language of the eastern islands than in the western more cultivated dialects, in which, however, they are not wanting, give it a peculiar and pleasing character.

Even the beginning student knows that Hawaiian has twelve pronouns (listed in section 8.2). Chamisso's *mamure* and *mamoa* are today's *mamuli* 'afterwards' and *mamua* 'before' (section 8.6).

After returning to Europe in 1819, Chamisso was employed as curator of the botanical gardens of Berlin; at this time he wrote his most famous poems—but none about Hawai'i or the Marshalls, his two greatest enthusiasms (for a vivid account of Chamisso in the South Seas, see Schweizer 1973, especially p. 43). In 1835 Wilhelm von Humboldt proposed his name for membership in the Berlin Academy of Science. During the next two years in spite of weakening health he busied himself with Hawaiian grammar, which was the subject of his acceptance speech into the Academy. This was published a year before his death in 1838. It was reprinted in 1969 with an introduction by Samuel H. Elbert. An English translation was made by Paul G. Chapin in 1973.

Near the beginning of his grammar, Chamisso lists his sources, which included a Tongan grammar of 1818, a Maori grammar and vocabulary of 1820, and an undated Tahitian grammar. There is no evidence that he corresponded with Hawaiian missionaries, but he did obtain translations into Hawaiian of portions of the Scriptures and other religious works, primers, geographies, and arithmetic manuals that had been brought to him in 1833 by a Dr. von Besser, who had journeyed to the Sandwich Islands (Schweizer 1973:26).

Chamisso may also have met a Hawaiian, Maitai, who had stowed away on the German ship *Mentor* in the hope of going to China; instead, he was taken to Germany and became a gardener on the Pfaueninsel, a small river island between Berlin and Potsdam. Humboldt (or Buschmann) met Maitai (Humboldt 1836–1839, vol. 3, pp. 438–439), and one would think that Chamisso too would have met him, since both lived in Berlin. Maitai married and had children and died in 1872.

Chamisso accepted the missionaries' orthography and expressed no doubts as to its accuracy as a true reflection of the language. It is perhaps not surprising that he did not recognize the glottal stop as a significant sound because it is present in neither German nor French, and was not at that time recognized as a speech sound. Chamisso also did not realize that vowel length under certain conditions is of unpredictable occurrence. These two lacks in his analysis made him see homonyms at every turn. He wrote in his 1837 study (p. 7) that many utterances in Hawaiian have no consonants at all and gives this example: *Ua oia au, e ue ae oe ia Ii, e ao ae oe ia ia. . . .* These are separate sentences and are decipherable today, but not always with Chamisso's translations. In this Grammar they would be written *Ua 'ō 'ia au* 'I am speared'. *E uē a'e 'oe iā 'Ī'ī* 'You must weep for *'Ī'ī* [a person]'. *E a'o a'e 'oe iāia* 'You teach him'.

In analysis of morphology and syntax Chamisso was on surer ground than he was in phonology, and for his time, remarkably enlightened. The only "sign of inflection," he said (1837:42), is in reduplications. (Today, reduplications are considered derivatives rather than inflections.) Chamisso realized that the Hawaiian language is distinguished by multifunctional words, and stated (1837:8) that no distinctions are made in the language in "head and modifier, substantive and verb, adjective and adverb, and the framework of our grammar can make no use of them; their value in this respect is always determined by their position in the sentence and by the accompanying particles, in which the life and flexibility of the language manifest themselves" (translation by Paul G. Chapin 1973:104).

This sounds very much like the statement of W. D. Alexander (1968:27) that "most words may be used either as nouns, adjectives, verbs or adverbs, their meaning being indicated by their position in the sentence, and by the accompanying particles."

Almost the same phraseology—had Alexander studied Chamisso? This question is discussed in section 1.4.

HUMBOLDT AND BUSCHMANN

1.2   Humboldt was probably the first scholar to establish unequivocally the existence of the Malayo-Polynesian language family (now usually called Austronesian). He based his findings on grammatical comparisons and tables listing 131 words in Malay, Javanese, Bugis, Malagasy, Tagalog, Tongan, Maori, Tahitian, and Hawaiian (vol. 2, pp. 241–256). Both Humboldt and his posthumous collaborator, J. E. Eduard Buschmann, avoided Latin models and emphasized 'particles' (vol. 3, pp. 602–634 and 654–662). Buschmann had seen Chamisso's gram-

mar of 1837 and he praised it as "clever" or "ingenious"
(geistreich).

Humboldt mentioned that he had met some Tahitians (vol. 2,
p. 302), and yet he did not recognize the glottal stop as a significant sound, an oversight all the more surprising in that Tahitian
has even more glottal stops than Hawaiian, replacing Proto-
Polynesian ng as well as k by this sound. (Humboldt wrote that
the first consonant of various words meaning 'to see', as in New
Zealand kitea, was "dropped" in Tahitian. Tahitian and
Hawaiian correspondences of kitea are 'ite and 'ike. Humboldt's
unfortunate term "dropped" is commonly used by laymen today
instead of an accurate statement that New Zealand k corresponds to a glottal stop in Tahitian and Hawaiian.) Humboldt
also stated (vol. 3, pp. 408–409) that in Berlin he met Harry
Maitai of "Owahu" in the Sandwich Islands and was saved by
him from many errors.

HALE

1.3   Horatio Hale's remarkable contributions, published in 1846,
were the result of his observations during three years in the
South Pacific with the United States Exploring Expedition. He
was apparently the first to recognize the importance of the glottal stop, which he described as "a hiatus or catching of the
breath" or a "guttural break." Not a slave to Latin grammars,
Hale declared (pp. 262–263): "The accidents of tense, mood,
voice, number, and person are in general denoted by particles
affixed to the verbs. The only inflection which it undergoes consists in the reduplication of the whole word. . . ."

This suggests Chamisso (previously quoted), yet Hale gave no
indication that he had ever seen Chamisso's study, and lists only
Andrews' 1836 vocabulary and 1838 article. Hale advocated
(pp. 129–136) a Marquesan origin of the Hawaiians, a theory
favored today by archaeologists. His sixty-page "Polynesian
Grammar" in the same volume considers seven Polynesian languages including Hawaiian and recognizes that "the dialects of
Polynesia have, properly speaking, no grammatical inflections."

ANDREWS AND ALEXANDER

1.4   Two nineteenth-century Hawaiian grammars were produced in
Hawai'i, one by the Reverend Lorrin Andrews and the other by
W. D. Alexander. Andrews (1795–1868) came to Hawai'i as a

missionary in 1828. His "Peculiarities of the Hawaiian Language" appeared in 1838 (the year after Chamisso's grammar) and contained twenty-eight pages. This brief account was expanded and padded out in his 156–page grammar of 1854. He acknowledged no sources.

Alexander (1833–1913), a missionary son and educator, published his concise and revolutionary fifty-nine-page grammar in 1864. He did not mention Chamisso, but acknowledged "obligations" to Andrews, from whom he took numerous examples. His sources seem revealed in his "Introductory Remarks" to Andrews' *A Dictionary of the Hawaiian Language* (1974, first published in 1865). In this rather lengthy essay he traced the development of Malayo-Polynesian studies. He identified (p. 9) Chamisso's grammar as "the earliest really scientific analysis of the structure of a Polynesian language" and "a work of rare ability, considering the meager materials which the author had at his command." Then follows a long description of Humboldt's studies, and finally some word comparisons from Hale.

As previously stated, in phonology Chamisso was at the mercy of the orthography. What of Andrews and Alexander, both of whom spoke Hawaiian fluently?

Andrews spoke of words differing only in "accent," a term he did not define. He listed words that are somehow pronounced differently (1854:14), as *a-i* 'food', and *a-i* 'neck' (actually *'ai* and *'ā'ī*). He attributed change of meaning to "change of accent" (p. 20), as *ma-là-ma* 'month' and *mà-la-ma* 'take heed' (actually *malama* and *mālama*). Andrews admitted that use of "accent" marks would be "very convenient" for those wishing to learn Hawaiian, but he explained that his writing was for people who already knew the language, implying that they could guess meaning from context, much as though in English one might write *pig* and *big* with the same spelling.

Alexander borrowed Hale's term "guttural" and wrote (p. 5), "this guttural is properly a consonant and forms an *essential* part of the words in which it is found" (italics his). Yet he recommended indicating it in only a few common words, as *ko'u* 'mine' to be distinguished from *kou* 'yours'.

Neither Andrews nor Alexander recognized the contrast between a word-initial glottal stop and its lack, as in *ala* 'path' and *'ala* 'fragrant'. (See section 2.1 for a discussion of initial glottal stops.) Nor did they mention important changes common in fast speech: *'a'o* to *'a'a* (as in *'a'ole* 'not' to *'a'ale*), *ai* to *ei* (as in *ikaika* 'strong' to *ikeika*), *au* to *ou* (as in *mau*, plural marker, to

5

mou), or *Hawai'i* to fast *Hawa'i* (loss of vowel before a glottal stop and like vowel). These changes were first described by Kinney in 1956 (see section 2.7). They may not have been in existence in the 1860s, or they may have been considered "corruptions" unworthy of comment.

Unlike Chamisso and Alexander, Andrews modeled his grammar on Latin and posited for Hawaiian ten cases, four moods, and twenty conjugations, filling nearly thirty pages with repetitive tables of "declensions" and "conjugations"; he wrote in summary "a Hawaiian verb has nearly 3,500 forms" (1854:124). Andrews' model verb was *lawe* 'to carry'. In the present analysis this base has *five* derivative forms instead of 3,499: *la-lawe, lawe-lawe, ho'o-la-lawe, ho'o-lawe-lawe,* and *lawe-na.*

Andrews' "conjugations" actually consist usually of particle + base + pronoun, as *ua huna au* 'I have concealed', *ua huna 'oe* 'thou hast concealed', *ua huna ia* 'he has concealed'.

Andrews attempted to introduce Hawaiian terms for his tenses and cases, and he even used these terms when writing in English. They seem not to have caught on and are not entered in Hitchcock's Dictionary of 1887, intended for use in the public schools. His term for case, *'aui* 'to digress, deviate, turn aside', parallels the English word, which is said to come from Latin *casus* 'falling, deviation', actually a quite fortunate choice.

Not all his inventions were so clever. He called the qualitative stative noun-verb *'ē* 'different, elsewhere, strange, beforehand' a pluperfect because it sometimes follows verbs and has the meaning 'beforehand' and in some few circumstances can be translated 'had'. The same *'ē*, however, follows nouns with different meanings, and follows imperatives, as in the saying:

I   kahi 'ē   ka   ua,   waele 'ē   ka   pulu.
in place elsewhere   the rain clear first   the   refuse
'When rain is elsewhere, first clear away the refuse. / Clear off the weeds and refuse before the rain comes so that it will soak in. / Make hay while the sun shines.'

PRIMITIVES AND EVOLUTION

1.5   The old grammarians and some not so old have entertained a patronizing attitude toward the subject and toward the people, although to both they devoted a large part of their lives. They believed that the Hawaiians were "primitives" or even "savages," that their "dialect" (hardly advanced enough to be called a language) was somehow in an early, child-like stage. Nearly all these writers made uncomplimentary innuendos about the Hawaiian people and their language and culture. In this respect Chamisso, perhaps because of Humboldt's influence, was relatively free of bias. He wrote nearly always of the Hawaiian *language (Sprache)*, whereas though Andrews and Alexander occasionally used that honorable term, they more often referred to the Hawaiian *dialect*, with the implication that Hawaiian could hardly be called a language.

It is not surprising that these scholars (mostly missionaries or their descendants), trained in Greek and Latin and convinced that heathens speak primitively, should have been dismayed at a language with so few sounds and without true inflections, almost without tenses, with no words "to have" or "to be," without comparative and superlative degrees and grammatical gender, without distinction of "he" and "she" and without an unequivocal "thou must."

A few of the unflattering remarks written by these gentlemen, products of their times, are quoted here:

Andrews (1838:396–397): "There is a great want of generic terms in the language. This is a peculiarity that distinguishes it from the English, but not from other uncultivated languages. No people have use for general terms until they begin to reason, and the language of the Hawaiians shows that they have never been a thinking people. They, however, have specific names to almost any extent." And sixteen years later he wrote (1854:96): "Interjections are numerous among the Hawaiians, as they are among all illiterate people."

Writing in 1865 Alexander wrote (Andrews 1968:13–14) of the Hawaiian language: "Its childlike and primitive character is shown by the absence of abstract and general terms . . . it still has the freshness of childhood. . . . "

Even Chamisso, enlightened as he was by 1837, remarked (p. 5) that as one proceeded eastward from the Asian mainland the languages became "simpler and at the same time more childlike in their structure and sounds."

Dr. Nathaniel B. Emerson, who devoted years of his life to collecting and translating Hawaiian legends, chants, and other traditions, wrote in a preface to his translation of David Malo's work that missionary endeavors in translating the Bible were at

the time of Malo's writing (about ten years before the publication of the translated Bible in 1839) as yet insufficient "to heal
the infirmities and make amends for the evolutionary weak-
nesses of the Hawaiian speech" (Malo 1971:xv).

In his *Unwritten Literature of Hawaii*, which, like his translation of Malo, is a Hawaiian classic, Emerson remarked (1909:8)
that the work "does nothing more than prove that savages are
only children of a younger growth than ourselves, that what we
find them to have been we ourselves—in our ancestors—once
were." And again (p. 13): "Those children of nature, as we are
wont to call them, in this regard [dancing] were less free and
spontaneous than the more advanced race to which we are
proud to belong."

THE LAST HUNDRED YEARS

1.6   After Alexander's 1864 grammar appeared, no advances in the
study of Hawaiian grammar were made for eighty-seven years,
when Helene Newbrand's phonemic analysis of Hawaiian was
issued as a master's thesis. Why such a dearth of interest in Hawaiian grammar? This is probably because no professional linguists were interested in the language. The missionaries' interest
had been pragmatic, and once the Scriptures were translated,
they were no longer concerned. The number of native Hawaiians was rapidly diminishing, and English was the official
language of instruction in the public schools. As early as 1878
the extinction of the Hawaiian language was feared. In
September of that year Lorenzo Lyons, a missionary who loved
the Hawaiians and who championed their language, wrote in
the *Friend* (September 1878):

> I've studied Hawaiian for 46 years but am by no means
> perfect. . . . It is an interminable language. . . . It is one of the oldest
> living languages of the earth, as some conjecture, and may well be
> classed among the best. . . . The thought to displace it, or to doom it
> to oblivion by substituting the English language, ought not for a mo-
> ment to be indulged. Long live the grand old, sonorous, poetical Ha-
> waiian language.

Now, in 1977, many persons are optimistic that the language
is *not* about to die. After all, it is the first language of some 300
people on or from Ni'ihau. Increased interest in the language is
attested by its introduction in the Kamehameha Schools (for
years, students there were punished for speaking Hawaiian) and

in several high schools and community colleges, and by increased enrollment in Hawaiian classes and in the Hawaiian Studies major at the Mānoa campus of the University of Hawai'i.

Increased interest has resulted in new analyses and texts, as the theses by Emily A. Hawkins and William H. Wilson previously mentioned, the brief reference grammars in the first three editions of Pukui and Elbert's Dictionary and in the *Pocket Hawaiian Dictionary* (Pukui, Elbert, and Mookini), and pedagogical grammars by Kahananui and Anthony and by Elbert. The Hawaiian Dictionary in 1977 was in the fourth printing of the third edition. The Committee for the Preservation of Hawaiian Language, Art, and Culture has for many years supplied teaching materials at many levels. It is now believed that the Hawaiian language may live at least as a second language for an unpredictable and perhaps long future. This optimism is strengthened by what a Hawaiian leader, George Kanahele, has called a "renaissance" or "rebirth of cultural interest" (*Honolulu Star-Bulletin*, March 24, 1977). Kanahele likens this "renaissance" to similar movements among Blacks, Indians, and Chicanos on the mainland. Some Hawaiians seem to attribute almost magic value to words such as *aloha* 'compassion, love', *'āina* 'land', *'ohana* 'family', and *ho'oponopono* 'settling to rights by family discussion and prayer'. They have come to regard the language as a sacred heritage that they are in danger of losing.

Even the vast and ever-increasing influx of tourists adds to the interest and value attached to the native language and culture. Some of the tourists want to know more than just to say Ka-lā-kaua and Wai-kīkī. They are interested in what *distinguishes* Hawai'i from the mainland, and this includes the Hawaiian language—so many vowels, so few consonants, such long words seen everywhere on maps and street signs.

Both the spirit of *aloha 'āina* and the tourist business, although so dissimilar, contribute to the survival of the language.

2　The Sound System

CONSONANTS *(p, k, ', h, l, m, n, w)*

2.1　　Both *p* and *k* are voiceless stops, the first bilabial, the other velar, pronounced about as in English but with less aspiration. (For substitution of *t* for *k*, see section 2.8.1.)

The glottal stop, ', is made by closing the glottis or space between the vocal cords, the result being something like the hiatus in English *oh-oh*. In Hawaiian the glottal stop is a consonant, the second most common in the language. It distinguishes such pairs as:

ala 'road, awake'	*'ala* 'fragrant'
kai 'ocean'	*ka'i* 'to lead'
kiki 'to sting'	*ki'i* 'picture'

It differs from other consonants in two ways:

(1) It is always heard before utterance-initial *a*, *e*, and *i*, but this is not considered significant because its occurrence in this position is predictable. A Hawaiian greets a friend " *'Aloha,*" but if he uses this word within a sentence, the glottal stop is no longer heard: *ua aloha* '[he] did [or does] have compassion'. Since the glottal does not occur in this word within a sentence, it is entered in the Dictionary *aloha*, and is so written in the present grammar.

(2) Words borrowed from English that begin with vowels *a*, *e*, *i*, *o*, and sometimes *u* are pronounced in Hawaiian with initial glottal stops, as *'Alapaki* 'Albert', *'elepani* 'elephant', *'Inia* 'In-

10

dia', and *'okomopila* 'automobile'. The initial glottal is written in these words in the present grammar.

In spite of the fact that the glottal stop has its own special symbol (a question mark without the bottom dot) in even the most elementary phonetics book, and although it is a phoneme in innumerable of the world's languages, it remains a source of mystery to many, who refuse to think of it as a Hawaiian consonant phoneme. One often hears and reads that the Hawaiian glottal stop represents a *k* in other Polynesian languages, as in Tuamotu *tiki* 'image' cognate with Hawaiian *ki'i*. One might as logically say that Hawaiian *k* represents *t* in Tuamotu. Actually, Hawaiian *k* and the glottal stop *correspond* to Tuamotu *t* and *k*; but that information is irrelevant in a description of Hawaiian sounds.

In early Hawaiian works, such as the translations of the Bible and the early grammars and dictionaries, the glottal stop was indicated by an apostrophe in such important words as *ko'u* 'mine' and *kou* 'yours'. A reversed apostrophe was apparently first used in Hawaiian by Judd, Pukui, and Stokes in 1943. Pratt's Samoan dictionary of 1862 uses the reversed apostrophe, as do later religious works in Samoan. Churchward's Tongan grammar (1953) and dictionary (1959) use a reversed apostrophe. Newspapers in Hawai'i today are beginning to use the ordinary apostrophe, which is quite acceptable. The possibility of confusing the apostrophe representing the Hawaiian glottal stop with the apostrophe representing the English possessive is almost nil.

The Hawaiian names for the glottal stop are *'u'ina* (literally, 'snap') and *'okina* ('break'). English writers have called the sound "guttural break" and "hamzah"—this based on its usage in Arabic as a *symbol* for the sound, whereas the preferable term "glottal stop" represents the actual sound.

The fact that most Hawaiian written before World War II does not contain any symbol for the glottal stop or for vowel length (see section 2.2) greatly complicates translation of texts and etymological analysis. The occasional but haphazard use of symbols such as a hyphen helps a little, but such writing as *Ka-u*, a district on Hawai'i Island, *pa-u* 'sarong', or *ka-i*, a kind of taro, indicates that the final vowel is long, but does not tell us whether the first vowel is long or short, or whether the two vowels are separated by glottal stops; such information is provided by the Dictionary spellings *Ka'ū, pā'ū, kaī*.

Context helps in deciphering, but in place names there is usually no context. So how, in the absence of context and of diacritical marks, could one distinguish between the district on Hawai'i called *Ka'ū* and a place in that district called *Kau*? How would one distinguish between *'Alae* ('mudhen'), the name of a crater and of a place on Hawai'i, and *'Ala'ē* ('strange fragrance'), the name of another place—when both are commonly written *Alae*?

A helpful clue in understanding texts in which the glottal stop is not indicated is that before initial *a* and *e* the definite article is always *ke*, but before *'a-* either *ke* or its alternate *ka* may occur (see also section 10.2):

ke ali'i 'the chief'	*ka 'ala* 'the fragrance'
ke aloha 'the love'	*ka 'ehu* 'the redhead'
ke ehu 'the spray'	*ke 'ano* 'the kind'

In a few words the glottal stop and *k* alternate. Common variants of *lau kī* 'ti leaf', *lau kō* 'sugarcane leaf', and *lau kalo* 'taro leaf' are *lā'ī lā'ō*, and *lā'alo*. These variations are not dialectal. Numerous nonproductive causative prefixes are *kā-* and *'ā-* (section 6.3); they are prefixed to different bases. Similarly, prefixes expressing quality or state are *kū-* and *'ū-*. The common word *mo'o* 'lizard' is *moko* in the place name *Moko-li'i*, literally 'little lizard'. Section 2.8.2 includes historical speculation about these variants.

The consonants *h*, *l*, *m*, and *n* are pronounced about as in English, except that *n* is dental-alveolar, and some Ni'ihau people occasionally replace *l* by an *r*-like sound.

The consonants *w* and *v* are variants (or alternants) of the same sound. A pattern seems to emerge, as shown in table 1. Speakers from Kaua'i and Ni'ihau tend to use the *w* variant always, whereas speakers from Hawai'i use the *v* variant; either is permissible.

Translators will find in old texts considerable inconsistency as to use of *w* or its omission. One finds *kaua* and *kauwa* (Dictionary *kauā*) for 'outcast'; *ui* and *uwiuwi* (Dictionary *'uwī'uwī*) for 'squeak'; *kauila* and *kauwila* (Dictionary *kauila*), a kind of tree; *koali* and *kowali* (Dictionary *koali*), 'morning glory'; *uala* and *uwala* (Dictionary *'uala*) 'sweet potato'. In every case, the *w* that is sometimes written and sometimes omitted follows *u* or *o*.

12

TABLE 1
The Vexing Hawaiian w

Pronunciation	Spelling	Explanation
iv– –ev–	*iwa* 'nine' *'Ewa*, a place name	The lips are not rounded in the production of *i* and *e*; hence the unrounded *v*-like sound is most common after *i* and *e*.
–uw– –ow–	*'auwa'i* 'ditch' *'o wai* 'who'	The lips are rounded in the production of *u* and *o*; hence the rounded *w*-like sound is most common after *u* and *o*. An exception for some people is *pu'uwai* 'heart' with a *v*-like sound.
–aw–, –av– w–, v–	*'awa*, a plant *wahine* 'woman'	After *a* and initially, both *w*-like and *v*-like sounds are heard.

Is *w* a phonetic and predictable glide following rounded vowels, or is it a significant sound?

The answer to this question is that *w* is significant after the unrounded vowels *i*, *e*, and *a*, as in *iwi* 'bone'; *'Ewa*, a place name; and *awa* 'harbor', or if following *o* or *u* and preceding a recognizable base, as in *'uwī'uwī* mentioned above (cf. *wī* 'to squeal') and in *kūwili* 'to move restlessly' (cf. *wili* 'to twist'). The *w* in the other words mentioned at the beginning of this paragraph is a nonsignificant glide; hence the definition in the revised Dictionary follows the forms without *w*. Both spellings are given for commonly used words.

In word-initial position the *w* is written even though it may be a barely perceptible glide, as in *'o wai* 'who'.

A similar *y*-glide occurs between *i* or *e* and a following *a*, and is particularly noticeable before *ā*, as in the particle *iā*. But unlike the *w*-glide, this sound occurs only in predictable environments and never serves to distinguish meanings. It is therefore not written, but is nevertheless pronounced.

Many speakers use English sounds in a few common words borrowed from English (section 2.9.1), as *Kristo* 'Christ', *tita* 'sister', *'ekalesia* 'church organization', and the common interjection of scorn written *kā* but usually pronounced *sā* or *chā*, often with a vowel sound suggesting that in English *hat*. The use of *b*, *d*, *f*, *g*, *r*, *s*, *t*, and *z* in the Bible translations and elsewhere has had little effect on the spoken language. Most people say *pila* 'fiddle', *Keoki* 'George', *loke* 'rose', *Kamuela* 'Samuel', *kaukani* 'thousand', and perhaps *kepela* for 'zebra'.

A consonant occurs only before a vowel; thus two consonants never occur in succession and a syllable always ends with a vowel.

VOWELS (i, ī, e, ē, a, ā, u, ū, o, ō)

2.2   In the description to follow, the terms *front*, *central*, and *back* refer to the position of the tongue in the mouth, as do the terms *lower* and *raised*. The Hawaiian vowels are front unrounded *i* and *e*, central *a*, and back rounded *u* and *o*. Values vary with stress. Unstressed *i* and *u* are slightly lower than stressed *i* and *u*. Stressed *a* suggests at times the sound of *a* in *father* but for some speakers it is slightly raised. Unstressed *a* usually suggests the *a* in *sofa*. According to Helene Newbrand (1951:9–10) *e* contiguous to *l* and *n* is usually similar to the *e* in *bell*; otherwise it suggests *ay* in *pay* except that the English off-glide is lacking (that is, it is not diphthongized): *hē* 'caterpillar' contrasts with *hei* 'snare'. Similarly *kō* 'sugarcane' contrasts with *kou*, a tree species. Long *ē* and *ō* are usually difficult for mainland Americans to pronounce because they do not exist in English without the off-glides.

All vowels occur with and without the macron, a symbol indicating both stress (or accent) and length, the amount of length depending on neighboring sounds and position within the utterance. (Long *i* seems less long than other long vowels.)

A glottal stop seems to shorten a preceding vowel, or at least it has done so in the history of the language. For example, the Proto Central Polynesian (PCP) singular *a*-possessives were *tāku* 'my', *tāu* 'your', and *tāna* 'his'. When the earlier *k* was replaced in Hawaiian by the glottal stop, and *t* by *k*, the glottal stop shortened the 'my' form to ka'u. (The other forms are *kāu* and *kāna*, with *ā* retained.) Similarly, the focus forms are na'u, *nāu*, and *nāna*. Significantly, the shape CV'V does not occur in the language except in longer words (*mā'ona*).

Stressed vowels, even those unmarked by a macron, may be slightly longer than unstressed ones. Isamu Abe, who studied spectograms, remarked (1970:108) that when two long vowels follow each other with a consonant between, the second vowel is longer than the first and the pitch level falls on the second, as in *pōwā* 'robber'. However, in a partial reduplication of a CVCV base, the length is retained in the reduplication but not in the base: thus *wāhi* 'to split' and its reduplicated derivative *wāwahi*. Utterance-final vowels marked with the macron and not preceded by long vowels are stressed but are usually not very long, as in the sentence *Ua kū* 'Standing'. This may not be related to the fact that short vowels at the ends of utterances are commonly voiceless, as, in fast speech, the final vowels in *ki'i, aku, Maka-pu'u*. They do not seem, however, ever to be completely dropped. Double vowels fuse into a single long vowel: *aloha 'ia aku* 'loved' becomes *aloha 'iaku. Ia'u* 'to me' is from *iā a'u*. Threefold repetition of the same vowel exists only as a means of imparting great emphasis, as in *hele aaa uka* 'went far far upland'.

Combinations of two unlike vowels are of two types. If the two vowels are pronounced in every environment with the stress on the first member, they constitute a **diphthong**. An example is *ai*: in *'aina* 'meal' the stress is still on the first member of the combination. The other type of combination of two unlike vowels may be termed a **cluster**. If the combination is followed by a single syllable, the stress is on the second member of the cluster. An example is *io* in *'iole* 'rat'. The diphthongs are *ai, ae, au, ao, ei, eu, oi, ou*. In each, the two vowels are not as closely knit as in English. Contrasts hard for the English ear to distinguish are such pairs as *kai* 'ocean' and *kae* 'to refuse'; *hau*, a tree, and *hao* 'iron'. The *o* in *oi* suggests the *o* in English *sole* (but not diphthongized *ou!*). In fast speech *a* before *i* may suggest the vowels in English *hat* or *set*, and *a* before *u* may suggest the vowel in *cut*.

The following sets indicate the role of vowel length in distinguishing otherwise homophonous words:

kanaka 'man'	*nana* 'to plait'
kānaka 'men'	*nāna* 'by him'
kohola 'reef'	*nanā* 'to snarl'
koholā 'whale'	*nānā* 'to look (at)
mala 'ache'	*hio* 'to blow'
māla 'garden'	*hiō* 'to lean'
'aina 'meal'	*kao* 'spear'
'āina 'land'	*kāō* 'crowd'

And how is one to translate *ii*? The four pronunciations follow, with the number of entries in the revised Dictionary in parentheses: *i'i* (1), *'i'i* (7), *'iī* (4), *īī* (2). The poor translator has a choice of 14 glosses!

The devoicing of utterance-final vowels has been mentioned.

In a few words, especially in place names, an entire second syllable is dropped, with lengthening of the vowel in the retained first syllable. *Moku* 'district' becomes *mō-* in the place name *Mō-kapu* 'sacred district'; similarly *moʻo* 'lizard' becomes *mō-* in the place name *Mō-ʻiliʻili* 'pebble lizard'. *One* 'sand' becomes *-ō-* in *Ke-ō-kea* 'the white sand'. *Limu* 'seaweed' becomes *lī-* in such seaweeds as *lī-pahapaha*. *Maka* 'eye' becomes *mā-* in *mākole* 'red-eyed', *mākahi* 'one-eyed', and probably *makaʻi* 'policeman'. *Mahaʻoi* 'rude' (literally, sharp head temple) is also *māʻoi*. The causative *hoʻo-* is shortened to *hō-* and *ho-* in certain environments (section 6.4).

(For use of hyphens, see section 2.12.)

WORD STRESS

2.3   Albert J. Schütz has suggested (1977) for Fijian that stress (or accent) can best be described for that language on the basis of what he calls "accent groups." The term "stress group" is used here. The stress in a stress group is always on the next to the last syllable or on a long vowel marked by a macron. In Fijian Schütz separates stress groups *within a word* by a period, as syllables are marked in some English dictionaries. Stress groups in Hawaiian consist most commonly of two syllables, often of one or three syllables, but never more than three except in proper names. Examples follow:

(1) Words containing a single stress group: *akaaka* 'clear'; *hale* 'house'; *Hanauma*, a place name; *kanaka* 'person'; *malama* 'light'

(2) Words containing two stress groups: *ʻekale.sia* 'church organization'; *ʻele.makule* 'old man'; *Hana.lei*, a place name; *hei.au* 'ancient temple'; *kā.naka* 'people'; *mā. lama* 'to care for'; *nenele.au* 'sumac'

(3) Words containing three stress groups: *hoʻo.lau.leʻa* 'celebration'; *kō.ʻele.ʻele*, species of seaweed; *kū.nā.nā* 'puzzled'

The stress in five-syllable reduplications is most commonly as in *mā.lama.lama* 'clear', but some are as in *luma.lumaʻi* 'to upset', or *huele.elo* 'having tails'.

If two or more stress groups occur in a single word, the last one as spoken is usually somewhat louder than the preceding one or ones.

Many proper names begin with the definite article *ka/ke*.

These are clitics; that is, they are pronounced as a part of what follows. Examples: *Kameha.meha, Kapi'o-lani, Kalā-kaua, Kai.mukī.*

In some long proper names, the breakup according to component words differs from the breakup according to stress groups:

Semantic Breakup	Stress-group Breakup
'Au-i-ke-kai-loa 'swim in the distant sea'	*'aui.kekai.loa*
Ka'elele-o-ka-wana'ao 'the messenger of the dawn'	*ka'e.lele.oka.wana.'ao*
Ka-mehameha 'the lonely [one]'	*kameha.meha*
Kau-i-ke-ao-uli 'place in the dark clouds'	*kaui.keao.uli* or *kaui.keouli*
Ke-one-'ō'io 'the bonefish sand'	*keone.'ō.'io*

The division by stress group is strange-looking and unfamiliar. We "feel" that *mehameha* is a unit and should not be cut in two, regardless of pronunciation. For these reasons, proper names in the revised Dictionary are written with hyphens separating the identifiable parts. All entries, however, are written with periods separating the stress groups.

The syllable following a period within a word is usually rearticulated (that is, it is separated from the preceding syllable by a slight pause). Thus in ordinary conversation one says *Kai.mukī*, not *Ka.imu.kī, hei.au,* not *he.iau;* and *ho'o.uli,* not *ho.ouli.* Singers are sometimes criticized for incorrect placing of this pause, as in such common words as *onaona* 'fragrant' (not *ona.ona*) and *i laila* 'there' (not *ila.ila*). The period is also "significant" if inserted between vowels otherwise pronounced as diphthongs:

a.i: *kana.iwa* 'nine', *kula.iwi* 'native'
a.e: *kama.ehu* 'strength'
a.u: *pala.uli* 'dark'
a.o: *kana.ono* 'sixty'
e.i: *'e.iwa* 'nine times'
o.i: *ho'o.ilo* 'winter'
o.u: *ho'o.uli* 'to darken'

In the present Grammar the stress groups are shown only if pronunciation is under discussion. The periods separating the stress groups are helpful in a glossary or pedagogical text and as a descriptive device, but are not needed in ordinary writing.

JUNCTURES

2.4   In spoken Hawaiian there are four types of pauses, sometimes called "junctures":

(1) The end of a sentence, marked by a period. The final vowel in the sentence may be voiceless or even inaudible, and the pitch and volume may decrease.

(2) The end of a question sentence, marked by a question mark (section 2.6).

(3) Pauses within sentences, ordinarily between phrases (section 3.2), marked by a comma.

(4) A pause between words within a phrase, or the pause between stress groups (called a plus juncture) within words explained in section 2.3. Of the four types of juncture, this is the least prominent.

STRESS IN PHRASES AND SENTENCES

2.5   Stress in sequences longer than words depends to a large extent on the junctures just described. The stress patterns of words usually extend to the phrases in which they are used (a **phrase** is a base and its modifiers). Phrases are usually (but not always) separated by junctures of some kind. Each of the two examples below consists of two phrases—a verb phrase and a noun phrase in (1), and two noun phrases in (2). Each phrase is pronounced as a unit, but there is a plus juncture /+/ between the phrases. Vowel sequences with intervening /+/, as $e + i$ in (1) and $a + o$ in (2) usually do not diphthongize. The /+/ in each sentence separates two unstressed syllables.

(1) *Ua hele + i laila.* '[He] went there.'
(2) *Nā maka + o Hina.* 'The eyes of Hina.'

Both (1) and (2) are **sentences,** which are phonologically defined as sequences bordered by /./ or /ʔ/. Sentences vary in length from a single word, such as *Kimo!* 'James!', to a long succession of phrases. In sentences, as in phrases, there is usually a single primary stress, with secondary stresses, if any, preceding the

18

primary stress. The placing of the primary stress is unpredictable. In sentences (1) and (2) above primary stress could be on
hele or *laila*, or on *maka* or *Hina*. The farther removed a secondary stress is from the primary stress, the louder it seems to be.

Proper names are sometimes very long and contain a succession of phrases. Unfortunately they are usually written as single
words, for example, Kaliokalanilapakauilakuikahekiliikama-
kaokaopua. This becomes pronounceable if the glottal stops,
macrons, and potential juncture points are marked (here, stress
is indicated also):

(Possessive phrase)

Ka	lí ‖ ò	ka	lani, ‖ lapa kà	uíla, ‖
the	chill of	the	sky	flash the	lightning

(Locative phrase)   *(Possessive phrase)*

kùʻi kà	hekíli, ‖ i	ka	máka ‖ ò	ka	ʻòpúa.
roar the	thunder in the	face	of	the	horizon cloud.

'The chill of heaven, the flash of lightning, the roar of thunder in the
face of the horizon cloud.' (This is a personal name and an indication
of high rank; nature was believed to pay tribute to royalty.)

In other less obvious ways the usual orthography (even with
glottal stops and macrons included) fails to reflect the pronunciation. For one thing, in ordinary fast speech, certain particles
called **clitics** (see Glossary) are always short and are not followed
by junctures. Common ones are the definite article *ka/ke*, the indefinite article *he*, and *i* 'at'. In fast speech and in personal
names they are pronounced without any plus junctures as
though they are a part of what follows.

> *ka ukana* 'the baggage' /kau.kana/
> *ka inoa* 'the name' /kai.noa/
> *ke aloha* 'the love' /kea.loha/
> *i laila* 'there' /ilaila/

In slow unnatural speech, or sometimes in acculturated speech,
the clitics are followed by plus junctures. And conversely, in fast
speech the given name *ʻAu-i-ke-kai-loa*, for example, may
become *ʻaui.kekai.loa*.

Monosyllabic words and particles present an added difficul-
ty, as some are always long, others are always short, and the
length of vowels in still others varies according to the environ-

ment. This seems to be the clearest explanation: Words (not particles) consisting of a single syllable are always long:

'ā 'to burn'
'ē 'different'
hā 'a stalk'
'ī 'to say'
kā 'to hit'
kō 'sugar cane'
kū 'upright'
lā 'sun'
mā 'faded'
nā 'to soothe'
'ō 'fork'
pā 'fence'
ū 'breast'
wā 'noise'

Such words have meanings in the real world and are intelligible
if used alone. Some of the **particles** (most of which tell grammatical relationships and are not intelligible if used alone) are
always short: *ka/ke*, singular articles; *i* 'at'. Other particles are
always long: *nā*, plural article; *nō*, intensifier. Other equally
common particles are usually short before short syllables and
long before long syllables (short syllables have short vowel
nuclei; long syllables have long vowels and diphthongs as
nuclei). A macron is not used in these particles. The native
speaker unconsciously lengthens them. Some examples:

a 'of'	*Hale-à-ka-lá* 'house-of-the-sun' (mountain name)
	'Umi-à-Lìlóa 'Umi-[child]-of-Līloa' (chief's name)
o 'of'	*Hale-o-Lóno* 'house-of-Lono' (place name)
	Pù'u-ò-Mänòa 'hill-of-Mānoa' (place name)
ma 'at'	*mà O'áhu* 'on O'ahu'
	má-uka 'inland'
	mà Kì-làu-èa 'at Kī-lau-ea'
na 'by, for'	*nà ke ali'i* 'by the chief / for the chief'
	nā làkòu 'by them / for them'
no 'for'	*no kè ali'i* 'for the chief'
	nō kou hale 'for your house'

It must be emphasized that the macron indicates both vowel
length and stress. Its role is threefold: (1) Every vowel with a

macron is somewhat lengthened, but (2) at the end of a word or particle the length is not as noticeable as the stress, and (3) every word-final vowel with a macron is usually followed by some kind of juncture. A sentence that illustrates the three functions is *'Ua kū + 'o Kímo.* 'Jim stood up.'

PITCH LEVELS

2.6   Of the four contrasting pitch levels, level 4 is the highest and least frequent, as for great emphasis. Utterances commonly begin with 2, and continue on this level with minor fluctuations until a marked change in level is made. The change in level is a definite step up or down, rather than a glide.

	2				3 1
(1)	*Hele*	*au*	*i*	*ka*	*hale.*
	go	I	to	the	house

	2				3 3
(2)	*Hele*	*au*	*i*	*ka*	*hale.*

'I go to the house.'

	2	3 2	2	3	1
(3)	*Ua*	*hele,*	*ā*	*ua*	*noho.*
	(perf.)	go	and	(perf.)	stay

'Went and stayed.'

	2		3 3
(4)	*Ua*	*hele*	*'oeʔ*
	(perf.)	go	you

	2		3 2
(5)	*Ua*	*hele*	*'oeʔ*

'Did you go?'

	2		3	3
(6)	*He*	*aha*	*kēlā*	*meaʔ*
	is	what	that	thing

	2		3	2
(7)	*He*	*aha*	*kēlā*	*meaʔ*

'What's that thing?'

Pitch levels in (1) and (3) suggest those in similar English sentences. Pitch levels in (2) are rather different from those in English. The last four sentences illustrate two ways to ask questions. *Aha* in (6) and (7) is a question word, but takes the usual

21

question intonations. Pitch levels in (5) and (7), with falling intonation, are commonly heard in Hawaiian Island English. It is
not certain whether Hawaiian has influenced Island English, or
vice versa. Or could we say that pitch levels in (4) and (6) have
been influenced by English?

In contrast to English, intonation with question words is the
same as that following other words. Abe (1970:110) diagramed
the sentence *Mahea kou wahi hānau?* 'Where is your birth-
place?' with medium pitch level on all syllables, except for a low
level on *Ma-* and a rise on final *-u*.

NATURAL FAST SPEECH

2.7   In any language natural fast speech is quite different from slow
artificial speech, and in Hawaiian there are many changes of
vowel values, losses of vowels, and stress changes. These were
studied at the Bishop Museum by Kinney (1956). She analyzed
tape recordings of the speech of fourteen speakers who ranged in
age from late middle age to eighty and ninety, and who, with
one possible exception, grew up speaking Hawaiian before
English. The results of her survey are given in table 2.

Kinney tabulated the varying pronunciations of nineteen
words, most of which occur frequently in the spoken language.
The second column in the table shows pronunciations that correspond to the traditional spelling, and the third column gives
pronunciations that show assimilation or reduction. The fourth
column gives the percentages of times that the fast pronunciations were noted, and the last column shows the number of times
each word was recorded.

Other changes include partial instead of complete reduplications *(makemake* to *mamake, kuikui* to *kukui),* loss of short *a*
(hele akula to *hele kula, e ia nei* to *ei nei, ke akua* to *ke kua),*
whispering of vowels or syllables before silence (as the final
vowel in *Punalu'u* or in reduplications (as the second and fourth
o's in *Nāpo'opo'o),* raising an *a* before *u* to sound like the vowel
in English *cut* (as in *Maui)* or to *ou* in the place name *Ke-au-hou*
(usually called *Ke-ou-hou*), and especially the fusion of like
vowels to a single vowel: *loa'a ana* to *lo'ana, loa'a aku* to *lo'aku,*
pua aloalo to *pualoalo, a hiki i kēia lā* to *a hiki kēia lā* (FS 273).

This fusion induced Bible translators to insert an apostrophe,
as in *loaa'i* instead of *loa'a ai.* This unfortunate use of the
apostrophe is discussed in some detail in section 2.12.

TABLE 2
Sound Changes in Fast Speech

Type of Change	Pronunciation According to Spelling	Fast Pro-nunciations	Percentages of Fast Pro-nunciations	Number of Citations
Assimilation				
ai to *ei:*	*laila* (there)	*leila, lila*	100	138
	kaikua'ana (sibling)	*keikua'ana*	100	6
	kaikunāne (sibling)	*keikunāne*	100	4
	kaikamahine (girl)	*keikamahine, keikimahine*	95	43
	ikaika (strong)	*ikeika*	92	13
	maika'i (good)	*meike'i*	63	34
	kaikaina (sibling)	*kaikaina*	56	7
	kaikuahine (sibling)	*keikuahine*	50	2
	maila (hither)	*meila*	49	41
	waiho (leave)	*weiho*	40	10
	mai (hither)	*mei*	37	242
	ai (linking)	*ei*	36	216
'a'o to *'a'a:*	*'a'ole* (no)	*'a'ale*	79	324
	'a'ohe (none)	*'a'ahe*	37	73
io to *iu:*	*lio* (horse)	*liu*	66	36
	'īlio (dog)	*'īliu*	48	42
au to *ou:*	*mau* (plural)	*mou*	29	75
Loss of *–a–*				
before *–'a:*	*loa'a* (get)	*lo'a*	100	62
	pua'a (pig)	*pu'a*	100	2

DIALECT VARIATIONS

2.8   Variations in Hawaiian dialects have not been systematically studied, but they appear to be not great if compared, for example, with those in the Marquesas. The dialect of Ni'ihau is the most aberrant and the one most in need of study.

Ni'ihau Dialect

2.8.1   Ni'ihau is the only area in the world where Hawaiian is the first language and English is a foreign language. Because of many sufficiently marked variations, Ni'ihau people, when visiting or living in Honolulu, substitute the O'ahu dialect for their own—apparently easy to do—saying that otherwise people in Honolulu have trouble understanding them. Ni'ihau people speak very rapidly; many vowels and entire syllables are dropped or whispered. Newbrand (1951:106) reported that a Kala-pana, Hawai'i, male read at the rate of 120 words per minute, and a Ni'ihau female, at the rate of 170 words per minute.

23

Reductions and changes noted by Newbrand include the following:

Standard Hawaiian	Niʻihau dialect	Changes
noho ʻana 'living'	*nooana*	h and ʻ dropped; the first *a* pronounced like *u* in English *cut*, and the second as in *sofa*
ʻelua oʻu tita 'two of my sisters'	*elu aʻu tita*	initial ʻ and final *a* in *ʻelua* dropped; *o* pronounced like *u* in English *cut*; *a* in *tita* pronounced as in *sofa*
hoʻokahi lumi 'one room'	*hoʻotaii lumi*	*k* replaced by *t*; *h* dropped; *a* pronounced like *u* in *cut*; the first *i* lengthened

Newbrand reported that her Niʻihau informant, reading from a text that she herself had prepared, sometimes read a written *k* as *t* and vice versa; *t* occurred 102 times, *k* 87 times. The informant used *t* consistently in the words *makuahine* 'mother' and *hiki* 'able'; *k* was used consistently in *akā* 'but', *no ka mea* 'because', and *like* 'like'; *t* was not used utterance initially. Some common examples of interchangeable use of *k* and *t* included *ke*, *ka*, *koʻu*, *kaʻu*, *keia* (usually *teia*), *kekahi*, *makemake*. Vowel assimilation was frequent: *mawaho* 'outside' was *mauwoho*; *ʻaʻohe wahi* 'no place' was *ʻaʻohi wahi*.

In the early 1950s Elbert collected four short stories in the Niʻihau dialect, all from the same informant, then the oldest man on the island but long since dead. In two of them the variant *k* was used 108 times, and the variant *t*, 107 times. In two others, *k* was recorded 178 times and *t*, 87 times. The first story had examples of 10 successive *k*'s and 10 successive *t*'s. The last story had one stretch of 21 successive *k*'s and 10 successive *t*'s. In the first story the common *kēlā* 'that' was recorded *kēlā* 11 times, *tēlā* 14 times, and *tērā* once.

William H. Wilson, who has worked extensively with the university Hawaiian-language radio programs, has noted that if a word has two *k*'s, the Niʻihau speakers pronounce the first as *k* and the second as *t*: *kātou* 'we', *kahatai* 'beach'. In the speech of informants from Kau-pō and Kī-pahulu in East Maui, and

Hālawa, Moloka'i, Wilson has noticed the *t* sound after the vowel *i*: *laiti* 'rice', *'ite* 'to know', *maita'i* 'good', *makahiti* 'year'. This might be attributed to an assimilatory fronting of *k* after a high front vowel.

Experienced chanters, too, randomly substitute *t* for *k* without realizing they are doing so.

These are a few lexical differences noted between the speech of Ni'ihau (or Kaua'i) and O'ahu:

Ni'ihau (or Kaua'i)	O'ahu	English Glosses
'a'ole o ke'a mai	*'a'ole o kana mai*	'there's no limit'
kali	*kohe*	'vagina'
kuikui	*kukui*	'candlenut'
mana'o nui	*mana'o*	'meaning'
nā'ele	*nahele*	'forest growth'
neki	*'aka'akai, nānaku*	'giant bulrush'
piaia	*'ōhua manini*	a small *manini* fish
pōkeokeo	*pelehū*	'turkey'

n FOR *l* AND GLOTTAL STOP FOR *l* AND *k*

2.8.2   The next most conspicuous dialect variation is substitution of *n* for *l*, especially, perhaps, on Moloka'i and Lā-na'i. Many of the changes are assimilatory; that is, *l* . . . *n* and *n* . . . *l* become *n* . . .*n*:

hālana, hānana	'to overflow'
kōnale, kōnane	'clear', and a game
kūlana, kūnana	'position'
kūlono, kūnono	'leaky'
lānahu, nānahu	'charcoal'
Lā-na'i, Nāna'i,	island name
lanaiea, nanaiea	'weak'
lanakea, nanakea	'pale'
lanalana, nananana	'spider'
lanau, nanau	'unfriendly'
luna, nuna	'above'
lunu, nunu	'greed'
malino, manino	'calm'
ulana, nana	'to plait'

Non-assimilatory changes include the following:

l . . . l to *n . . . n*	*'ele'ele, 'ene'ene* 'black'
	kolili, konini 'to flutter'
	kūlokuloku, kūnokunoku 'to flow'
	lahilahi, nahinahi 'thin'
	uluulu, unuunu 'entangled, to singe'
li to *ni*	*kūlihi, kūnihi* 'steep'
	lihi, nihi 'edge'
	lili, nini 'jealous'
	lipo, nipo 'to yearn'
lo to *no*	*kūlokuloku, kūnokunoku* 'to flow'
	kūlou, kūnou 'to bow'
	loku, noku 'downpour'
	loulu, noulu, palm species
lu to *nu*	*kūkulu, kūkunu* 'border'
	lupa, nupa 'lush' (of vegetation)
-lū to *-nū*	*hakalū, hakanū* 'silent'

Of these, the *l . . . n* forms are in more general use except for *kōnane, nihi,* and *kūnihi; kōnane* (the game) may be a reflex of Proto Central Polynesian (PCP) *nane;* the other two, of Proto Polynesian (PPN) *nifi.*

A number of the *l*-forms are reflexes of PPN, indicating that most of the *n*-forms may be Hawaiian innovations. These include PPN *lalanga* (Hawaiian *ulana*), *lili* (Hawaiian *lili*), *tuulanga* (Hawaiian *kūlana*), and *tulou* (Hawaiian *kūlou*). In a few words, some speakers replace *l* by the glottal stop:

kūlou, kū'ou (?) 'to bow'
mālamalama, mā'ama'ama 'light'
malaulauā, ma'au'auā 'peddler'
malauea, ma'auea 'lazy'
palanehe, pa'anehe 'dainty'
pūliki, pū'iki 'to embrace'

Both Ulu-koa and Ulu'oa are listed in the Dictionary as names of an unknown star. In three words *l* is omitted without replacement:

'a'ole, 'a'oe 'not' (poetic)
huli, hui 'to turn' (poetic)
māilo, māio 'thin'

Some persons say *lōkihi* 'long' and *kūlepe* 'harelip' for common *lō'ihi* and *'ūlepe*. *Haki* and *ha'i* 'to break' seem equally common, as are *he'a* and *heka* 'inflamed' and *mu'umu'u* and *mukumuku* 'to cut'. *K* instead of the current glottal stop also occurs in the O'ahu islet name *Moko-li'i* 'little lizard', commonly known as Chinaman's Hat. The prefixes *kā*- and *kū*- have *'ā*- and *'a*- and *'ū*- and *'u*- variants (sections 6.3.1 and 6.3.2).

Some names of plants of little use vary according to locality, but these have not yet been systematically studied.

LOAN WORDS

2.9

ENGLISH AS A SOURCE

2.9.1   Words taken from one language into another are called **loan words.** Hawaiian has hundreds of loan words, mostly from English. The Hawaiian Bible is filled with them. The Hawaiian uses loan words when he gets married, baptizes his baby, reads the Scriptures, eats his lunch, goes to San Francisco, or uses soap. The spelling of some Hawaiian loan words is not fixed. In the Hawaiian Bible are found the letters *t, d, g, s,* and *z* (all of which the Hawaiians usually pronounce *k*), *b* (usually pronounced *p*), *r* (usually pronounced *l*), and *v* (sometimes pronounced *w*). Many words are spelled with either English or Hawaiian letters, as *dala* and *kālā* 'dollar', *ti* and *kī* 'tea', *mare* and *male* 'to marry'. For the sake of consistency and ease of reference, words in the Dictionary are listed according to the usual pronunciation of old-time Hawaiians, with variant spellings following the entry word. Thus, the Biblical *bapetema* 'baptism' is entered in the *p*'s, as follows: **papekema, bapetema.** Some substitutions for English consonant sounds in Hawaiianized loan words are shown in table 3.

We see that *k*, the most common Hawaiian consonant, is substituted for ten English consonant sounds. The Hawaiian word spelled *kika* has four variant spellings (*tita* 'sister', *sida* 'cider', *tiga* 'tiger', and *kika* 'cassia')—all from English. The only native *kika* means 'slippery'. The Hawaiian word spelled *kini* has two variant spellings, *gini* 'gin' and *tini* 'tin'; it also is the Hawaiian for king, kin, zinc, Guinea, Jean, Jane, and Jennie. The native Hawaiian meaning is 'multitude'.

Post-vocalic *r* is usually omitted in loans, as in the last syllable of *kolopā* 'crowbar'. This conforms with the pronunciation of New England missionaries to Hawai'i in the 1820s.

27

TABLE 3
Hawaiian Substitutions for English Consonants

English	Hawaiian	Examples
p, b, f	p	*Pika* 'Peter', *pia* 'beer', *palaoa* 'flour'
v, w	w	*welaweka* 'velvet', *waina* 'wine'
hw	hu, w, u	*huila* 'wheel', *wekekē* 'whiskey', *uapo* 'wharf'
h, sh	h	*home* 'home', *Halaki* 'Charlotte', *hipa* 'sheep'
l, r	l	*laiki* 'rice', *laki* 'lucky'
m	m	*mākeke* 'market'
n, ng	n	*Nolewai* 'Norway', *kini* 'king'
t, d, th		*kikiki* 'ticket', *kaimana* 'diamond', *kipikelia* 'diphtheria',
s, sh, z	k	*kopa* 'soap', *palaki* 'brush', *kokiaka* 'zodiac',
ch, j, k, g		*pika* 'pitcher', *Keoki* 'George', *kolokē* 'croquet', *Kilipaki* 'Gilbert'
j	i	*Iesū* 'Jesus'

The vowel correspondences in loan words are based on the English vowels and diphthongs listed by Gleason (1967:34–35), and on Elbert's dialect of American English (see table 4). Hawaiian adaptations of English words beginning with *a-, e-, i-, o-,* and sometimes *u-* begin with glottal stops (cf. section 2.1).

As there are no consonant clusters in Hawaiian, English adjoining consonants are separated in Hawaiian by a vowel (*pūlumi* 'broom' and *palaki* 'brush'), or one of the English consonants is dropped:

English:	steel	San F ranc isco
Hawaiian:	*k i l a*	*Ka pa la ki k o*

A vowel is added at the ends of the words, very often *a*. Many of the missionary introductions were based on English spelling rather than on pronunciation, as *koma* 'comma', *liona* 'lion', *hīmeni* 'hymn', and *poloka* 'frog'. In a highly readable article, Schütz (1976) contrasts these introductions with those recorded by early visitors, who were less interested in English spelling than in the way the Hawaiians attempted to pronounce the foreign words. Thus Campbell listed, probably in 1809 (quoted by Schütz 1976:83) the following:

bikete 'biscuit'	*lummee* 'rum'
tabete 'cabbage'	*Lookeene* 'Russian'
Pritane 'Britain'	*tookeine* 'stockings'
peepe 'sheep'	*Itseeke* 'Isaac'
teakete 'jacket'	*Keeme* 'James'

TABLE 4
Hawaiian Substitutions for English Vowels

English		Hawaiian	
Sound	Example	Sound	Example
i	hymn	ɪ	*hīmeni*
	Finland	i	*Pinilana*
iy	heel	i	*hila*
e	bell	e	*pele*
ey	bail	e	*pela*
æ	baptize	a	*papekiko*
ɨ	story	e	*kole*
ə	bucket	a	*pākeke*
a	March	a	*Malaki*
	papa	ā	*pāpā*
ay	pie	ai	*pai, pae*
aw	crown, town	au, ao	*kalaunu, kaona*
aH	palm	ā	*pāma*
u	book	u	*puke*
uw	blue	ū	*polū*
	Jew	iu	*Kiu*
	school	u	*kula*
ow	home	o	*home*
ɔy	boil	ay	*paila*
	Boyd	oe	*Poe*
ɔH	George	o	*Keoki*

The final vowel in these words *(e)*, according to a key to pronunciation, was pronounced as the first *e* in *eloquence* or the *y* in *plenty*, and *ee* as in *keep*. Yet the missionaries preferred to end their introduced words with *a*. Just why is not clear, except that they may have wished to keep the foreign words separate from the native ones (which is certainly why they introduced so many consonants). The inserted vowels are now established, Schütz says, and he concludes his article: "Thus are preserved the whims of those who were linguistically naive, but influential."

Just as the Hawaiians pronounced the introduced consonants with their own sounds, so they usually kept their stress on the next to the last syllable, regardless of English stress, in the introduced words: *'enemi* 'enemy', *kokomi* 'sodomy', *pekana* 'pagan'. Other three-syllable words derived from English words with primary stress on the first syllable tend to have stressed and lengthened vowels in that syllable, as *lāpaki* 'rabbit', *nōkali* 'notary', and *pāloka* 'ballot'.

The integration of much-used loan words is illustrated by their use with affixes: *kula* 'school', *kukula* 'to go to school'; *male* 'to marry', *ho'omale* 'to marry off'.

A number of loans are hybrids, either Hawaiian plus English or English plus Hawaiian:

haukalima 'ice cream', lit., cream ice
nī'au pulumi 'broom straw', lit., broom coconut-leaf midrib
nīoi 'pepper': *nīoi pekela* 'betel nut', *nīoi pepa* 'chili pepper'
nūpepa puka lā 'daily newspaper', lit., newspaper issuing day
'ohe puluka 'flute', lit., bamboo flute
pipikaula 'salted, dried beef', lit., rope beef
wilikī 'engineer', lit., key turning

The Dictionary lists 13 words beginning with *mīkini* 'machine', from English. In all except *mīkini 'aiana* 'clothes presser' (English, iron) the word or words following *mikini* are Hawaiian. The Dictionary lists nine sequences beginning *loke* 'rose', as well as *'ohi'a loke* 'rose apple'. *'Ō'ō* 'digging stick' is followed by *halo, hou, palau,* and *pē*—all from English.

For a fascinating comparison of adaptation of English loan words into Hawaiian and Japanese, see Carr (1964).

THE WORD FOR HORSE

2.9.2   The Hawaiian words for 'horse' and 'goat' have long been puzzling. 'Goat' is *kao*, which sounds like English *cow*. Why should a goat have been called a cow, and why the strange word *lio* for 'horse'? Could it have been because a horse's ears are sometimes pulled back "tightly" *(lio)* as some suggest?

Schütz has suggested that early word lists might provide clues. These were examined, with results as shown in table 5 (today's spellings of the words used by the early writers are in parentheses).

Lisianski wrote today's *l, u, eu,* and *w* as *r, oo, eo,* and *v.* Campbell was less consistent. He wrote *e* and *ee* for today's *i,* and *c* and *k* for today's *k.* His *d, a,* and *oo* correspond to today's *l, o,* and *u.* His word for goat should probably have been *peepe kao—koa* is perhaps a misprint. Arago was the only one to write *t* for today's *k.*

Schütz has pointed out (oral communication) that *rio* and *edea* are different spellings of the word for 'dog', and that they served as generic terms for nonnative quadrupeds, just as the Tahitians and Marquesans used their words for 'pig'. In Tahitian 'horse' is *pua'a horo henua* (quadruped runs ground), and in Marquesan it is *puaka piki 'enata* (quadruped man rides). Lisianski's quadruped is *lio* and Campbell's is *edea.* Lisianski's

TABLE 5

Spellings of Hawaiian Words for Animals

Animal	Lisianski 1804	Campbell (1809–1810)	Arago 1819	1976
Dog	*rio* (*lio*)	*edea cao* (*ʻīlio kao*)		*ʻīlio*
Goat	*riokao* (*lio kao*)	*peepe koa* (*pipi kao*)	*tao* (*kao*)	*kao*
Horse		*edea nooee* (*ʻīlio nui*)		*lio*
Sheep	*rio hooloo* (*lio hulu*) or *rio veoveo* (*lio weuweu*)	*peepe* (*pipi*)		*hipa*

goat is therefore a "cow quadruped" and his sheep a "hairy quadruped" (or a "fuzzy quadruped"). Campbell called his dog a "cow quadruped," his goat "cow beef," his horse a "big quadruped," and his sheep "beef." By Arago's time 'goat' had lost its preceding generic classifier. 'Sheep' has become *hipa* from English. *ʻĪlio* still serves as a generic classifier:

ʻīlio hae 'wolf' (fierce quadruped)
ʻīlio hohono 'skunk' (smelly quadruped)
ʻīlio holo a ka uaua 'seal' (quadruped running in the rough [sea])
ʻīlio hulu pāpale 'beaver' (quadruped [used for] hat fur)

Schütz suggested that the strange word for today's horse *(lio)* is a shortening of the word for dog *(ʻīlio)*.

BIBLICAL TERMS

2.9.3   The missionaries introduced many words from Hebrew, Greek, and Latin in the course of their monumental task of translating the Bible into Hawaiian. They had access to the Masoretic (Hebrew) texts of the Old Testament, the Septuagint (Greek) Bible, and the Latin Vulgate, as well as Bible dictionaries. Most of the introductions were of plants, animals, and cultural items not found in Hawaiʻi. Aside from the Christian names so beloved by Hawaiians, the only words from these sources used with much frequency are *ʻekalekia, hepekoma,* and *meli.* In the lists that follow, the first spelling is with Hawaiian letters, the second with the letters introduced by the missionaries. If two glosses are given, the first is from the Revised Standard Version of the Bible and the second from the King James Version.

From the Hebrew:

'aleka, areza 'cedar, fir': Hebrew *erez*
kikala, tidara 'plane tree, pine': Hebrew *tidhar*
kinola, kinora 'harp': Hebrew *kinnur*

From the Greek:

'ekalekia, ekalesia 'church organization': Greek *ekklesia*
hepekoma, hebedoma 'week': Greek *hebdomas*
meli 'honey': Greek *meli*

From the Latin:

lana 'frog': Latin *rana*
lepu 'hare': Latin *lepus*
mukuela, mutuela 'weasel': Latin *mustela*

Glottal stops rarely occur in Hawaiian loan words other than in initial position. Exceptions are *Kana'ana* 'Canaan', probably from Greek; *'Ikela'ela* 'Israel', and *le'ema* 'reem', from Hebrew; and such personal names as *'A'alona* 'Aaron', *'Ika'aka* 'Isaac', and *Lapa'ela* 'Raphael'. Could these have been reflexes of Semitic glottal stops? It seems more likely that the Hawaiians were used to inserting glottal stops as they read, since few were then written; hence they read medial *aa* as *a'a*, *ae* as *a'e*, and *ee* as *e'e*.

Non-Biblical words from the Greek are the names for the letters *m* '*mū*' and *n* '*nū*'. Lists of Biblical words from the three ancient languages (other than proper names) may be obtained from Samuel H. Elbert.

A few Hawaiianized Christian names used by Catholics differ from those used by Protestants, and also from those used by both Catholics and Protestants. In the following list, which is far from exhaustive, the non-Hawaiian consonants sometimes used are listed below the Hawaiianized consonants:

Catholic Only	Protestant Only	Catholic and Protestant	English
'Ekualo		*'Elewaka*	'Edward'
d r		d d	
'Iokewe		*'Iokepa*	'Joseph'
s		s	
Kalolo		*Kale*	'Charles'
r			

Catholic Only	Protestant Only	Catholic and Protestant	English
Kelekuluke		*Kekaluka*	'Gertrude'
G rt r d		G t r d	
Keokolo		*Keokoa*	'Theodore'
T d r		T d	
Kepano	*Kekepana*		'Stephen'
T	S t		
Malaka		*Maleka*	'Martha'
r t		r t	
Pelenalako	*Pelenako*		'Bernard'
B r r d			

OTHER SOURCES

2.9.4   Few words have been introduced from other immigrant groups, the largest number probably being from the Chinese, who were the first to arrive in Hawai'i after the Europeans. The following words from Cantonese have been identified by Robert L. Cheng of the Department of East Asian Languages at the University of Hawai'i:

> *konohī* 'Chinese New Year' from *kong-hee* 'congratulations'
> *pakalana* 'Chinese violet' from *pak-lan* 'white orchid'
> *Pākē* 'Chinese' from *pak ye* 'father's older brother'

Kamakū, the name for a rice wine, is said to come from Cantonese *samshu* (or *samshoo*), identified by Knowlton (1955) as a Cantonese term written with two Chinese characters meaning 'thrice' + 'burned', referring to the fiery taste of the drink.

Others of uncertain origin are *kīpā*, a gambling game, said to be *chee-fa*, and *mikilana* 'Chinese rice flower' said to come from *mei-sui-lan*.

Mexican cowboys introduced the word *paniolo* from Spanish *Español*, with the meanings 'Spain, Spanish, cowboy'. From Portuguese *bacalhau* comes *pakaliao* 'codfish', and perhaps from Portuguese *Pascoa* came the Catholic name for Easter, *Pakoa*. From Portuguese or Spanish *rosario* 'rosary' may have come Hawaiian *lōkālio*. Loans from French include '*elemita* 'hermit', *Kalema* 'Lent', *livere* 'book', *poma* 'apple', and perhaps *Luwele* 'Louvre'. '*Anemoku* 'peninsula' is a translation of French *presqu'île*. None of the French loans except *Kalema* seems to have been much used.

Several loans come from Tahiti. Two of them may be recognized by the occurrence of a glottal stop in place of *ng* in other Polynesian languages such as Samoan:

Samoan *(ng)*	*manongi* 'fragrance'	*Lalotonga* 'Rarotonga'
Tahitian *(')*	*mono'i* 'perfume'	*Laloto'a* 'Rarotonga'
Hawaiian *(n)*	*mano'i* 'perfume'	*Lalato'a* 'Rarotonga'

(Vowel assimilation is common in Polynesian languages: note that Samoan *manongi* is *mono'i* in Tahitian; *Lalo-* in Samoan and Tahitian is *Lala-* in Hawaiian.) A famous wild banana in Tahitian is *hē'ī*; the same name is in Hawaiian as a variant of *mai'a Polapola* 'Tahitian banana'. A possible fourth Tahitian loan is *ka'aka* 'fellow, chap', an old slang term that may have come from Tahitian *ta'ata* 'man' that is cognate with Hawaiian *kanaka*.

The ancient name for Samoa is *Ha'amoa*, dating from Proto Polynesian times. Present-day *Kāmoa* must be a loan from English or from modern Sāmoa; the form inherited from Proto East Polynesian would have been *Hāmoa*.

RELATIVE FREQUENCIES OF SOUNDS

2.10   A computerized count of 3,347 sounds taken from legends in Elbert's *Fornander Selections*, prepared by Robert Hsu of the University of Hawai'i, revealed the following percentage frequencies:

a	22.2 %		
ā	2.7		
i	11.3	*k*	8.0 %
ī	0.7	'	7.2
o	7.9	*l*	6.6
ō	1.1	*h*	5.8
e	7.6	*n*	5.6
ē	0.1	*m*	3.9
u	5.8	*p*	2.1
ū	0.3	*w*	1.4
Totals	59.7 %		40.6 %

The frequency of the glottal stop (7.2%) is comparable to the frequency of *n* in English (7.24%), as found by Dewey in 1923 (quoted by Trnka 1966, p. 125) in a count of sound frequencies in 100,000 English words in connected writing.

34

Certain combinations of sounds are absent or rare. No base exists in the shape CV, but of course CV particles are common *(ka, ke, no, . . .)*. No base exists in the shape CV̄'V (cf. section 2.2). The sequence CV̄CV is not common, but does occur: *hāna, kāna, kāne, kōhi, kōmi, māhu, māka, māki, māla, māna, māno, māpu, nāna, pāka, wāhi.* Of these, *māka, māki,* and *pāka* are English loans.

According to Krupa (1971:670), the most common shape for morphs in any Polynesian language is (C)V(C)V (by "morphs" he seems to mean bases or parts of bases). One or both of the vowels in CVCV words may be long. A study was made of the utilization of CVCV, CV̄CV, CVCV̄, and CV̄CV̄ in native words, but only those utilizing *three* or *four* of the four possible shapes were counted. Only one series was found with all four: *nana, nānā, nanā, nāna.* For CVCV, CV̄CV, and CVCV̄ shapes see in the Dictionary the following entries and the two entries just below each of them: *'a'a, hehe, huhu, 'i'i, keke, kika, kiki, koki, koko, kuku, mo'i, na'u, paku, papa, pa'u, pipi, 'uki.* Two series consist of CVCV, CV̄CV̄, and CV̄CV shapes: *hana, hānā, Hāna;* and *mana, mānā, māna.* Two series consist of CVCV, CVCV̄, CV̄CV shapes: *mano, manō, māno;* and *wahi, wahī, wāhi.* Only one was noted with CV̄CV, CV̄CV̄, and CVCV̄ shapes: *māhu, māhū, mahū.*

Krupa (1966:463–464) found 1,029 CVCV forms in the Hawaiian Dictionary, which is 50.81 percent of the 2,025 possible Hawaiian bi-vocalic forms. He found that most frequently the same vowels occurred, but different consonants. (He was not distinguishing long and short vowels.) Note that in the 15 CV̄CV words the same vowels exist in 7 forms, different consonants in all except *nāna.* Of the 17 forms taking CVCV, CV̄CV̄, and CVCV̄ shapes, 10 have the same vowels, but only 6 have different consonants.

DRIFT

2.11   Drift is taken to mean the direction in which changes in the language are going. Certain changes from inherited forms are not complete, but are on-going. Some of these have been mentioned before; they are summarized in table 6. The "most common forms" in the table, except for *l,* represent Hawaiian innovations.

A glottal stop is called a vestigial form of common *l* on the premise (by no means proven) that there existed a Proto

35

TABLE 6
Hawaiian Drift

Proto Central Polynesian	Hawaiian		Reference Section
	Most Common Form	Vestigial Form†	
*t	k	t	2.8
*k	'	k	2.8
*l	l	'	2.8
*te (article)	ka	ke	10.2
*faCa- (in caus-ative *faka- and in *fanga- 'bay')	hoʻo-, Hono-	haʻa-, Hana-	6.3.1, 6.4, 8.1

†In place of "vestigial" Chen and Wang (1975:257) used the terms *drift, retarded remnants,* and *belated cases.*

Marquesan–Hawaiian stage before the separation of the two languages, that is, that at one time Marquesan and Hawaiian were one language, until finally the Hawaiians moved north. Marquesan today has only the glottal stop as a reflex of Proto East Polynesian (PEP) *l* and sometimes *k* (if we can believe the Dordillon dictionary), but in Proto Marquesan–Hawaiian time perhaps the two reflexes of PEP *l* existed side by side (cf. section 2.8.2).

Another feature apparently shared only with Marquesan consists of the rare possessives *kā ia, kō ia,* and *nā ia* 'by him', now almost entirely replaced by reflexes of Proto Central Polynesian *taana, toona,* and *naana.*

NOTES ON ORTHOGRAPHY

2.12   Differences between common pronunciations and orthography as used in this Grammar and in the Dictionary are mentioned frequently in this study. Important deviations will be summarized here, as well as some general spelling rules.

(1) The changes mentioned by Kinney (1956) and discussed in section 2.7 are not reflected in the spelling, even those that occurred in 100 percent of her informants' speech, as *leila* or *lila* for *laila, keikuaʻana* for *kaikuaʻana,* and *keikunāne* for *kaikunāne.* Such pronunciations are never sung, and have never appeared in print, according to our observations.

(2) The *w*-glides after *o* and *u,* described in section 2.1, are predictable, but have appeared in the Hawaiian Bible and other published matter.

(3) The Hawaiian Bible *(Ka Baibala)* uses an apostrophe to indicate a glottal stop in a few words, for example, *ko'u, ka'u, o'u, a'u* 'mine', *ia'u* 'me', and *no'u, na'u* 'for me', and the same symbol as indication of a dropped vowel, in the manner of English *can't*. This is common (a) with the directionals *aku* and *a'e* (section 7.2): *e lawe pio ia'ku* [that is, *'ia aku*] (Ieremia 28.6) 'capturing', *i ka ninau ana'e* [*'ana a'e*] (Na Lii I 1.6), 'the questions'; (b) with the anaphoric *ai* (section 7.3): *ka olelo maikai ia e hooluoluia'i* [*hō'olu'olu 'ia ai*] (Na Solomona 12.25), 'a good word maketh it glad'; (c) with the common nouns *akua* 'god' and *ali'i* 'chief': *na'kua* [*nā akua*] 'the gods', *na'lii* [*nā ali'i*] (Isaia 32.11) 'the chiefs'. (The apostrophe was not used in the title of the Book of Kings.)

Andrews (1854:21) recommends such use of the apostrophe as a marker of elision, but it is frowned upon in the present study because of confusion with the glottal stop. One rule in Hawaiian will take care of the dropped *a:* *a+a* becomes *a* (as in the sequences illustrated above: *'ia aku, 'ana a'e, 'ia ai, nā akua, nā ali'i*).

For another, somewhat different but equally unsatisfactory use of the apostrophe, see section 6.6.2.

(4) Hyphens are used in proper names in the Dictionary and in this Grammar to separate the component parts in order to facilitate pronunciation and comprehension, but the pauses they mark do not necessarily occur in fast, natural speech (see section 2.3) and need not always be used. The Dictionary uses hyphens also to separate the component parts in names of winds, rains, stars, *lua* fighting holds, and tapa and mat designs:

Kuehu-lepo,   a wind associated with Ka'ū, Hawai'i (lit., dust-stirring)
Kani-lehua,   a rain associated with Hilo (lit., *lehua* rustling)
Hōkū-pa'a   'North Star' (lit., unmovable star)
'Alapa'i-a-ka-'ōpae,   a *lua* fighting hold (lit., ladder of the shrimp)
iwi-puhi,   a tapa design (lit., eel bone)
hōkū-helele'i,   a mat design (lit., falling star)

Most of these names are descriptive, poetic, or fanciful. Wind and rain names are frequently, but not always, preceded by *makani* and *ua*.

The names of plants and animals are written as single, unhyphenated words if the meaning of the whole is not decipherable from the meaning of the parts:

> *manulele,* a variety of sugarcane (lit., flying bird)
> *nūkea,* a mudhen (lit., white bill)
> *pānini* 'cactus' (lit., fence wall)
> *po'ouli,* a honeycreeper (lit., black head)

Similarly with many other words:

> *kūkaepele* 'match' (lit., volcanic excreta)
> *laholio* 'rubber' (lit., horse scrotum)
> *ulepua'a* and *wilipua'a* 'corkscrew' (lit., pig penis and pig twist)

Hyphens are inserted, however, in names of plants that consist of more than a single phrase:

> *'ai-a-ka-nēnē,* a plant (lit., food of the goose)
> *mo'opuna-a-ka-līpoa,* a seaweed (lit., grandchild of the *līpoa* [another seaweed])

(5) The parts in names of plants and animals that consist of a single base followed by one or more than one qualifier are written as separate words:

> *maile lau li'i* 'large-leafed *maile*'
> *maile lau nui* 'large-leafed *maile*'
> *'iole li'ili'i* 'mouse' (lit., small quadruped)
> *'iole pua'a* 'guinea pig' (lit., pig quadruped)
> *koa'e kea* 'white-tailed tropic bird'
> *koa'e 'ula* 'red-tailed tropic bird'

The same rule applies to place names, such as Mauna Kea and Mauna Loa and Ko'olau Loa and Ko'olau Poko.

Other orthographic conventions. The subject-marking preposition *'o* is separated from a following head word, except that it is joined to the third person singular pronoun *('oia),* and usually but not always to the second person singular pronoun. The object-marking preposition *iā* is joined to the first person singular pronoun *(ia'u),* usually to the third person pronoun *(iāia),* and sometimes to the second person pronoun *(iā'oe).* The passive/imperative *'ia* is often written joined to a preceding base, but this is not done in the Dictionary for reasons given in section 6.6.3.

As mentioned in section 2.3, *ho'o-* and *Hana-* form a separate stress group, but conventionally they are written joined to a following head word. Similarly we write *kanaono (kana.ono)* 'sixty' and *kanaiwa (kana.iwa)* 'ninety'.

38

3   From Sentence to Affix

3.1   Sentences are sequences bordered by periods, question marks, or exclamation points. In Hawaiian they can be thought of as **simple, verbless,** or **complex.** The most common simple sentence consists of verb phrase ± noun phrase(s). Verb phrases contain verbs as their heads; verbs are defined on the basis of potential occurrence with the particles marking aspect, especially *ua* (perfective aspect). Noun phrases contain nouns or substitutes for nouns; these are names of persons or places, or are defined on the basis of potential occurrence after the article *ka/ke* (definite), or the preposition *ma* 'at'.

     Five simple sentences follow. Each of them begins with a verb phrase followed by a noun phrase which functions as subject. The functions of the noun phrases are defined. (Double bars separate phrases; alternate translations are separated by slashes.)

(Verb phrase)		*(Subject phrase)*		*(Locative phrase)*	
(1) *Ua*	*hele*‖	*ke*	*kanaka*‖	*i*	*Maui.*
(perf.)	go	the	man	to	Maui

'The man went to Maui./The man has gone to Maui.'

(Verb phrase)		*(Subject phrase)*		*(Object phrase)*		
(2) *Ua*	*'ai*‖	*ke*	*kanaka*‖	*i*	*ka*	*poi.*
(perf.)	eat	the	man	(obj.	the	poi
				marker)		

'The man ate the poi./The man has eaten the poi.'

(Verb phrase)				*(Subject phrase)*	
(3) *Ua*	*'ā-*	*pono*	*'ia*‖	*kēia*	*pila.*
(perf.)	(caus.)	proper	(pas/imp.)	this	bill

'This bill was approved./This bill has been approved.'

(Verb phrase)			*(Subject phrase)*	*(Agentive phrase)*		
(4) *Ua*	*'ai*	*'ia*‖	*ka poi*‖	*e*	*ka*	*wilikī.*
(perf.)	eat	(pas/imp.)	the poi	by	the	turnkey

'The poi was eaten by the engineer./The engineer ate the poi.'

(Verb phrase)		*(Subject phrase)*		*(Agentive phrase)*		
(5) *Ua*	*loa'a*‖	*ke kumu*	*kula*‖	*i*	*ka māka'i*	*'eleu.*
(perf.)	catch	the teacher	school	by	the policeman	alert

'The school teacher was caught by the alert policeman./The alert policeman caught the school teacher.'

Sentences (3), (4), and (5) are translated by the passive voice. In (3) and (4) the passive is marked by the particle *'ia*, but in (5) the passive is unmarked. *Loa'a* in this sentence is neither intransitive nor transitive, unlike the verbs in the other sentences, but is *stative*. The distinction is discussed at some length in chapter 4.

The usual order for simple sentences, as illustrated above, is verb phrase ± noun phrase(s). The initial verb phrase of any of the sentences above (or the verb alone) could constitute a sentence without the noun phrase. The second noun phrase in sentences (1), (2), (4), and (5) could directly follow the verb phrase, perhaps with attendant focus upon them, but this order is less usual than that shown above. *Wilikī* at the end of sentence (4) is a compound, and its meaning is not obvious from the meanings of its two constituents (*wili* 'to turn' and *kī* 'key', a loan from English).

Another type of sentence may be called **verbless** or **equational**. It contains one or more noun phrases and no verb phrase:

(6) *He*	*kumu*	*au.*
a	teacher	I

'I'm a teacher.'

The last noun phrase, *au*, could be deleted.

Complex sentences have more than one verb phrase, or contain noun phrases that can be most effectively explained as *underlying* verbless sentences. In English "That's the thing I wanted" would be considered a complex sentence consisting of two underlying simple sentences: "That's the thing. I wanted the thing." In Hawaiian "That's the thing" would be a verbless sentence *('Oia ka mea)*, and the second sentence would be *Ua makemake au i ka mea.* The two together would be *'Oia ka mea a'u i makemake ai.* Although the sentence contains only one verb phrase *(i makemake ai)*, it nevertheless would be considered

40

TABLE 7
Hawaiian Phrases

Preposed Elements

	± Prepositions (9)	± Determiners:* Articles (10.2) Demonstratives (8.3) Possessives (8.4) Others (10.1)	± Numerals (10.3)	± Particles (7.1, 7.5)	± φ-possessives (8.4)	± Plurals + (10.4)
Noun phrase						
Verb phrase	Verb markers (5)					

Nuclear Elements

	Noun (8.1) Substitutes:* Pronouns (8.2) Demonstratives (8.3) Possessives (8.4) Interrogatives (8.5)	± *mā* (8.7.5)	± Vocatives (9.10)	± Compound members or qualifiers (8.7)	±
Noun phrase					
Verb phrase	Verb (4)				

Postposed Elements

	Particles (7.1) including *'ia* (6.6.3)	± *'ana* (6.6.2)	± Directionals (7.2)	± *ai* (7.3) or φ-Demonstratives (7.4)	± Particles (7.5)
Noun or verb phrase					

* Items listed under Determiners and Substitutes are mutually exclusive. Numbers in parentheses refer to sections of this Grammar.

complex because the initial noun phrase is most effectively explained as outlined above. Such processes are explained in section 11.2.

PHRASES

3.2   Table 7 is a diagram of a Hawaiian phrase. The three possible elements in a phrase may be termed preposed, nuclear, and postposed. Every phrase contains a noun or noun substitute or a verb as its head or nucleus and may be flanked on both sides as indicated in the diagram.

Some phrases consist of single words, especially in verbless sentences, as illustrated below. Double bars separate the phrases.

Ma'ane'i‖ ka hale.
here   the house
'The house is here.'

Pēlā‖   kāna   kama'ilio   'ana.
like that   his   chat   (nominalizer)
'That's the way he chatted.'

Examples follow of long phrases taken from Moses Nakuina's rewriting (1901) of the legend of Pāka'a. This important work was influenced by English literary style; perhaps this is one reason for his many long phrases. These two phrases have been selected to illustrate postpositional elements in noun phrases (ho'i, ho'okahi, 'ia, mai, nei, kā, ho'i) and in verb phrases (mua, 'ia, a'e, nei). The order of these elements does not change. The grammatical categories, in parentheses, can be found in table 7.

Noun Phrases

1		2	3		
'Oia'i'o	ho'i‖	'o	ka	ho'oku'u	ho'okahi
(noun)	(particle: intensifier)	(prep.: subj. marker)	(article)	(noun)	(qualifier)
truth			the	permit	alone

				2	
'ia	mai	nei	kā ho'i	‖ ia	
(part.)	(directional)	(φ-demonstr.)	(particles)	(φ-demonstr.)	
		here			

4			
o	ke	keiki . . . (Nakuina 11)	
(prep.: possessive)	(article)	(noun)	
of	the	child	

'So actually, the child was permitted to be alone . . .'

This portion of a longer sentence contains four noun phrases. Phrase 3 is embedded within phrase 2.

42

Verb Phrases and Noun Phrase

1		2		3	
. . . e	*like*	‖*me*	*ia*‖	*i*	*ha'i*
(verb	(verb)	(prep.: sim.)	(φ-	(verb	(verb)
marker: mood)			demonstr.)	marker: perf.)	
		like		this		tell

mua	*'ia*	*a'e*	*nei* . . . (Nakuina 7)	
(qualifier)	(particle:	(directional)	(φ-demonstr.)	
	pas/imp.)			
before			recently	

'. . . as has just been told . . .'

Phrases 1 and 3 are verb phrases; phrase 2 is a noun phrase.

WORDS

3.3   The next smallest element, after the phrase, is the word, or **lexical item**. These may be classified as follows:

> **Nouns:** names of persons, places, or things; potential occurrence after the articles *ka/ke*, *nā*, and *he*, or after such prepositions as the locative *ma*.

> **Verbs:** potential occurrence after the aspect markers *ua* and *e* (+verb + *ana*). Verbs are subdivided into five classes, as outlined in section 4.

> **Noun-verbs:** verbs commonly used as nouns without the nominalizer *'ana*.
> **Substitutes**
>   Pronouns
>   Demonstratives
>   Possessives
>   Interrogatives
> **Prepositions**
> **Conjunctions**
> **Numerals**
> **Interjections**
> **Idioms:** words not otherwise classifiable

Readers new to linguistics may be shocked to learn that adjectives and adverbs are lacking in the analysis just presented. The shock is due to the fact that most persons think in terms of their mother tongue. In English, adjectives are formally determined: they inflect for comparative and superlative degree *(big, bigger, biggest)* or may be preceded by *more* and *most (serious, more serious, most serious)*. No such criteria exist in Hawaiian. *Big* is an adjective in English; but this does not make it an adjective in Hawaiian. It is easy to understand that the need to analyze in terms of the Hawaiian language rather than in terms of one's mother tongue is a major yet not unsurmountable hurdle.

PARTICLES

3.4   An important category in Hawaiian is the particle. Particles are not called lexical items because most of them are not intelligible if used alone. Particles, furthermore, do not occur as nuclei of phrases, but are nearly always subordinate to nuclei. They may be classified as follows, according to position within phrases: (1) particles at or near the beginnings of noun phrases, (2) particles at the beginnings of verb phrases, (3) particles following nouns and verbs.

Particles of types (1) and (2) usually denote grammatical meaning. They are the machinery of the language and indicate whether accompanying words are nouns or verbs; whether action is completed or going on; whether a noun is subject, object, agent, possessor, locative, or instrumental—the sort of information that in Latin or Greek is often given by inflected endings. Particles of type (3) have either grammatical meaning *('ia, 'ana)* or meanings in the real (as contrasted with the grammatical) universe. Perhaps they are less troublesome to students than are the others.

AFFIXES

3.5   The only grammatical process in Hawaiian is affixation, that is, the addition of prefixes, infixes, and suffixes to bases. (Bases occupy the nucleus position in phrases.) Only sentence (3) in section 3.1 contains an affix, the causative prefix *'a*. Suffixes are discussed in sections 6.5 and 6.6. The only infix in the language is a lengthening of the third from the final vowel in ten kinship terms (section 8.1). Another type of affixation is by reduplication (section 6.2).

Affixes, like particles, are unintelligible when used alone, but

44

differ from particles in that they are closely bound to bases. Other bases or particles may intervene between base and particle: both *hoe wale* 'just paddle' and *hoe wa'a wale* 'just canoe paddle' are grammatical. But the verb *ho'o-hā-like-like* 'to resemble' contains the base *like* and three prefixes. No base or particle can separate these prefixes.

Bases plus affixes are called **derivatives**.

4 Classification of Verbs; Verblike Idioms

BASIS OF THE CLASSIFICATION

4.1   The classification presented in table 8 is similar in most respects to that of Wilson (1976), which itself was a modification of the classification used by Pukui and Elbert (1957). A classification prepared by Hawkins (1975) resembles the present one in that her major division is between action-marking and condition-marking verbs (her terms are *process* versus *state*), but the subdivisions are somewhat different. The subdivisions we propose are briefly illustrated below, but fuller explanations of the diagnostic particles and bases are given in the sections listed in the table. Hawkins pointed out that the subdivisions are arbitrary and represent a continuum, rather than sharp cuts. This is clearly indicated in section 4.4: some of the *loaʻa*-stative verbs are action-marking. Hawkins also suggested that the verbs in the leftmost major division tend to indicate time, whereas those on the right tend to be timeless.

Probably all verbs can be followed by the nominalizer *ʻana*, which transforms them into nouns, as *kona hele ʻana mai* 'his coming'. Many verbs, however, function as nouns without nominalizers, as *ʻaʻā* 'to burn' and a type of lava; *ʻaʻahu* 'to put on clothing, clothing'; *makaʻu* 'to fear, fear'; *mele* 'to sing, song'; *ʻōlelo* 'to speak, language'; *oli* 'to chant, chant'; *pilikia* 'to be in trouble, trouble'. These are called noun-verbs.

The following new abbreviations are used in table 8.

	Model	Section
vi: intransitive verb	*hele*	4.2
vtd: deliberate transitive verb	*ʻai*	4.3
vtsp: spontaneous transitive verb	*aloha*	4.3
vsadj: adjectival stative verb	*maikaʻi*	4.4
vsl: *loaʻa* stative verb	*loaʻa*	4.4

TABLE 8
Classification of Verbs

	Action-marking		Condition-marking		
	vi *(hele)*	vtd *('ai)*	vtsp *(aloha)*	vsadj *(maika'i)*	vsl *(loa'a)*
Preceded by					
imperative *e/ø, ō, mai* (5.4)	+	+	+	rare	+
possession *a* (9.6.2)	rare	+	−†	−	−, +
possession *o* (9.6.2)	+	+	+	+	+
na, agentive (9.11)	rare	+	+	−	−
ua as present (5.2)	−	−	+	+	+, −
ua as perfective (5.2)	+	+	−	−	−
mai 'almost' (5.4)	rare	rare	rare	rare	+
Followed by					
pas/imp. *'ia* (6.6.3)	+	+	+	rare	rare
i/iā, direct object (9.3.1)	−	+	+	rare	rare
i/iā, agent, cause (9.3.1)	−	−	−	+	+
Occurrence with place names					
i, direct object (9.3.1)	−	−	−	−	−
iā, direct object, causal (9.3.1)	−	+	+	−	−
Occurrence with following bases					
Nui, intensifier (8.7.5)	−	+	+	rare	rare
loa, intensifier (8.7.5)	−	+	rare	+	+

NOTE: Model verbs follow the five subheadings in parentheses. Numbers in parentheses in the first column refer to sections of this Grammar.

† But does occur with nominalizer *'ana.*

The salient features of this rather confusing table may be summarized as follows:

(1) v (all types): may be preceded by *ua*; v + noun is classified as v *(hoe wa'a).*

(2) vi: may be preceded by *ua* as perfective marker; not followed by object marker but may be followed by *'ia*; nvi (noun + vi) may take possessive *a* (*ke kani a ka moa* 'the crowing of the chicken'); action-marking.

(3) vtd, vtsp: may be preceded by *ua* and followed by object marker; take *'ia*; vtd is action-marking, vtsp condition-marking.

(4) vsadj, vsl: may be preceded by *ua* as present marker; rarely followed by *'ia* or object marker; takes possessive *o* (*ka nani o ka moa* 'the beauty of the chicken'); condition-marking.

Full comprehension of table 8 and the above will not be possible until the sections of this Grammar referred to in the table have been studied.

INTRANSITIVE VERBS (vi)

4.2   By definition intransitive verbs do not take direct objects. They do take affirmative and negative imperative markers (*E hele 'oe.* 'Go.' *Mai hele 'oe.* 'Don't go.') and the passive/imperative (*Ua hele 'ia ke ala e ke kanaka.* 'The road was traveled by the man.'). They most commonly take the *o*-class possessive (*kona hele 'ana* 'his going'), but see section 9.6.2 for use with *a* possessives. *Ua hele aku* is usually translated by a past tense: '[He] went away.' Intransitive verbs take neither *nui* nor *loa* as intensifiers (*hele loa* means 'to go far', *not* 'to go a great deal').

The intransitive verb *hele* in the previous sentences may be replaced by such verbs of motion as *'au* 'to swim', *ho'i* 'to go back', *iho* 'to go down', or *pi'i* 'to climb'.

For use with *mai* 'almost', see section 5.4.

TRANSITIVE VERBS (vt)

4.3   The most obvious characteristic of transitive verbs is that they take direct objects (*'Ai 'oia i ka poi* 'He ate the poi.') The transitive verbs are divided into two classes labeled **deliberate** (vtd) and **spontaneous** (vts); alternant names are **voluntary** and **involuntary**. Their principal difference concerns possessives: the deliberate transitives most commonly take the possessive *a (kāna 'ai 'ana* 'his eating', *kāna wehewehe 'ana* 'his explanation'; the spontaneous possessives take *o (kona aloha* 'his love', *kona mana'o* 'his opinion'). Deliberate transitives include such action-marking verbs as *hana* 'do, make', *inu* 'drink', *nānā* 'look at'. Spontaneous transitives include *makemake* 'want', *no'ono'o* 'think', *'ike* 'see, know'. *Ua inu 'oia i ka lama* would usually be translated by a past tense: 'He drank the rum.' *Ua makemake 'oia i ka lama* might be translated by a present tense: 'He likes rum.'

The two types agree in usage as follows:

(1) After imperatives: *E 'ai 'oe i ka poi.* 'Eat the poi.' *E aloha 'oe i kou mau mākua.* 'Love your parents.'

(2) After *na*, agentive: *Na ke Akua i hana i nā mea.* 'God made the things.' *Nāna i no'ono'o pēlā.* 'He thought that way.'

(3) After *'ia: 'ai 'ia* 'eaten', *aloha 'ia* 'loved'.

(4) After directionals: *Inu iho i ka lama.* 'Drink the rum.' *No'ono'o iho i ka pānina.* 'Think about the answer.'

(5) Before place names: *Ha'alele iā Ni'ihau.* 'Leave Ni'ihau.' *Aloha iā Ni'ihau.* 'Love Ni'ihau.'

(6) Before *nui:* '*ai nui* 'eat a lot', *aloha nui* 'much aloha'.

For use with *mai* 'almost', see section 5.4.

STATIVE VERBS (vs)

4.4   This term was probably first used with reference to a Polynesian language when Buse in 1965 applied it to Rarotongan. The term caught on with other Polynesianists. Lyons (1969:315) says that the "most striking characteristic" of stative verbs is that "they refer to a state of affairs, rather than to an action, event, or process." In Hawaiian the statives are the most common of all verbs.

As previously mentioned, there is no formally distinguished class of adjective or of adverb in Hawaiian. Words performing as English adjectives and adverbs are stative verbs in Hawaiian. Good, well, happy, happily, sick, sickly, red, hot, cold, are verbs: all can occur after the perfective *ua*, which is diagnostic for verbs (section 3.3). Statives also frequently follow noun and verb bases: *he kanaka maika'i* 'a good man', *ua hana maika'i* 'did work well', *he keiki hau'oli* 'a happy child', *ua pā'ani hau'oli nō lākou* 'they played quite happily'. Such words are called **adjectival statives** (vsadj).

A much smaller class of stative verbs, but of much-used ones, is called **loa'a-type** (vsl). It is illustrated below.

The most easily identifiable characteristic of stative verbs is that ordinarily they are not followed by the passive/imperative '*ia* (section 6.6.3); this is especially true of the adjectival statives. A few examples will be given later of *loa'a*-type statives taking '*ia*. Another diagnostic feature is that both types of statives usually take the *o*-possessive (*kona maika'i* 'his goodness', *kona make* 'his death'). But as shown in table 8, vsl verbs sometimes take the possessive *a*, as in *kāna make* 'his killing [of someone]'. Both types of statives may be followed by agentive or locative phrases introduced by *i/iā*.

The three most common *loa'a*-type verbs are probably *hiki* 'able', *loa'a* 'find, get', and *maopopo* 'understand'. *Ola* 'to live, save' is also common.

　　　(Agentive phrase)
Hiki ‖　*ia'u* ‖　　　*ke　hele.*
able　　to-me　　　　to　go
'I can go.'

(Agentive phrase)
Loaʻa ‖ *ka*   *ʻaihue* ‖ *i*   *ka*   *mākaʻi*.
catch   the thief   by   the   policeman
'The policeman caught the thief.'

(Agentive phrase)
Maopopo ‖ *kēlā*   *mea* ‖ *iāia*.
understand that (far) thing   to-him
'He understands that thing.'

(Agentive phrase)
Ola ‖ *ka*   *mōʻī* ‖ *i*   *ke*   *Akua*.
live   the   king   by   the   god
'God save the king.'

A few other examples of common *loaʻa*-statives follow. Their English translations vary according to context, sometimes using passive voice and sometimes active, and sometimes both transitive and intransitive. Usually the preposition *i/iā* is translated as agent. *Ua ʻeha au* 'I'm in pain' and *ʻeha au iāʻoe* 'you hurt me'. *Ua hina ʻoia* 'he fell' and *ua hina ʻoia i ke kanaka ikaika* 'the strong man threw him' or 'he was thrown by the strong man'; *ua make ʻoia* 'he died' and *ua makeʻoia iaʻu* 'I killed him'. *Eo* can mean either 'win' or 'lose': *nā ʻai eo* 'the winning points' and *eo au iāʻoe* 'you defeat me'.

Other common *loaʻa*- statives include *hemo, hewa, kū, lilo, makala, pā, paʻa, pau, punahele, puni*. See examples in the Dictionary.

Traditionally the passive/imperative marker *ʻia* was not used with *loaʻa*-statives, which are inherently passive. Some examples: *puni i ka makaʻu* 'overcome with fear', *pau i ka ʻai ʻia* 'consumed by being eaten', *ua nalowale ka poi i nehinei* 'the poi was lost yesterday'.

Some Hawaiian speakers seem now to be treating some of the *loaʻa*-stative verbs as transitives. They may say *maopopo au* 'I understand' instead of *maopopo iaʻu*, *hiki nō ʻoe* 'you can' instead of *hiki nō iāʻoe*, and might translate the *loaʻa*-sentence (previously cited) *loaʻa ka ʻaihue i ka mākaʻi* 'the thief caught the policeman'. This change is perhaps common on Niʻihau, and is noticeable in Guy and Pamela Buffet's story of Kama-puaʻa (1972), as told mostly by a lady from Niʻihau.

Another way in which some speakers transitivize statives is by use of *ʻia: ʻEha ʻia koʻu lima.* 'My hand was hurt.' This may be a response to the English need of a passive voice. Both are examples of leveling (regularizing of anomalies). Other examples noted with *'ia:*

> *Ua wela 'ia kona 'ā'ī i ka pauka* (Kelekona 95). 'His neck was burned with powder.'

> *Ua nui loa 'ia kona inaina* (Kelekona 147). 'His wrath was very great.'

> *Ua lo'ohia 'ia au me kekahi pō'ino* (Kelekona 110). 'I was overtaken by a misfortune.'

> *Ua 'ikea wale 'ia nō* (Kelekona 111). 'I was just seen.'

Statives take *loa* rather than *nui: make loa* 'completely dead', *maika'i loa* 'very good'.

For use of statives with directionals, see section 7.2.

It is sometimes difficult to distinguish statives and intransitives. In general, as previously noted, intransitives are time words and mark actions, and statives are timeless and mark conditions or states. Statives usually take the possessive *o;* intransitives take *a* and less commonly *o* (see section 9.6.2); or one may test with the nominalizer *'ana:*

Statives: *ka nani o ka wahine* 'the beauty of the woman', *ka 'eha 'ana o ko'u lima* 'the pain of my hand'.

Intransitives: *ka lele a ka wahine* 'the jump of the woman', *ka hele 'ana a ka wahine* 'the woman's going'.

Sequences of verbs (or noun-verbs) are classified as having the part of speech of the last verb. The sequence *'imi ā loa'a* 'to keep looking until found' consists of the deliberate transitive verb *'imi* and the stative *loa'a*. The sequence is a stative, as shown by the lack of an object marker in the sentence *'imi ā loa'a ka waiwai* 'strive until [you] obtain wealth'.

MULTIPLE-CLASS VERBS

4.5   A few verbs belong to more than one class. A conspicuous example is the common word *aloha*. In its meaning 'to greet' it is a deliberate transitive; in its meaning 'to love, have compassion or pity' it is a spontaneous transitive, and as a greeting it is a *loa'a*-stative.

> vtd: *Aloha au iā'oe.* 'I greet you.' *Aloha 'o 'Aukai iā Maka.* ' 'Aukai greets Maka.' *Aloha 'ia nō 'o Maui.* 'Maui is indeed greeted.'

51

vtsp: The same sentences would be translated 'I love you./I pity you.' ' 'Aukai loves Maka./'Aukai has pity for Maka.' 'Maui is indeed loved./Maui is indeed pitied.'

vsl: As a greeting, *aloha* is followed by a subject that is the object of the love, as (1) *Aloha 'oe!* (2) *Aloha kāua!* (3) *Aloha kākou!* The verbs *aloha* in these three sentences have passive meanings and are followed by pronoun subjects: (1) 'May you (sing.) be loved! Hello!' (2) 'May there be love between the two of us! Greetings (to one person, as in the opening of a letter).' (3) 'May there be love among us (more than two)! Greetings (to more than two)!'

The lecherous pig-god, Kama-pua'a, ends thus a mocking chant addressed to his antagonist, Pele:

Aloha   ka   wahine   o   ka   lua (FS 225).
be greeted the lady   of the pit
'Greetings, lady of the pit.'

Komo and *mama*, illustrated below, occur most commonly as deliberate transitives. The stative uses are idiomatic.

Deliberate transitive use of *komo:*

> *(Object phrase)*
> *Komo‖   i   ka   lole.*
> put on   (obj.) the dress
> 'Put on the dress.'
> *Komo‖   'ia   ka   lole.*
> put on   (pas.) the dress
> 'The dress was put on; put on the dress.'

Loa'a-stative use of *komo:*

> *(Agentive phrase)*
> *Komo‖   ka   wa'a‖   i   ka   i'a.*
> fill   the canoe   by the fish
> 'The canoe is filled with fish.'

Deliberate transitive use of *mama:*

> *(Object phrase)*
> *Mama‖   i   ka   'awa.*
> 'Chew the kava.'

Loaʻa-stative use of *mama:*
   Mama‖ ka ʻawa.
   chew   the   kava
   'The kava is chewed.'

It may be that such utterances as *komo ka waʻa, mama ka ʻawa,* and *kālua ka puaʻa* 'bake the pig' are a stylistic device that imparts terseness and, semantically, a sense of admirable speed. Or the entire utterance may be thought of as a compound; there may be a drift in the language toward elimination of object markers.

The common verb *lilo* seems to behave as a deliberate transitive with the meaning 'to become' and as a *loaʻa*-stative with the meaning 'to accrue':

Transitive:

Mai lilo i ʻaihue. 'Don't become a thief.'

E lilo i kumu. 'Become a teacher.'

Ua lawe a lilo ʻia ka ipo. 'The sweetheart was carried off and lost.'

Stative:

Ua lilo ke kālā i ka ʻaihue. 'The money accrued to the thief./ The thief got the money.'

Mai lilo ke kālā i ka ʻaihue. 'The thief almost got the money.'

Ua lilo ʻoia ke poʻo . . . i ka home (Kelekona 122). 'She became the head . . . of the home.'

Make 'die' is a *loaʻa*-stative verb:

                            (Agentive phrase)
Ua   make‖   ke   keiki‖   iā   Pele.
(perf.) die   the   child   by   Pele
'The child was killed by Pele./ Pele killed the child.'

However, in a long chant in which the pig man Kama-puaʻa lists his victories (FS 234–239), *make* is used as a deliberate transitive verb 'to defeat': *Make ke kaua iā ʻOlopana.* 'The warrior defeats ʻOlopana.' (Perhaps the chanter whispered the causative *[hoʻo-]* part of *hoʻo-make,* the transitive transformation!)

VERBLIKE IDIOMS

4.6   The few members of this class generally occur at the beginning of sentences as do verbs. Most of them do not follow aspect markers, nor do they reduplicate, and most of them do not passivize. They do not take the verb affixes listed in section 6.1. Some of them, however, are followed by particles that follow verbs, especially the intensifier *nō*, as illustrated below. They can be called idioms.

Lyons (1969:177) avoided the term *idiom*, and borrowed from de Saussure the term *ready-made utterances*, described as "a further category of utterances or parts of utterances which resemble 'incomplete' sentences in that they do not correspond directly to sentences generated by the grammar, but differ from them in that their description does not involve the application of the rules established to account for the vast mass of more 'normal' utterances. These are what de Saussure has called 'ready-made utterances' *(locutions toutes faites)*, expressions which are learned as unanalysable wholes and employed on particular occasions by native speakers. An example from English is *How do you do?*"

Some Hawaiian examples:

(1) *Aia* 'there is'
    Aia ka hale ma'ō. 'There's the house over there.'
    Aia nō ia iā'oe. 'That's up to you' (lit., there indeed it to you).
    Aia ka'u puke iā Kū. 'Kū has my book' (lit., there is my book to Kū).

(2) *Eia* 'here is, here'
    Eia a'e 'o Pua. 'Here comes Pua.'
    Eia 'oe ke hō'ike 'ia aku nei . . . 'You are hereby notified . . .'
    Kō mākou noho 'ana me Pua mā, eia aku nō ā eia mai. 'Our home and that of Pua and [her] family, close by.'
    Eia ho'i, ua hewa! 'Behold, there's sin!'

(3) *'Auhea* means 'where' in questions, but is used idiomatically as a command, 'listen': *'Auhea wale ana 'oe.* 'Now listen.'

(4) *'Ānō* 'now' is described in section 7.5. Followed by *iho* and *iho nei* it occurs as an idiom:
    'Ānō iho, e hiki mai ana. 'Soon, [he] will come.'
    'ānō wale iho nei nō 'just a short time ago, recently'

(5) *'Akahi* 'first time, never before, to have just' is followed by an optional subject and an optional verb phrase introduced by the conjunction *ā* or by a verb marker:

'Akahi nō 'oe ā hiki ma'ane'i? 'Is this the first time you have come here?'

'Akahi nō ā pau ka'u ha'awina. 'My lesson is just finished.'

'Akahi nō au i hele i laila. 'This is the first time I've gone there./I've never gone there before.'

'Akahi ka le'a o ku'u inoa iā'oe (FS 235). '[I've never heard] you [sing] my name song so amusingly before.'

Compare *'akahi 'akahi* 'inexperienced'.

(6) *Kainō* and *kainoa* 'I thought, I supposed, why not' are followed by verb phrases:

Kainō ua hele 'oe. 'I thought you had gone.'

Kainō ho'i e hele mai 'olua? 'Why don't you two come?'

(7) *Aho* 'better' occurs only after the imperative/exhortative *e:*

E aho ia. 'That's better.'

E aho nō ia, hala nō ka lā. 'It's good enough, the day passes (It's good enough for the needs of the day).'

E aho ka hele 'ana mamua o ka noho 'ana. 'Going is better than staying.'

(8) The interrogative *aha* 'what' is most commonly a noun, but idiomatically, it occurs as an intransitive verb that can be passivized but is not used with imperative markers.

E   aha   ana   'oe ?
     what   you
  (imperfective)
'What are you doing?'

E   aha   'ia   ana   'oe ?
     what   (pas/imp.)   you
  (imperfective)
'What was happening to you?'

(9) The common word *apau* 'all, entirely' is like a qualifying stative verb in that it follows nouns, but, unlike the members of this class, it does not follow verb markers; neither does it occur as a noun.

Hele mai lākou apau. 'They all came.'

(10) *'Ehia* (see Dictionary) might be considered a verblike idiom in its meaning 'no matter how much'.

(11) A fairly common idiom is *'a'ohe i* (or *o*) *kana mai ka* + noun, expressing the superlative: *'A'ohe i kana mai ka nani* 'ever so beautiful'.

(12) *Alia* 'wait' is used without verb markers.

(13) *Nao:* a rare intensifier following *'a'ole* or *'a'ohe* and followed by words expressing damage, havoc, distress, pain. See the Dictionary for examples.

5   Verb Markers

CLASSIFICATION OF VERB MARKERS

5.1   The three semantic categories of verb markers are aspect, tense, and mood (see table 9). Some of these have alternants depending on whether they occur at the beginning of a sentence or in the middle.

The discussion to follow will be clearer after the *ϕ*-demonstratives (section 7.4) and the anaphoric *ai* (section 7.3) have been studied. The reader may wish to refer to these sections beforehand.

ϕ in table 9 means 'zero' or 'nothing', that is, the absence of a form. The slash, appearing twice in the column headed "Initial," means that zero (no form at all) is possible, as well as the forms (here *ua* and *e*) preceding the slashes. They may be called zero-alternants.

ASPECT MARKERS

5.2   Both the aspect markers in table 9 are commonly used in writing, but only *e* (verb) *X*, usually *e* (verb) *ana*, is common in conversation. "Aspect" never means "tense." Hall (1964:158) says, "Under aspect are included such contrasts as those of completed (perfective) action vs. incomplete (imperfective)."

Since *ua* does not mark tense, tenses must by supplied in English translations of sentences containing *ua* + verb. As shown in table 8, the action-marking verbs (vi, vtd) often indicate single past acts, whereas the condition-marking verbs (vtsp, vsadj, vsl) may often be translated by present tenses. However, context is decisive. Some legends are best translated entirely in the past tense. Similarly, some *loa'a*-stative verbs are

TABLE 9
Classification of Verb Markers

Category	Initial	Mid-utterance After 'a'ole	Mid-utterance After Noun Phrase
Aspect marker			
Perfective/inceptive	ua/ø	i	i (verb) ai
Imperfective	e (verb) X†	e (verb) X	e (verb) ai
Tense marker			
Present	ke (verb) X	e (verb) X	e (verb) X
Mood marker			
Affirmative imperative/intentive	e/ø, ō		e (verb) ai, i
Negative imperative/intentive	mai, 'a'ole		
Purposive	i		
Infinitive	ke		
Imminence	mai		

†X=ø-demonstratives *nei, ana, ala, lā.*

usually action-marking (*loa'a* 'get') and others condition- marking ('*eha* 'to hurt'):

> *Ua loa'a ke kālā ia'u.* 'I got the money.'
> *Ua 'eha ko'u lima.* 'My hand hurts.'

Time words may make past tense of any verb: *Ua maika'i au i nehinei, akā, ua ma'i i kēia lā.* 'Yesterday I was well, but today I'm sick.'

In all these examples *ua* may be omitted, but with loss of the nuance of inceptiveness. The unusual sentence *Ua hale mākou!* may be understood as meaning 'At last we have a house!' The inceptive nuance may distinguish such pairs as *ua lō'ihi ke ala* 'the road is (now) long', *he lō'ihi ke ala* 'the road is a long one'.

Dorothy M. Kahananui has pointed out (oral communication) the importance of the inceptive meaning of *ua*. She would not accept the sentence **Ua hou ka puke.* 'The book is new'. A book could not *become* new. But she would accept *Ua kahiko ka puke.* 'The book is (now) old'. Also unacceptable is **Ua kalakala ka limu kala. Limu kala* is always rough *(kalakala)*, and only in a legend could it have been smooth and then made newly rough.

The meaning of *ua* is clearly inceptive in this conclusion to a prayer for resuscitation: *'Aina ka 'ai, hume 'ia ka malo, ua ola* (FS 273). 'Eat food, gird on the loincloth, [you] are alive.'

In a complicated sentence in Nakuina 34, *ua mākaukau* must

be translated by a future tense: *E a'o kāua i nā hana a kō haku a loa'a iā'oe, malia ō noho mai ā hū a'e ke aloha, 'imi mai iā kāua, ua mākaukau 'oe.* 'We (dual) will study the activities of your lord, and when [they] are mastered *(loa'a)* by you, wait a bit *(ō noho mai)* and [your lord] may *(malia)* feel compassion and search for us, and you will be prepared.'

In negative sentences *ua* + verb is replaced by *'a'ole i* + verb. A pronoun subject follows *'a'ole:*

> *Ua hele ke kanaka.* 'The man has (just now) gone.'
> *'A'ole i hele ke kanaka.* 'The man did not go.'
> *Ua hele 'oia.* 'He has (just now) gone.'
> *'A'ole 'oia i hele.* 'He didn't go.'

'A'ole is nearly always pronounced in an assimilated form, *'a'ale,* but is not written or sung in this fashion. It is commonly used alone, as in answer to a question, with the meaning 'no'. *E hele ana 'oe? 'A'ole.* 'Are you going? No.'

'A'oe is a rare variant of *'a'ole: Kapu ke kanaka, 'a'oe hele; kapu ke 'īlio, 'a'oe 'aoa; kapu ka moa, 'a'oe kani; kapu ka pua'a, 'a'ole e holo* (FS 29). 'People are taboo, [they] do not go [anywhere]; dogs are taboo, [they] do not bark; chickens are taboo, [they] do not crow; pigs are taboo, [they] do not run about.' For more about *'a'ole,* see section 10.2, 11.1, and chapter 12.

In the following utterance, the perfective *ua* is replaced after a noun phrase by *i* (verb) *ai: i ka manawa i hele mai ai ke kanaka* 'at the time the man came'. Here, the time word at the beginning *(manawa)* is in focus (it is emphasized). With the verb first the sentence would read: *Ua hele mai ke kanaka i kēlā manawa.* 'The man came at that time.'

For other examples of the alternant *i* (verb) *ai* after noun phrases, see sentences labeled (b) in section 7.3.

The imperfective aspect marker *e* (verb) *ana* is, like *ua,* diagnostic for verbs; it marks continuing or durative action and is commonly translated in conversations by a present progressive tense, as in the common way to announce one's departure: *E ho'i ana au.* 'I'm leaving.' In legends, however, the translation is often by a past progressive tense:

> *iā lāua e kama'ilio ana* (FS 71) 'while they were chatting'
> *iāia e 'au aku ana* 'while he was swimming away'

Hā'awi maila ia i mau wa'a no Ka-welo . . . no ka mea, e noho ana nō 'o Kākuhihewa me ka maka'u iā Ka-welo (FS 63). 'He gave Ka-welo some canoes because Kākuhihewa was afraid of Ka-welo.'

In table 9 the imperfective aspect is shown by *e* (verb) ∅-demonstrative. The most common ∅-demonstrative in this structure is *ana*, as has been illustrated. Note that in table 12 (section 8.3.3), which shows spatio-temporal relationships, *ana* is in the column headed "far." *Ana* in some instances is replaced by *ala* or *lā*, perhaps to indicate greater distance in time or space:

E kau lā ke ao i ke kuahiwi (FS 25). 'The cloud is resting there on the mountain.'

'Oia ia lepo 'ula au e 'ike ala. 'That's the red dirt you see.'

He lae ia e nānā ala iā Hawai'i (FS 21–25). 'That's a headland facing Hawai'i.'

TENSE MARKER

5.3   *Ke* as the marker of the present tense is followed by verb + ∅-demonstrative, usually *nei*:

Ke kali nei au.

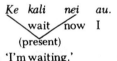

wait now I
(present)
'I'm waiting.'

Ke pi'i lā lā, ke pi'i lā (FS 237).
climb there (refrain) climb there
(present) (present)
'Climbing there, tra-la, climbing there.'

In noninitial position, *ke . . . nei* is replaced by *e . . . nei* or *e . . . lā*:

'A'ole nāu ke keiki āu e pepehi mai nei (FS 119).

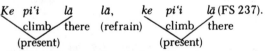

not for-you the child your beating here now
(present)
'The child you are beating now is not yours.'

Ke (verb) *lā* (or *ala*) seems to emphasize present time less emphatically than does *ke* (verb) *nei*. Note in table 12 that *lā* indicates the greatest distance from the speaker in time and space.

'A'ohe wahi ahe makani e ho'okanaaho a'e ai,' ke 'ike ala au i ka wela
malōhāhā o ka pu'u (Kelekona 106). 'Not even a slight breeze
brings relief as I look over at the dry heat of the hill.'

Ke koni iho, koni aku, koni a'ela (from the song "Ke Ka'upu," Elbert
and Mahoe 65). 'Throbbing here, throbbing there, throbbing
near.'

MOOD MARKERS

5.4   The imperative/intentive markers are *e/ø*, *ō*, and *i*. The common
(second person only) negative imperative marker is *mai*.

The second person imperative is commonly a direct command with the subject expressed. (It is usually awkward to translate the subject in English.) In the first and third persons, the
meanings, subsumed as "intentive," include a vague desire,
need, purpose, necessity, or probability. *Ō* is milder and politer
than *e*.

E hele 'oe! 'Go!/ You should (must, ought to) go!'
Ō ho'i ā 'ōlelo aku . . . (FS 129). 'Better go back and say . . . '
Pono e hele. 'Really ought to go; necessary to go.'
Ō hele kāua. 'Let's go.'
Malia ō hele au. 'Maybe I'll go.'
Hele akula 'o Ka-welo e 'au'au (FS 55). 'Ka-welo went to bathe.'
Mai uwē 'oe. 'Don't cry.'

The *ø*-alternant is rather common in informal speech: *Ho'i
aku kāua i ka hale* (FS 21). 'Let's the two of us go back to the
house.'

E is commonly used before certain subordinate verbs:
Makemake au e hele. 'I want to go.' *E* is sometimes replaced by
a'e in songs: *'A'ole mākou a'e minamina . . .* (Elbert and Mahoe
64). 'We do not cherish . . . '

Near the end of section 7.3 (page 98) is an example of mid-
utterance *e* (verb) *ai*, with *e* the imperative/intentive. Here is
another example (FS 125):

*Lilo ia i hala no Pai'ea e make ai iā 'Umi i ka wā e puni ai 'o Hawai'i
iā 'Umi.* 'This became a fault for Pai'ea for which 'Umi would kill
him when 'Umi should have conquered Hawai'i.'

Note that *make ai* in this sentence is translated 'would kill' and
that *e puni ai* is translated 'should have'. Also near the end of
section 7.3 (page 98) is a long sentence in which *e ka'apuni ai* is
translated 'in order to go around it' and *e huli ai* is translated 'to
search there' (purpose). Thus the mood marker *e* has many

meanings, ranging from 'must' to 'should' to 'in order to' to merely a purposeful 'to'.

Andrews (1854:112) discusses a pidgin-like use of *'a'ole* by foreigners in direct commands, as *aole hana pela* (Andrews' spelling) 'do not do so' and adds that "this is intelligible to Hawaiians; but where the prohibition is direct and positive they always use *mai.*"

Mai also is used alone with the meanings 'Don't! Stop it!'

I may mark purpose in either main or subordinate clauses:

'Ī ihola ke Akua, "I mālamalama" (Ka Baibala, Kinohi 1.3). 'God said, "Let there be light." '
I uhi pākaukau hou, i hele loa aku kēia lumi i ka maika'i 'By-means-of-a new tablecloth, this room will be fine.'
Hā'awi 'oia i kālā i kāna keiki e hele i ke kula i loa'a ka na'auao. 'He gave money to his child to go to school and get an education.'

In the following, *i* may be considered as either a passive/imperative or purpose marker: "He aha kā 'olua huaka'i o ka hiki 'ana mai i O'ahu nei?" 'Ī mai nā makuakāne: "I ki'i mai nei māua iā'oe (FS 55)." ' "What is the reason for your trip here to O'ahu?" The uncles said: "We came to fetch you." '

Ke as an infinitive may introduce a verb after *hiki* 'can, able' or *pono* 'right, should, must', and seems a substitute for the imperative/intensive *e*, but it is used only after these two very common verbs.

Hiki nō ke hele. 'Certainly possible to go.'
Hiki ia'u ke 'ai. 'I can eat.'
Pono ke hele. '[It's] fine to go. / [It's] a good idea to go.'
Pono e hele 'It's necessary to go / [you] must go' is stronger.

The imperative markers are rarely used with adjectival statives, although one can say *e maika'i kāu hana* 'may your work be good'. Frequently the stative is preceded by a transitive. 'Be still' is *e noho mālie* (lit., sit quietly). 'Be honest' is *e hana pono* (lit., work honestly). 'Don't be noisy' is merely *kulikuli* (lit., noisy). A poetic way to say 'don't be cruel' is *he 'ole manawa 'ino* (FS 245).

One can say *e lilo 'oe i kumu* 'become a teacher', or *mai lilo 'oe i 'aihue* 'don't become a thief'. Here, however, there is ambiguity. The last sentence might be translated, 'You almost became a thief.'

Another *mai* must be introduced here, a rarely used particle *mai* that was listed in both the Andrews and the Andrews and Parker dictionaries as an adverb, but is not found in either Alexander's grammar or Andrews'. In his *Tongan Grammar*, Churchward (1953:205) lists Tongan *mei* 'nearly' among his "moderative adverbs." The usual translation of this particle, which directly precedes verbs, is 'almost'. It seems always to indicate something unpleasant, and this suggests the awkward term *imminence*, since, according to English dictionaries, this word is applied usually to danger or evil that hangs over one's head. This *mai* is used with all types of verbs, most commonly perhaps with *loaʻa*-statives:

vi: *Mai hāʻule ke keiki.* 'The child almost fell.'
Mai piholo i ke kai. '[He was] almost drowned in the sea.'

vtd: *Mai hoʻokuʻi ʻia ʻoia e ke kaʻa.* 'He was almost hit by the car.'

vtsp: *mai ʻike ʻole ʻia nō* 'almost not seen at all'

vsadj: *Mai pakika a ʻeha.* '[He] almost slipped and got hurt.'
I hoʻolohe ʻia e ʻoe, mai maikaʻi kāu hana. 'If you had listened, your work would have been fairly good.'

vsl: *Mai make ʻoia i ke kālā ʻole.* 'He almost died from lack of money.'
Ka pakele mai make iā Ka-welo (FS 51). 'The narrow escape from death at Ka-welo's [hands].'
Mai nalo ke kālā. 'The money was almost lost.'
Mai pā ʻoe i ka lāʻau pālau. 'You were almost hit by the club.'
(Cf. *Mai hoʻopā ʻoe i ka lāʻau pālau.* 'Don't touch the club.')
Mai pilikia mai nei lākou. 'They almost got into trouble.'

Since both *mai*, negative imperative, and *mai*, imminence, directly precede verbs, is there ever any confusion? Perhaps. *Mai hina* is usually 'don't fall' but in some contexts might possibly be 'almost fell'.

6 Verb Affixes and Thematic Consonants

6.1   The many prefixes to verbs and verb/nouns are listed in table 10, in the order in which they occur with reference to **bases**. (Bases are words without affixes.)

Examples of bases taking prefixes from more than one of the vertical columns in table 10 follow. The bases that they precede are in boldface type.

ho'o	hā		like	**like** 'resemblance'
ho'o		mā	'aka	**'aka** 'to cause laughter'
ho'o	ha'a			**heo** 'proud'
ho'o	kā		hili	**hili** 'to fan gently'
ho'o		mā	'oki	**'oki** 'streaked'
ho'o		mō	aka	**aka** 'explanation'

Prefixes in the column in table 10 headed "Other" are mutually exclusive (that is, each occurs with a different base). A few examples have been noted of more than one prefix in each of the three leftmost columns occurring with a single base:

ho'oikaika, hō'ikaika 'to strengthen'
hākuma, 'ōkuma 'thick'
hākia, kākia 'to nail, fasten'
ma'ewa, pa'ewa 'crooked'

REDUPLICATIONS

6.2   Reduplication consists of repetition of all of a base or part of it. Most partial reduplications are commonly pronounced in the same stress group (see section 2.3: the reduplicated vowel is short, as in *kali, kakali* 'to wait'); but complete reduplications

64

TABLE 10
Hawaiian Prefixes

Causative/Simulative		Qualitative/ Stative	Other	Reduplications
(6.4)	(6.3.1)	(6.3.2)	(6.3.3)	(6.2)
hoʻo-, hoʻ-, hō-, ho-, hō-	hā-, haʻa-, ha- ʻā-, ʻa-, kā- ʻō- hai-	mā-, ma-, mo-, mō- nā-, na-, nō-, no- pā-, pa-, pū-, pu- kū-, ku-, u-, ʻu-, ʻū-	aka- ala- u- hau- Hau- ele- kī-	

are pronounced in separate stress groups, as *pī.pī* 'to sprinkle', *kau.kau* 'to chant', and *ʻio.ʻio* 'to peep'. Complete reduplication of vowel-consonant-vowel bases are usually pronounced as a single stress group, as *ikiiki* 'stifling' and *onaona* 'softly fragrant'. (*I laila* 'there' is not a reduplication at all, but is sometimes sung *ila.ila* or *ilaʻila*.)

All types of verb bases may be reduplicated, as for example:

vi: *ʻau, holo, lele, piʻi*
vtd: *ʻaki, ʻapo, hoe, hula, kālai, lawe, wehe*
vtsp: *aloha, lohe, manaʻo, noʻo*
vsadj: *kea, liʻi, nui, ʻōpio, pailua, pono, nīele, pule, uli*
vsl: *hiki* 'able', *kaʻa, make, pā*

Many nouns can be reduplicated, including names of fish (*ʻāhole, aʻu*) and *ʻeke, helena, lāʻau, lau, lima, mahina, naʻau, nahele, wēlau*.

TYPES OF REDUPLICATION

6.2.1   (1) Complete reduplication: *ʻaki, ʻaki-ʻaki; hoe, hoe-hoe; pā, pā-pā.*

(2) Reduplication of the first syllable: *ʻaki, ʻa-ʻaki; kaʻa, ka-kaʻa; kea, ke-kea; lele, le-lele; make, ma-make; nui, nu-nui; pilikia, pi-pilikia.* The vowel of the reduplicated first syllable in this type is short and stressed weakly or not at all. The short vowel contrasts with a long vowel of a few otherwise homophonous pairs, as *ka-kau*, reduplication of *kau* 'to place' and *kā-kau* 'to write, tattoo' (causative *kā- + kau*); *pa-paʻi*, reduplication of *paʻi* 'to slap' and *pāpaʻi* 'crab'; *pa-pale*, reduplication of *pale* 'to ward off' and *pā-pale* 'hat' (*pā* 'flat surface' + *pale*). A long vowel in the first syllable is retained in the

reduplication, but is shortened in the base, as *kōhi*, *kō-kohi* 'to break off'; *wāhi*, *wā-wahi* 'to smash'.

(3) Reduplication of all but the first syllable: *āhole*, *āhole-hole*; *'ānai*, *'ānai-nai*; *'īniki*, *'īniki-niki*; *'ōpio*, *'ōpio-pio*. A short first syllable is usually lengthened: *aloha*, *āloha-loha*; *nahele*, *nāhele-hele*. Reduplications of this sort are suffixes.

(4) Double reduplication of the first syllable or first two phonemes of the first syllable: *hiki*, *hi-hi-hiki*; *komo*, *ko-ko-komo*; *pau*, *pa-pa-pau*; *pono*, *po-po-pono*.

(5) Reduplication of the first two phonemes of the first syllable: *pailua*, *pa-pailua*; *pau*, *pa-pau*.

(6) Reduplication of a first syllable (usually with shortening of long vowels in the base) and of a truncated second syllable: *kālai*, *kala-kalai*; *lā'au*, *la'a-lā'au*; *na'au*, *na'a-na'au*; *nīnau*, *nina-ninau*. A glottal stop is added in *ālai*, *ala'-alai*.

(7) Reduplication of the first two syllables, with shortening of long vowels in the base: *nīele*, *nie-niele*; *pīna'i*, *pina-pina'i*; *unahi*, *una-unahi*; *welelau*, *wele-welelau*.

Several types of reduplication exist for some words, as *'ānai*, *'a-'anai* (formal), *'ānai-nai*; *hula*, *hula-hula*, *hu-hu-hula*; *make* 'to like', *ma-make* (colloquial), *make-make*; *pau*, *pa-pau*, *pa-pa-pau*.

A prefix or suffix is not reduplicated with the base: *'awa-'awa-hia*, *hā'-uli-uli*, *hele-helena*, *ho'-āloha-loha*, *holo-holo-na*, *ho'o-mākau-kau*, *kū-pina-pina'i*, *'ō-pule-pule*.

Some reduplicated forms are used so commonly as to nearly or totally exclude an unreduplicated base: *'ao-'ao*, *hila-hila*, *ika-ika*, *ki'e-ki'e*, *lehu-lehu*, *make-make*, *mina-mina*, *moko-moko*, *mo-mona*, *nahe-nahe*, *nā-nā*, *no'o-no'o*.

MEANINGS OF REDUPLICATIONS

6.2.2   By far the commonest meanings of reduplicative affixes are **frequentative, increased,** or **plural action.** These terms are to be construed broadly. For example, *hoe* 'to paddle', *hoe-hoe* 'to paddle continuously, frequently, or for a long time; for many persons to paddle'. *Make*, 'death, to die'; *ma-make* 'deaths everywhere, many deaths'. *Nīnau* 'to question', *nina-ninau* 'to question repeatedly, interrogate; for many persons to be asking questions'. *Niho* 'tooth', *niho-niho* 'toothed, notched, serrated'.

In some instances there is little difference in meaning between the reduplicated and base forms, as *'ōpio* and *'ōpio-pio*, both meaning 'young'. Frequently it is difficult to carry over into English the subtle semantic force that the reduplication conveys to the Hawaiian.

A few reduplications are diminutives. For example, *āhole* is the adult stage of a species of fish (about 6 to 8 inches long), and *āhole-hole* is the young stage of the same fish (about 2 inches long); *a'u-a'u*, young stage of the *a'u* (a fish); *ma'i* 'sick' and *ma'i-ma'i* 'sickish'; *mana* 'branch' and *mana-mana* 'tiny branch, finger, toe'. Compare also the unreduplicated bases of the following (see the Dictionary): *'eke-'eke, ho'o-pa-pailua, li'i-li'i, māhina-hina, na'a-na'au.*

In general, the part of speech of the reduplicated form is the same as that of the base. These exceptions have been noted:

> *ho'i* (vi) 'to go back'; *ho'i-ho'i* (vtd) 'to return something' (Hawkins believes that the reduplicated form is assimilated from a causative **ho'o-ho'i*, a nonexistent form.)
>
> *kui* (vtd) 'to string' (as a lei); *kukui, kui-kui* (Ni'ihau form), (n), a tree whose oily nuts were strung to provide lights
>
> *kuli* (n) 'knee'; *ku-kuli* (vi) 'to kneel'
>
> *mana* (n) 'branch'; *mana-mana* (vsadj) 'branched'
>
> *niho* (n) 'tooth'; *niho-niho* (vsadj) 'notched'

A few reduplicated forms have meanings rather different from the meanings of the bases, as *'ākau* 'right (not left)' and *mā-kau-kau* 'prepared', or *lau* 'leaf' and *lau-lau* 'leaf package of steamed food'. See also in the Dictionary *'apo, 'a-'apo; 'au, 'au-'au; 'awa, 'awa-'awa; hema, hema-hema; ho'i, ho'i-ho'i; ho'o-kama, ho'o-kama-kama; ho'o-puni, ho'o-puni-puni; hula, hula-hula; kea, ke-kea, kea-kea; kui, ku-kui; kuli, ku-kuli; lawe, lawe-lawe; lima, lima-lima; pi'i, pi-pi'i;* and *wehe, wehe-wehe.*

Etymology of such words may be difficult to determine. Is *wai-wai* 'wealth' related to *wai* 'water', as is generally believed, or to *wai*, a rare form for *waiho* 'to leave, deposit', as seems more probable?

Reduplications of many words in the Dictionary are not defined, and the reader is referred to the base. This is an indication that the reduplicated meaning is frequentative, increased, or plural action.

PREFIXES TO VERBS: MIDDLE LAYER

6.3

PREFIXES WITH CAUSATIVE/SIMULATIVE MEANINGS

6.3.1   Of the prefixes to verbs listed in section 6.1 in the second column
in table 10, *hā*- and its alternants are probably the most common. Before bases beginning with vowels, the prefix is *hā-:*

ehu 'vigorous'	*hā-ehu* 'vigorous'
iki 'small'	*hā-iki* 'narrow'
inu 'to drink'	*hā-inu* 'to give to drink'
uli 'dark'	*hā-uli* 'darkish'

Before bases beginning with consonants there is a lack of
complementation (no rules describe which of the three alternants will occur with any given base); the prefixes are *hā*- (the
most common), *haʻa*, and *ha:*

ʻāpuka 'to cheat'	*ha-ʻāpuka* 'to cause to cheat'
ʻawe 'to carry'	*hā-ʻawe* 'to carry'
ʻele 'black'	*hā-ʻele* 'blackish'
kea 'white'	*hā-kea, haʻa-kea* 'whitish'
lewa 'to float'	*haʻa-lewa* 'to float'
laʻi 'peace'	*hā-laʻi* 'calm'
liu 'to turn'	*hā-liu, hoʻo-hā-liu* 'to cause to turn'
lulu 'to shake'	*haʻa-lulu, hoʻo-haʻa-lulu* 'to cause to shake'
nini 'to pour'	*ha-nini* 'to overflow'
	hoʻo-ha-nini 'to cause an overflow'
nui 'large'	*haʻa-nui* 'to brag, exaggerate'
	hoʻo-haʻa-nui 'to pretend to brag; to cause to brag'

(Analysis of *hā*- and its alternants was aided by study of
Russell Makanani's unpublished paper on the *haʻa*-type prefix.)
The prefixes *ʻā*-, *ʻa*-, and *kā*- have meanings similar to those of
the causative/simulative *hoʻo*- (section 6.4). A few bases take
both *ʻā*- and *kā*-. *ʻĀ*- and *kā*- seem to occur before each of the
eight consonants. *ʻĀ*- also has been noted before *-o*, as in *oʻo*, and
-u, as in *uli*, listed below. Only a few of the Dictionary glosses
are given in the following list, and no reduplications. Only two
of these examples occur with the common *hoʻo*- or its variants:
ʻā-pono (ho-ʻā-pono) and *kā-huli (hoʻo-kā-huli)*.

68

'ele 'black'	*kā-'ele* 'darkened'
hele 'snare; to tie'	*'ā-hele* 'to snare' *kā-hele* 'decoration, as a lei'
hewa 'mistake'	*'ā-hewa* 'to condemn' *kā-hewa* 'to miss, not find'
ka'a 'to roll'	*'ā-ka'a* 'to peel' *kā-ka'a* 'to roll'
muku 'cut short'	*'ā-muku* 'to cut off' *kā-muku* 'to diminish'
ne'e 'to hitch along'	*'ā-ne'e* 'to hitch along'
o'o 'mature, elderly'	*'ā-o'o* 'elderly'
papa 'flat surface'	*'ā-papa* 'stratum' *kā-papa* 'stratum'
pono 'proper'	*'ā-pono* 'to approve'
pi'i 'curly'	*'ā-pi'i* 'curly' *kā-pi'i* 'curly'
uli 'dark'	*'ā-uli* 'darkish'
wili 'to twist'	*'ā-wili* 'to mix' *kā-wili* 'to snare'

A few of the *kā-* forms are extremely common:

hea 'to call'	*kā-hea* 'to call'
hili 'to strike'	*kā-hili* 'to brush; feather standard that waves behind a chief'
hinu 'lustrous'	*kā-hinu* 'to anoint'
huli 'to turn'	*kā-huli* 'to change'
kau 'to place'	*kā-kau* 'to write, tattoo'
ko'o 'prop'	*kā-ko'o* 'to support'
lepa 'flag'	*kā-lepa* 'merchant' (merchants raised white flags before their goods)
lua 'pit'	*kā-lua* 'to cook in a pit'
ma'a 'to tie'	*kā-ma'a* 'sandals, shoes'
ma'i 'genital'	*kā-ma'i* 'to prostitute'
nuku 'beak'	*kā-nuku* 'funnel'

69

The ‘a- forms noted are the following:

kiu 'spy'	‘a-kiu 'to spy'
kuku 'to beat tapa'	‘a-kuku 'to beat tapa'
lohi 'to shine'	‘a-lohi 'to shine'
nu‘a 'heap'	‘a-nu‘a 'heaped'
‘ole 'not'	‘a-‘ole 'no'
pahū 'explode'	‘a-pahū 'explode'
pai 'a fish trap'	‘a-pai 'a fish trap'

Of the three causatives (kā-, ‘ā-, and ‘a-), kā- is the most frequent (53 examples noted in the Dictionary), followed by ‘ā- (43 examples), and ‘a- (7 examples).

The meanings of the prefix ‘ō- relate to approximation, 'somewhat', rather than to causation, but in some cases, little semantic difference is noticed between a base and a base with ‘ō-. ‘Ō- has been noted before bases beginning with every phoneme except the glottal stop, o-, and the long vowels. Search revealed 81 examples in the Dictionary; reduplications were not counted. Some examples follow:

a‘a 'fibrous'	‘ō-a‘a 'somewhat fibrous'
ehuehu 'animated'	‘ō-ehu 'to romp'
heke 'best'	‘ō-heke 'somewhat modest'
hepa 'idiot'	‘ō-hepa 'moronic'
hewa 'mistake'	‘ō-hewa 'incoherent'
huku 'protrude'	‘ō-huku 'protrude'
hulu 'feather'	‘ō-hulu 'to feather out'
ilo 'to germinate'	‘ō-ilo 'to germinate'
kai 'ocean'	‘ō-kai-kai 'rough (as the sea)'
kū 'erect'	‘ō-kū 'erect'
ku‘e-ku‘e 'elbow, knuckles'	‘ō-ku‘e-ku‘e 'knuckles'
kuma 'rough (skin)'	‘ō-kuma 'rough (skin)'
la-lau 'astray'	‘ō-la-lau 'somewhat astray'
la‘o 'to weed'	‘ō-la‘o 'to weed'
ma‘i 'sick'	‘ō-ma‘i 'sickly'
niho 'tooth'	‘ō-niho 'toothed'
pule-pule 'crazy'	‘ō-pule-pule 'somewhat crazy'
ūpē 'crushed'	‘ō-upē 'beaten down'
waka 'to flash'	‘ō-waka 'to flash'

Only 7 examples of use of the prefix hai- were found in the Dictionary. (Hai is probably a reflex of fai 'to do' in other Polynesian languages, but here the meaning can be subsumed as causative/simulative):

70

kea 'white'	*hai-kea* 'pale'
lawe 'to carry'	*hai-lawe* 'to exchange'
lepo 'dirt'	*hai-lepo* 'gray pallor'
luku 'to destroy'	*hai-luku* 'to stone'
pule 'prayer'	*hai-pule* 'religious'
'ula 'red'	*hai-'ula* 'reddish'
wā 'space'	*hai-wā* 'to plant far apart'

PREFIXES WITH QUALITATIVE/STATIVE MEANINGS

6.3.2   It is impossible to predict which of the many prefixes of this group are used with which base, and in most instances there is little difference between meaning of base and prefix-plus-base. The part of speech of the derived *mā-* form is the same as that of the base. (Exception: *hele* [vtd] 'to cut' and *mahele* [n] 'division'.) Some bases take several of these prefixes, as indicated below. Some common forms with *mā-* and *ma-* have no bases at all: *mahalo* 'thanks', *maka'u* 'fear', *mānalo* 'sweet, potable', *mana'o* 'think'. Of these, *maka'u* can be traced back to Proto Austronesian *takut*. In these words, *ma-* and *mā-* cannot be considered prefixes.

The prefix *mā-* was counted in 51 words in the Dictionary, not counting reduplications or plant names. The bases taking *mā-* begin with any of the sounds except *a-* and *p-*. Examples:

ea, mā-ea 'to rise up'
hune, mā-hune 'poor'
ihi, mā-ihi 'to peel'
koi, mā-koi 'fishing pole'
la'e, mā-la'e 'calm'
mio, mā-mio 'to disappear'
nae, mā-nae 'short of breath'
ohiohi, mā-ohiohi 'to grow vigorously'
'olu 'soft', *mā-'olu* 'squashy'
ui 'to ask', *mā-uiui* 'to ask repeatedly'
wehe, mā-wehe 'open'

Use of the prefix *ma-* was noted 33 times in the Dictionary; bases begin with the vowel *i-* and all the consonants except *w-*. Examples:

hili, ma-hili 'to turn, wander'
kala, ma-kala 'to loosen'
lama 'torch', *ma-lama* 'light'

nene 'to stir', *ma-nene* 'to quake'
'oki, ma-'oki 'to cut'

Examples with *mā-* and *mō-:*

'ali, mā-'ali, mō-'ali 'scar'
ho'o-lili 'rippled'; *mā-lili, mō-lili* 'withered'
ka'oka'o, mā-ka'o, mō-ka'oka'o 'arid'
koi, mā-koi, mō-koi 'fishing pole'
mio, mā-mio, mō-mio 'to disappear; narrow'
wae, mā-wae, mō-wae 'to separate'

For *mō-*, see also in the Dictionary *mō-akaaka, mō-hai, mō-halu, mō-hio, mō-'iu, mō-lio.* Some of these words are rare today.

For *mo-*, see in the Dictionary *mo-aka, mo-ani, mo-'au, mo-kala, mo-kapu, mo-lohi, mo-luhi* (also *mā-luhi*), *mo-'oni.*

For *nā-*, see in the Dictionary *nā-hili, nā-ki'i, nā-kolo, nā-pele, nā-uki, nā-wā, nā-wele, nā-weo.*

For *na-*, see in the Dictionary *na-hae, na-holo, na-kele, na-koa, na-ku'e, na-kulu, na-luli, na-ue.*

For *nō-*, see in the Dictionary *nō-'ā, nō-kea, nō-la'e-la'e* (also *mā-la'e-la'e*), *nō-lino-lino, nō-weo.*

For *no-*, see in the Dictionary *no-hae* (also *na-hae*), *no-kule, no-'olu.*

The base *hae* may carry any of the prefixes *ma, na, no,* and also *u,* all combinations meaning 'to tear'.

Pā- occurs before bases beginning with the vowels *o-* and *u-* and all the consonants. In the Dictionary 39 instances were noted. Examples:

ola 'life', *pā-ola* 'quick recovery'
uma 'curve', *pā-uma* 'curved'
'ao'ao 'side', *pā-'ao'ao* 'sideways'
ha'o, pā-ha'o-ha'o 'surprising'
koni, pā-koni 'to throb'
leo 'voice', *pā-leo* 'to converse'
malō, pā-malō 'dry'
na'i 'to conquer', *pā-na'i* 'reciprocity'
pi'o, pā-pi'o 'arch'
wai 'water', *pā-wai* 'to have water'

Pa-: 16 words with this prefix were noted. See in the Dictionary *pa-he'e, pa-hele, pa-hemo, pa-hio, pa-hiwa, pa-hole, pa-*

hū, pa-'iha, pa-kele, pa-keo, pa-kī, pa-kika, pa-kohana, pa-laka (?), pa-ne'e, pa-noa.

Pū-: A few of the 36 examples noted include *pū-hanu, pū-hene, pū-hili, pū-kai, pū-ko'a, pū-koko, pū-lale, pū-lama, pū-lawa, pū-lewa, pū-liki, pū-niho, pū-nono.*

Pu-: A few of the examples noted include *pu-'aki, pu-ehu, pu-ha'u, pu-hemo, pu-hole, pu-mahana.*

The stative prefix *kū-* differs from those previously listed in that it also occurs as a verb meaning 'to resemble' (*kū nō i ka makuahine* 'resembling indeed the mother, having the mother's character'). Why, one may ask, is *kū* not considered a verb rather than a prefix, and the *kū-* forms listed in the Dictionary considered compounds rather than derivatives? Probably because such sequences (as *kū-'ena* 'burning' and *kū-paoa* 'strong fragrance') are indivisible: *kū i ka 'ena* 'resembling the heat' and *kū i ka paoa* 'resembling the fragrance' seem impossible. *Kū-* is extremely common, and approximately 80 examples have been counted, one of them even with the loan word *hapa* 'half, partially' (*kū-hapa* 'partially resembling'). *Kū-* has been noted before bases beginning with *a-, o-,* or any of the consonants.

amu-amu, kū-amu-amu 'to curse'
'ena 'red-hot', *kū-'ena* 'burning'
o'o 'mature', *kū-o'o* 'dignified'
like, kū-like 'resembling'
moe 'to lie down, sleep', *kū-moe* 'bedstead'
napa 'flexible', *kū-napa* 'insecure'
pau 'finished', *kū-pau* 'entirely finished'
waho, kū-waho 'outside, foreign'

Kū- differs from the other qualitative/stative prefixes in that it may precede *hā* and *ha'a: hā-iki, kū-hā-iki* 'narrow'; *ha'a-liki, kū-ha'a-liki* 'to brag'.

Ku- occurs as a prefix most commonly before bases beginning with the vowels *a-* (*ku-ahu, ku-ahua, ku-ali, ku-anea, ku-awa*), *e-* (*ku-ehu, ku-emi, ku-ewa*), and *o-* (*ku-oha, ku-olo, ku-oni*). See also *ku-'āwa'awa'a, ku-hua, ku-kane, ku-newa, ku-wā, ku-wala, ku-walo.*

The prefix *u-* occurs with 22 bases, *'ū-* with 12, *'u-* with 8, and *ū-* with only 2:

ha'i, u-ha'i 'to break'
kali 'to wait', u-kali 'to attend'
nahe, u-nahe 'soft'
oki, u-oki 'to stop'
wa'a 'canoe', u-wa'a 'to dig a furrow'

hini 'feeble', 'ū-hini 'tapering'
ke'e 'crooked', 'ū-ke'e 'twisted'
lina, 'ū-lina 'soft'
malu, 'ū-malu 'shade'
poho, 'ū-poho 'hollow'
See also 'ū-kele, 'ū-lepe, 'ū-li'i, 'ū-melu, 'ū-pī, 'ū-pili, 'ū-po'i.

hane 'ghostly', 'u-hane 'soul'
kemu, 'u-kemu 'to absorb'
wehe, 'u-wehe 'to open'
See also 'u-hene, 'u-wā, 'u-walu, 'u-wa'u, 'u-weke.

pē, ū-pē 'crushed'
kō, ū-kō 'fulfilled'

OTHER PREFIXES

6.3.3   *Aka-* 'carefully, slowly'

'ai 'to eat'	aka-'ai 'to eat slowly'
hana 'to work'	aka-hana 'to work slowly'
hao 'to pick up'	aka-hao 'to pick up carefully'
hele 'to go'	aka-hele 'cautious'
hoe 'paddle'	aka-hoe 'to paddle carefully'
holo 'to sail, run'	aka-holo 'to sail or run cautiously or slowly'
ku'u 'to leave'	aka-ku'u 'diminished'
lewa 'to float'	aka-lewa 'to sway hips languidly'
luli 'to sway'	aka-luli 'to move slowly'
nahe 'soft'	aka-nahe 'cautious'
noho 'to sit'	aka-noho 'to sit quietly'
'ōlelo 'to speak'	aka-'ōlelo 'to speak cautiously and slowly'

It is possible that the common word *akahai* 'modest' is made up of the prefix *aka-* and *-hai*, which has no meanings in Hawaiian related to 'modest', but which has cognates elsewhere in Polynesia meaning 'to make, do'. The same *hai* may also occur in Hawaiian *hai-pule* 'religious' (cf. *pule* 'prayer').

Ala- 'quickly'

heo 'depart'	*ala-heo* 'gone'
mimo 'quick, deft'	*ala-mimo* 'quick'
pinepine 'often'	*ala-pine* 'quick'
wiki 'quick'	*ala-wiki* 'hurry'

U-, a plural marker. Examples: *u-haele* 'to go'; *u-heʻe* 'to slide, drip, hang'; *u-lawaiʻa* 'to fish'; *u-noho, u-no-noho* 'to sit, live, stay'.

(Purpose phrase)			*(Comitative phrase)*			
no	ke	kāne	‖ā	me	ka	wahine‖
for	the	man	and	with	the	woman

e	u-	kaʻawale	ai (Kep. 65)
to	(pl.)	separate	(anaphoric)

'for the man and the woman to be separated'

E		aho	e	u-	haele	kāua
(intentive)		better	to	(pl.)	go	we two

'It is better for us to go.'

Hau-, an intensifier with meaning 'unpleasant, dirty', occurs with the passive/imperative suffixes *-mia* and *-na*, and with bases with similar meanings *(hau-ʻeke, hau-halakī, hau-hili, hau-kaʻe, hau-na)* and with less specific meanings, usually unpleasant *(hau-la-lapa, hau-naku, hau-ʻopo, hau-walaʻau, hau-wawā)*. But compare *ʻoli* 'joy' and *hau-ʻoli* 'happy'. It is doubtful that native speakers recognize *hau-* as a prefix. It occurs also in South Marquesan as *faufau* 'disgusting, bad'.

Hau- 'ruler', as a prefix, is even less recognizable to native speakers, as it occurs principally in names of female deities, the most famous being the earth mother, *Hau-mea*, probably literally 'red ruler' (red is a sacred color in Polynesia). Others are *Hau-lani, Hau- maka-puʻu, Hau-nuʻu, Hau-wahine*. The same prefix occurs in two common names now used by females, *Hau-lani* 'royal ruler' and *Hau-nani* 'handsome ruler'. Hawaiian *hau-* is cognate with Tahitian *hau* 'government' and Rennellese *Sau-* 'to have abundance of gifts from the gods' (a prefix to male names). The Proto Polynesian form is *sau*.

'Ele- 'old'. See in the Dictionary *'ele-hine, 'ele-kule, 'ele-makule, lā-'ele.*

Kī-, ki-, an intensifier. Many examples occur in the Dictionary. Some derivative meanings are rather different from those of the base. The prefix *ki-* was noted only in *ki-ani.* Examples: *ki-ani, kī-apu, kī-au, kī-helu, kī-kaha, kī-kākala, kī-laha, kī-lepa, kī-lepe, kī-lou, kī-mana-mana, kī-mo'o, kī-'o'e, kī-'ohu-'ohu, kī-'ōnaha, kī-pa'i, kī-papa, kī-pau, kī-pe'a, kī-pehi, kī-poko, kī-pa'i, kī-pola.*

THE CAUSATIVE/SIMULATIVE *ho'o-* AND ITS ALTERNANTS

6.4   As pointed out in section 2.3, *ho'o-* and a following base are in distinct stress groups; there is always a slight pause between *ho'o-* and the ensuing base, as in *ho'o.ikaika* 'to strengthen', which is never pronounced *ho'oi.kaika.*

Words beginning with *ho'o-* and its alternants are entered in the Dictionary *under the bases* and not with the *h*'s. This is because their meanings are much clearer if studied in connection with the meanings of the bases, and repetition is avoided. *The user of the Dictionary should search for such forms under the bases.*

The distribution of the alternants follows:

Ho'o-: before any consonant other than the glottal stop *(puka, ho'o-puka)* and usually before bases beginning with *i* and *u* and with a plus juncture before the vowel *(ilo, ho'o.ilo; una, ho'o.una).* (An apparent exception is the common word *ho.oulu* 'to grow, inspire'.)

Ho'-: before bases beginning with *e-, a-,* and *o-,* and sometimes *i-* and *u-,* with lengthening of the stressed vowel of the stem *(emi, ho'-ēmi; ala, ho'-āla; ola, ho'-ōla; ilo, ho'-īlo; ulu, ho'-ūlu).* These forms are in the same stress group.

Hō'-: sometimes before bases beginning with *i- (ikaika, hō'-ikaika).*

Ho-: before a glottal stop followed by a long vowel *('ā-puka, ho- 'ā-puka)* or by a base containing the nominalizing suffix *-na ('ike, ho-'ike-na).*

Hō-: before a glottal stop followed by a short vowel *('ike, hō-'ike)* or by a single long vowel *('ā, hō-'ā)* or by two long vowels *('ā-'ā, hō-'ā-'ā; 'ō-'ō, hō-'ō-'ō; 'ōpā, hō-'ōpā).*

A contrasting pair: *ho-'ōki* (from *oki* 'to stop'), *hō-'oki* (from *'oki* 'to cut').

Words with *ho'o-* and its alternants, unless used as nouns, are transitive verbs, most commonly deliberate transitive verbs regardless of the class of the base:

> vi base: *hele* 'to go', *ho'ohele* 'to set in motion'
> vtd base: *'ai* 'to eat', *hō'ai* 'to give to eat'
> vtsp base: *maka'u* 'to fear', *ho'omaka'u* 'to frighten'
> vsadj base: *'ula'ula* 'red', *ho'o'ula'ula* 'to redden'
> vsl base: *pa'a* 'firm', *ho'opa'a* 'to make firm'; *ola* 'alive', *ho'ōla* 'to save'. (*Hō'ōla ke Akua i ka mō'ī.* God save the King.)

A vtsp *ho'o-* form is *ho'omaopopo*, from *maopopo* (vsl). *Hō'ike* 'to show' is a deliberate transitive; the base *'ike* 'to see, know' is a spontaneous transitive.

Hawkins (1975, section 2.3.5) has pointed out that with transitive verbs, the primary function of *ho'o-* is to make the agency deliberate:

> *Ua peku 'o Kale i ke kinipōpō.* 'Charles kicked the ball.'
> *Ua ho'opeku 'o Kale i ke kinipōpō.* 'Charles deliberately kicked the ball.'

The same is true with *loa'a*-stative verbs:

> *Make ke ali'i i ke kanaka.* 'The chief died because of the man.'
> *Ho'omake ke kanaka i ke ali'i.* 'The man (deliberately) killed the chief.'

Ho'o- is also prefixed to verb-nouns, sometimes with similitude meanings: *haole* 'white person' and *ho'o-haole* 'to act like a white person'; *hula*, a dance, and *ho'o-hula* 'to cause someone to dance a hula, to pretend to dance a hula'; *kanaka* 'person' and *ho'o-kanaka* 'human'.

Some words occur only with initial *ho'o-* or its alternants. Nevertheless they are entered in the Dictionary under the elements following these causatives. Thus for *ho'ālaala* and *ho'omā'aka'aka*, see *-alaala* and *-mā'aka'aka*. Some rare *ho'o-* forms are not included in the Dictionary; in such cases, a translator can himself usually calculate the meanings.

The productivity of *ho'o-* within historic times is attested by its use with loan words, as *keonimana* 'gentleman' and

>*ho'okeonimana* 'to act the gentleman', and *male* 'to marry' and *ho'omale* 'to marry off'.

RARE SUFFIXES

6.5   One rare suffix is *-kīkē* 'back and forth':

pā 'to touch'	*pā-kīkē* 'to answer rudely'
wala 'to tilt backwards'	*wala-kīkē* 'to toss back and forth, as spears'
'ōlelo 'to speak'	*'ōlelo-kīkē* 'dialogue, repartee; to engage in such' (This form is metathesized /kīkē-'ōlelo/ with the glosses 'to argue, talk back'.)

A suffix noted in several forms is *-ea* (perhaps cognate with an identical suffix in Rennellese labeled pejorative):

hana 'to do'	*hana-ea* 'wilful, disobedient'
lu-a'i 'to vomit'	*lu-ea* 'seasickness'
poluā 'nausea'	*polu-ea* 'seasickness, dizzy'
pulu 'moist'	*pulu-ea* 'body odor'

-Hine 'female' is noted in *'ele-hine, kai-kama-hine, kai-kua-hine, lua-hine, wa-hine*.

A pejorative ending occurring usually with bases that cannot stand alone is *-ā*. In the traditional literature this is usually written *-wā* after *-u-* and *-o-*, but as mentioned in section 2.1, this is a predictable glide; the form without *-w-* is preferred. Both forms are entered in the Dictionary. Examples:

'a'ahuā or *'a'ahuwā* 'to deride'	*makoeā* 'tedious'
'aiā 'wicked'	*ma'oeā* 'lazy'
'ainā 'aching'	*moemoeā* 'fantasy'
haiā or *haihaiā* 'wicked'	*na'auauā* or *na'auauwā* 'grief'
hainā 'cruel'	*noneā* 'distaste for food'
huā or *huwā* 'jealous'	*nonohuā* or *nonohuwā* 'jealous'
kauā or *kauwā* 'outcast'	*pāleoleoā* or *paleoleowā* 'noisy'
lonoā or *lonowā* 'rumor'	*poluā* or *poluwā* 'nausea'

Of these forms, *lonoā* is derived from *lono* 'to hear', and *noneā* is derived from *none* 'tedious'. The PPN form is *-ha'a*.

-Kī and *-kikī* are intensifying suffixes. See *hili-kī, holo-kikī*,

kupaka-kī, maka-kī, mōkā-kī, paʻa-kikī, wala-wala-kī. Pukalakī seems indivisible.

-Kai 'swollen, bloated' has been noted in *kuakaikai, kūhākakai,* and *ʻuʻulukai.*

-Poni 'suddenly, without warning' has been noted in *kaʻiliponi* and *leleponi.*

THEMATIC CONSONANTS AND THE SUFFIXES AND PARTICLES THEY INTRODUCE

6.6

INVENTORY

6.6.1   An inventory of the suffixes and particles beginning with thematic consonants is given in table 11. The two particles in the right-hand column are in such common use that they are apparently driving out the increasingly rare nonproductive suffixes other than the passive/imperative marker *-a*. Examples of *ʻana* are given in section 6.6.2, examples of *ʻia,* in sections 6.6.3.

    The consonants represented by *C* in table 11 include all the consonants except *p* and *w* (i.e., *h, k, l, m, n,* ʻ, *ø*). They may be called **thematic consonants.** (The term "thematic" was used in descriptions of Latin vowels that end the stem and precede the inflectional endings, as in *aud-i-o* 'I hear'. Milner [1966:xxxiv] used the term for Samoan.)

NOMINALIZERS

6.6.2   The single nominalizing particle is *ʻana*. It is not considered a suffix because of its potential separation from a preceding base.

TABLE 11
Thematic Consonants, Suffixes, and Particles

	Suffixes	Particles
Nominalizers	*-na* *-Cana (C = -h-, -k-, -l-)*	*ʻana*
Passive/imperative markers	*-a* *-na* *-Cia (C = -h-, -k-, -l-,* *-m-, -n-, -ø-)*	*ʻia*
Transitivizers	*-Caʻi (C = -k-, -l-, -n-, -ø-)* *-Ci (C = -h-, -k-, -ʻ-, -ø-)*	

Examples:

> *ka   hele   'āwīwī   'ana   mai*
> the   come   quick   (nominalizer)   here
> 'the quick coming'

> *ma   kēia   noho   ka'awale   'ana*
> at   this   stay   apart   (nominalizer)
> 'at this staying apart'

Directionals (such as *mai* in the first example) *follow* the nominalizer *'ana*, but they *precede* the ∮-demonstrative *ana* in the refrain:

> *ha'ina   'ia   mai   ana   ka   puana*
> tell   (pas/imp.)   here   then   the   refrain
> 'then tell the refrain'

After words commonly used as nouns, *'ana* seems to give a verblike meaning to the noun head, which of course remains a noun:

> *'āina* 'land':   *ka 'āina 'ana* 'the giving /or forming or distribution/ of land'
>
> *mahi'ai* 'farmer':   *ka mahi 'ai ('ia) 'ana o ka 'āina* 'the farming of the land'

Of the nominalizing suffixes listed at the beginning of section 6.6.1 (table 11), *-na* is by far the most common. Only a few of the many bases taking *-na* are listed below, but effort is made in the last part of this section to list *all* the bases taking the nominalizing suffix symbolized *-Cana*.

What is the difference between the nominalizing particle *'ana* and the suffix *-na*? In the first place, *'ana*, as has been shown, can be separated from its base, but *-na* cannot; further, *'ana* cannot be followed by a qualifier, as can *-na* (one can say *kalai-na ki'i* 'image carving' but not **kālai 'ana ki'i*). The semantic difference is that *-na* words usually designate a single act or object (Alexander [1968:25] calls it "the result or the means of the action . . . [rather than] the action itself"), whereas the combination verb + *'ana* usually represents an ongoing process, frequently translated into English by the present participle. For example, *Pehea kāna hāuna lā'au?* 'How is his club-stroke?' *Pehea kāna hāuna la'au 'ana?* 'How is his club-fighting?'

The meanings of *-na* derivatives are in some instances quite different and unpredictable from the meanings of the bases (see

80

in the lists that follow *hā'awi, hānau, hiki, holoholo, waiho, kahu, kuhi, 'ohā*). Meanings of bases change but little when followed by *'ana*. Wilson (1976:60) subtly contrasts *nui kona 'eha* 'he has much pain' and *nui kona 'eha 'ana* 'he has a lot of pain'; *kona 'ike 'ana i nā mele* 'his knowing songs' and *kona 'ike i nā mele* 'his knowledge of songs'; *pehea kāna hana 'ana?* 'how does he do it? and *pehea kāna hana?* 'what's his job?' *'Ana* may follow a great number of verbs, including loan words: *hīmeni 'ana* 'hymn singing'. (Note the many examples of *'ana* in 9.6.2 following intransitive and *loa'a*-stative verbs.) *-Na*, however, is suffixed to only a few verbs and not to loan words (it is not productive). Both *-na* and *-'ana* may occur with the same base *(hāpai 'ana, hapai-na)*, both meaning 'carrying', but not within the same phrase. *Hāpai 'ana* has a wider range of meanings, including 'pregnancy', but *hapai-na* has a much more restricted range of meanings.

In spite of these strictures, many persons have equated the two. Nakuina (1901:104) writes *i ka hapai'na waa* 'canoe carrying'. The apostrophe was believed to represent a lost *a* in *'ana*; *-na* was considered a shortening of *'ana*. But such a sequence as **hāpai 'ana wa'a* is ungrammatical. (A more common use of the apostrophe as a marker of elision is described in section 2.12; the apostrophe described herein is the result of a misunderstanding of Hawaiian grammar.)

A few examples of *-na* nouns follow.

-Na, nominalizer, with bases losing vowel length with suffixation:

hā'awi 'to give'	*ha'awi-na* 'allotment, lesson'
hānau 'to give birth'	*hanau-na* 'generation'
hāpai 'to carry'	*hapai-na* 'carrying'
kālai 'to carve'	*kalai-na* 'carving'
māka'i 'policeman'	*maka'i-na* 'guard'

-Na, nominalizer, with bases retaining long vowels with suffixation or losing only the second of successive long vowels:

'alalā 'to squeal'	*'alalā-na* 'squealing'
hālō 'to peer'	*hālo-na* 'peering'
hiō, hiōhiō 'to lean'	*hiōhio-na* 'leaning'
kōhi 'to split'	*kōhi-na* 'splitting'
lūlā 'calm'	*lūla-na* 'calm'
papā 'to sound'	*papā-na* 'sounding'

81

-Na, nominalizer, with bases lengthening a vowel with suffix-ation:

'ali 'to scar'	*'āli-na* 'scar'
'alu 'to descend'	*'ālu-na* 'descent'
hau 'to strike'	*hāu-na* 'a blow'
koi 'to urge'	*kōi-na* 'urging'

-Na, nominalizer; forms with meanings unpredictable from meanings of the bases:

hiki 'to arrive'	*hiki-na* 'east'
holoholo 'to run about'	*holoholo-na* 'animal'
waiho 'to leave'	*waiho-na* 'depository'

-Na forms that have no bases:

'oi'oina 'resting place' (cf. Rennellese *'oki'oki* 'to rest')
pā'ina 'meal'

The nominalizer *-na* in some words indicates 'person':

kahu 'guardian'	*kahu-na* 'priest, expert'
kuhi 'to show'	*kuhi-na* 'councilor'
'ohā 'taro shoot'	*'oha-na* 'family'

The alternants *-hana* and *-lana*, like *-na*, are closely bound to bases (except *mana'o*), but only a few have been noted, and the meanings of base and derivative in some cases are rather different:

haki 'to break'	*haki-hana* 'broken place'
hau- (in *hauhoa* 'to lash')	*hau-hana* 'lashing'
kilo 'to watch'	*kilo-hana* 'lookout post, best'
komo 'to enter'	*komo-hana* 'west'
kumu 'source'	*kumu-hana* 'topic'
pou 'post'	*pou-hana* 'post supporting ridgepole'
kau 'to place'	*kau-lana* 'resting place'
kū 'to stand'	*kū-lana* 'place, situation'
mana'o 'to think'	*mana'o-lana* 'hope'
wai 'to place'	*wai-lana* 'banished'

Of these forms, *wai-lana* is a possible, rather than a certain, derivative.

Mana'o-lana 'hope' differs from all the others in that the constituent elements may undergo transposition and particle insertion: *ua lana ka mana'o* 'there is hope'.

Two *-kana* nominalizers have been noted: *pale* 'to ward off, protect' and *pale-kana* 'protection'; *pili* 'to cling' and *pili-kana* 'relative'.

A possible *-ɸana* alternant is *māpuana* (from *māpu*), both meaning 'fragrant'. Common *kuleana* 'land holding, responsibility' might possibly be another example.

PASSIVE/IMPERATIVES

6.6.3   The passive/imperative particle *'ia*, like the particle *'ana*, is written as a separate entity because it too can be separated from its base. The alternants of *'ia* (see discussion of *-a*, below) are inseparable.

Some examples follow of *'ia* separated from its head.

Ua   hānai   maika'i   'ia.
(perf.) feed   good   (pas/imp.)
'[He] was well fed.'

Ua   'ā-pono   wale   'ia   ke   kānāwai.
(perf.) approve unnecessarily (pas/imp.) the law.
'The law was approved unnecessarily.'

Ua   'ike 'ole 'ia   ke   keiki.
(perf.) see   not (pas/imp.) the child
'The child was not seen.'

A stative qualifier or noun may intervene between transitive verb and *'ia: Ho'onoho niho 'ia.* 'Stones are set in place.' *'Ia* occasionally qualifies two verbs, as in the sequence *ka pua i hi'ikua ā hi'ialo 'ia* 'the beloved child carried on the back and carried in the bosom'.

'Ia is rarely used with stative verbs and seems to have no effect on the meaning. Examples (from Wilson 1976:68–69):

Ua wela 'ia kona 'ā'ī (Kelekona 95). 'His neck was burned.'

Ua pūhā 'ia o loko (Nakuina 83). 'The inside was rotten.'

Ua aloha 'ia au iā Ka-lalau (Kelekona 76). 'I love Ka-lalau.'

'Ia has six alternants that begin with thematic consonants; common *-a* and rare *-na* also are variants; see table 11 in section 6.6.1.

The suffix *-a* is attached to a long list of bases and is perhaps productive. In some instances, little semantic difference exists between base and base + *-a (ulu, ulua)*, and in other instances the meanings are quite different, with the -*a* derivatives having the widest semantic domains: *hihi* 'entangled', *hihi-a* 'entangled, law suit'; *nane* 'riddle', *nane-a* 'pleasant, relaxed'. Many -*a* forms have imperative meanings, as *huki-a: Huki-a mai ka waha o ka 'upena.* 'Pull the opening of the net.' A few have passive meanings, as *hui-a: 'O 'oe ka i hui-a ihola, ē ke aloha* (song). 'You are the one who was met, my love.'

Some of the many bases that take -*a* are the following: *'a'e, ahe, ahu, 'aihue, 'aki, ale, ano, 'aui, 'awe, 'eli, hae, hai, haki, hali, haliu, hanu, hao, haohao, hau, ha'u, hauhaua, hehe, hehi, hihi, hiki, hili, hoe, ho'i, hō'ike, hole, holo, holu, honi, hopu, hu'e, hui, huki, hume, 'ike, koni, kuhi, lohe, nane, 'ohi, pahu, peku, pelu, pepehi, pili, puku, pu'ō, uhi.*

Following are lists of entities taking other passive/imperatives.

-*hia:*

'aihue	holehole	komo	lo'o-	olo
auhuli	hopu	kono	ma'ama'a	pa'a
'awa	huli	kualo	makala	palu
'awa'awa	ili	kuko	maka'u	pa'u
'āwa'a	iliili	kulu	make	ulu
hae	'imi	kūmalolo	mala	wa'awa'a
hahau	inu	kunikuni	mali	walo
hao	kani	kuolo	malu	walu
hau	kania'ā	la'a	moku	wele
hā'ule	kapu	lana	nalo	
hiolo	kilo	lanalana	nono	
hola	kolo	loa'a	oho	

Most of the words with -*hia* are rare. Only *malu-hia* and *la'a-hia* are in common use. Most or all of them may take a causative as well as -*hia*.

-*kia:* after *holo, kū, mala, 'ohā.*

-*lia:* after *'aihue, au, 'au, hīki'i, ho'opuka, ho'owa'a, ka'a, kāmau, kau, kō, kū, kūlō, ku'u, ku'upau, maka'u, mana'o, moku, nānā, nau, nu'a, pa'a, paka, pau, pō, puku, pūlō, wa'awa'a.* These words are rare except for *kau-lia* and *kū-lia*. Most or all of them take causatives as well as -*lia*.

-*mia:* after *hau-, inu.*

-*na:* after *aho, 'ai, ha'i, hau, ki'i, lua-.*

-nia: after *'aihue, kuhi, kuhikuhi, manoni, wala-*.
-ϕia: after *mala*.

A few bases take more than one alternant: *-hia* and *-lia* are used with *ho'owa'a, wa'awa'a, maka'u*, and *moku; -hia* and *-kia* with *mala; -hia, -lia*, and *-nia* with *'aihue*. Perhaps this indicates that *-hia* as well as *'ia* are driving out the rarer *-lia, -mia*, and *-nia*.

Some forms have both *-a* and *-Cia: -a* and *-hia* follow *hao, hau, hopu; -a* and *-lia* follow *ku'u, nau, puku; -a, -hia, -lia*, and *-nia* follow *'aihue*.

One *-a* and *-na* has been noted: *hau-*.

The usual meaning of *'ia* and its alternants is 'passive voice'. The imperative meaning is rarely heard today except in the common next-to-the-last line in songs: *Ha'ina 'ia mai ka puana*. 'Tell the refrain.' An imperative *'ia* occurs occasionally in chants: *'Aina ka 'ai, hume 'ia ka malo, ua ola* (FS 273). 'Eat food, put on [your] loincloth, [you] are saved.' *Ē Kāne-wahine-iki-a-Oha ē, lawe 'ia mai ka moena* (FS 41). 'O Kāne-wahine-iki-a-Oha, bring the mat.' The subject of the verbs *'aina, hume*, and *lawe* is translated by an English object. A rare instance of verb + *'ia* + agentive phrase translated by an imperative is *E hele 'ia e kāua*. 'We should go. / Let's go.' The imperative meaning of *'ia* seems weak: note the redundancy above of *ha'ina 'ia* and *e hele 'ia*.

The term "passive/imperative" is not altogether appropriate for the alternants of *'ia* for three reasons:

(1) Bases with alternants of *'ia* are sometimes followed redundantly by *'ia:*

'Aina 'ia ke aku e lākou. 'The bonitos were eaten by them.'
'O ka puana, ua ha'ina 'ia e Pua. 'The refrain was sung by Pua.'
Ua hāuna 'ia ka lā'au e ke kanaka. 'The blow was struck by the man.'
Ua ki'ina 'ia aku nei ka 'ulu. 'The breadfruit was fetched.'

(2) Some have passive meanings only if prefixed by *ho'o-:*

Ua ho'ohaehia ka 'īlio e ka 'aihue. 'The dog was made angry by the thief.'
Ua ho'ohahauhia (or *ho'ohahaulia*) *ka lā'au e ke kanaka*. 'The stick was struck by the man.'
Ua ho'okapuhia ka heiau e ke kahuna. 'The temple was sanctified by the priest.'

(3) Some are used as regular vi, vtd, and vsadj:

Ua haehia ka 'īlio. 'The dog was angry.'
E inuhia (or *inumia*) *iho 'oe i ka wai.* 'Drink the water.'
Ua komohia ka mana'o i loko ona. 'The thought occurred to him.'
E ho'okapuhia aku 'oe i ka heiau. 'Sanctify the temple.'
he wahi maluhia 'a peaceful place'
e luana wale ana nō 'just relaxing'

Factors such as these led Milner (1966:xxxii) to call similar words in Samoan "perfective suffixes." This is not done here because so many of them still retain passive or imperative meanings. (It is their infrequent use that has caused many of them to become more like ordinary verbs.) Some examples:

Kūlia i ka nu'u. 'Strive for the summit.'
Kaulia Kristo i ka lā'au ke'a. 'Christ was hung on the cross.'
Ua la'ahia au i ke kuhihewa. 'I am cursed by illusion.'
Ha'ina hou. 'Sing the refrain again.'
'Aina ke aku (FS 127). '[We would] eat bonitos.'
po'e e uluhia e nā kaimonia (Ka Baibala, Mataio 4.24) 'people possessed of demons'

TRANSITIVIZERS

6.6.4   Two suffixes have been labeled transitivizers: *-Ca'i* and *-Ci*. *-C* in *-Ca'i* may be any of the consonants *k*, *l*, *n*, and *ø*; in *-Ci*, it may be *h*, *k*, ', and especially *ø*. The transitivizer label is not to be taken too literally. Churchward (1953:241) says that *-Ci* in Tongan is suffixed to some verbs that are already transitive, and explains the suffix as expressing "more definitely, or more emphatically, the idea of carrying the action through to completion. It becomes *executive*, we might say, as well as transitive." Of *-Ca'i* (*-Caki* in Tongan) he says (p. 244): "The transitiveness of such verbs, however, is secondary or incidental rather than primary or fundamental. I mean that the true function of these suffixes is not to make intransitive verbs transitive, or to make transitive verbs more emphatically transitive, but to form new verbs with new meanings—meanings which, in some cases, happen to be transitive."

Both comments seem in general to be applicable to Hawaiian. Of the two suffixes, *-Ca'i* is the more common in Hawaiian and, being longer, is easier to recognize. It has been noted as follows:

C = -*k*-
  ala-ka'i 'to lead' (cf. *ala* 'road')
  hui-ka'i 'to combine' (cf. *hui* 'to join')
  kau-ka'i 'to depend on' (cf. *kau* 'to place')
  kū-ka'i 'to exchange' (cf. *kū* 'to extend' and Rennellese *tu'u-taki* 'to connect')

C = -*l*-
  kau-la'i 'to hang' (cf. *kau* 'to place')
  ku-la'i 'to overthrow' (cf. *kū* 'to extend')

C = -*n*-
  hili-na'i 'to believe, trust' (cf. *hili* 'to wander')
  pī-na'i 'to fill a crack' (cf. *pī* 'to sprinkle')

C = -ø-
  hū-a'i 'to pour forth' (cf. *hū* 'to rise up, swell')
  Kau-a'i, island name (cf. *kau* 'to place')
  lu-a'i 'to vomit' (cf. *lu-ea* 'nausea' and Tongan *lua* 'to vomit')
  lum-a'i 'to drown' (cf. *luma* 'to drown')
  māk-a'i 'to inspect' (cf. *maka* 'eye')
  n-a'i 'to conquer' (cf. *nā* 'to soothe, pacify')
  p-a'i 'to slap' (cf. *pā* 'to hit')
  pu-a'i 'to vomit' (cf. *pua* 'to pour forth')

  Possible others: *luma-ha'i* 'twist of fingers in making string figures', *hi-na'i* 'fish trap' (cf. *hī* 'to fish for bonito').

Words with the suffix -*Ci* have been noted as follows:

C = -*h*-
  kilo-hi 'to observe' (cf. *kilo* 'to gaze')
  uku-hi 'to pour out, as water' (cf. Samoan *utu*)

C = -*k*-
  'ini-ki, 'ini 'to pinch'

C = -'-
  'ekeke-'i 'short, as a dress' (cf. *'eke* 'to shrink')
  mū'ekeke-'i 'to recede; tight-fitting dress' (cf. *mū'e'eke* 'to shrink')
  nāku-'i 'to rumble' (cf. *naku* 'to suffer gas pains')
  pana'i 'to revenge' (cf. *pana* 'to shoot, snap')
  pūku-'i 'to collect' (cf. *puku, puku-a, puku-lia* 'to gather, collect')

6.6.5   THEMATIC CONSONANTS

$C = \phi$

hau, hau-i 'to strike'
hoa-i 'joint, suture' (cf. *hoa* 'to tie')
holo-i 'to wash' (cf. Samoan *solo* 'to wipe, as the body')
kala-i 'to carve' (cf. *ho'okala* 'to sharpen')
kalele-i 'to listen' (cf. *kalele* 'to lean upon, trust')
ho'okina, kina-i 'to persist'
lahu-i 'to prohibit' (cf. Samoan *lafu* 'to prohibit')
mino-i 'to pucker' (cf. *mino* 'creased')
mū, mu-i 'crowded, silent'
olo, olo-i 'to grate'

$C = -', -\phi$

helele'i, helelei 'to fall, scatter' (cf. *lele* 'to fly' and Samoan *felelei* 'flying')

Suffixes beginning with thematic consonants are most commonly added to action-marking verbs; a few are added to adjectival-stative verbs (*'awa'awa'*, *makala*) and *loa'a*-statives (*make, pau*).

In a few instances, the same *C* is present in two or more of the possible forms (*-Cana, -Cia, -Ca'i, -Ci*): *kilo-hana, kilo-hia, kilo-hi; komo-hana, komo-hia; kau-lana, kau-lia, kau-la'i, kū-lana, kū-lia, kū-la'i; mana'o-lana, mana'o-lia.*

POSSIBLE ANALYSES

6.6.5   Interpretation of bases ending in *-a* and taking *-a'i* or *'i* as a suffix is perhaps arbitrary. Is *lua'i* to be divided *lu-a'i* or *lua-'i*? What of *luma'i, māka'i, na'i, pa'i, pua'i*? The *-a'i* division has been made in every case; *-a-a* commonly shortens to *a* elsewhere in the language (e.g. *alohai* [*aloha* plus *ai*], *pua aloalo* 'hibiscus flower', usually pronounced *pualoalo*).

Bloomfield (1933:219), Nida (1949:76), and Gleason (1955:31), with reference to Samoan, recommended that bases be reconstructed ending in the first phoneme of the suffix, as **kiloh-, *komoh-, *kaul-, *kūl-,* and **mana'ol-,* and that the suffixes be *-a'i, -ana,* and *-ia.* In general this solution is more "economical" (high praise to many linguists); that is, it is simpler to posit for the passive/imperative only one suffix, *-ia,* but this would mean that Hawaiian *'ia* would not be treated as a particle, and that many bases would have alternants. 'Thief', for example, would be **'aihue', *'aihuel,* and **'aihuen* (to obtain

88

the active form the final consonant would have to be deleted). The base for 'drink' would be *inuh-*, *inum-* (*inum* happens to be the Tagalog form, but this fact is irrelevant in a description of Hawaiian). The overriding reason, however, that no specialist in Polynesian languages has made such a recommendation is that no Hawaiian words end in consonants, and such forms as *aihueh-* are disquieting.

Nineteenth-century Hawaiian grammarians were not very familiar with other Austronesian languages. Chamisso and Andrews attributed what they considered anomalous passives to euphony. Cautious Alexander (1968:21) merely says, "Sometimes another letter is inserted between the verb and *ia.*"

7   Postposed Phrasal Elements

SOME POSTPOSED PARTICLES

7.1   In table 7 (chapter 3) postposed particles occur in two positions. Those that belong to the set to the left in the table are discussed below. The particles occurring at the *ends* of phrases (at the right in the table) are examined in section 7.5.

'Ino is an intensifying particle most commonly used after *aloha* and *nui:*

> *Aloha 'ino!* 'What a shame!'
> *Nui 'ino.* 'Very very many.'
> *Nani 'ino ku'u makemake!* 'How much I want [it]!'
> *Ua lele 'ino a'ela kō Pāka'a hauli* (Nakuina 64). 'Pāka'a was terribly shocked.'

Pū, a modifier of both verbs and nouns has two meanings: 'together with, entirely, also with', and 'inactive, sluggish, quiet, bored'. Context determines which translation is appropriate; the second meaning is quite rare. In isolation, *ū* in *pū* 'together with' may be longer than *u* in *pū* 'inactive'. The difference, if any, may be lost in connected speech.

> *Like pū.* 'Just the same.'
> *Me 'oe pū.* 'You too./Same to you.'
> *Noho pū wale nō.* 'Just living together.'
> *Noho pū wale ihola nō 'o Kimo.* 'James just sat there dejectedly.'

Wale means 'just, quite, alone; without reason; reward, pay'. Many examples are in the Dictionary. The sequence *wale nō* usually means 'only' (*'elua wale nō* 'only two'), but may be a mild, almost negative, intensifier: *He maika'i wale nō kāu mau kūkaliki i painu'u mai nei* (Kelekona 135). 'What you've been bragging and boasting about here is all right, I suppose.' The fol-

90

lowing long noun phrase is acceptable: *Lākou mā wale mai nei nō.* 'Just all of them.' (For more about *mā*, see section 8.7.5.)

Koke 'quickly' occurs in both noun phrases and verb phrases: *No kona hele koke 'ole mai* 'because of his not coming quickly'. *E hele koke mai nō 'oe.* 'Come quickly.' (Cf. *kokoke* 'near', a qualifying verb.)

'Ole, a common negative from which *'a'ole* is derived, occurs in the following positions:

    verb/noun pū wale koke 'ole 'ia (directional)

Examples:

> *i kona hele koke 'ole mai* 'because of his not coming'
> *'ai 'ole 'ia* 'not eaten'

'Ole is more commonly used as an adjectival stative verb, as in *maika'i 'ole* 'not good', and also as a noun (see Dictionary).

Honua, glossed 'suddenly, abruptly and without reason', is less common than the other particles in this position. *Huhū honua ihola nō* 'suddenly angry and without reason'.

Kū as a particle, glossed 'abruptly, rudely, defiantly', is not to be confused with its many homonyms, all of which may be classed as noun, verb, or noun-verb: *'Ai kū* 'to eat informally, carelessly; to break taboos'. *Kā'ili kū* 'to snatch ruthlessly'.

The passive/imperative *'ia* is next in line (see example above under *'ole*), but has been discussed in section 6.6.3.

DIRECTIONALS

7.2   The four directionals, all very common, are the following:

Near or toward the speaker
    (1) *mai,* 'to me', toward the speaker
    (2) *iho* 'downward, self', reflexive, near future

Visible, sometimes near addressee
    (3) *a'e* 'up, nearby, adjacent, adjoining, next' in space or time

Far or away from the speaker
    (4) *aku* 'away', future

Examples of directionals with the common verb *hele:*

Hele mai! 'Come!'	*Hele iho!* 'Go down'
Hele a'e! 'Go up!'	*Hele aku!* 'Go away!'

A parallelism exists between the directionals and the pronouns, possessives, and demonstratives discussed in chapter 8: all of them more or less express relative distance between speaker and addressee in place and/or time. See table 12.

The ∅-demonstrative *nei* after *iho*, *a'e*, and *aku* adds the meaning 'past', with *aku nei* being more remote than *iho nei* or *a'e nei*. *Mai nei* indicates past time and present place: *Inā 'oe i hele mai nei me ka maika'i* . . . (FS 225). 'If you had come here with good [intentions] . . . .' Compare *i ka pō nei* 'last night' and *nehinei* 'yesterday', *i kēia mau lā iho nei* 'these last few days' and *i kēia mau lā iho* 'the coming few days', and *hele mai nei nō 'oia* 'he came here.'

The time scale with directionals with and without following *nei* is more or less as follows:

Distant past: *aku nei*
Recent past: *a'e nei, iho nei*
Adjoining the present: *a'e*
Near future: *iho*
Distant future: *aku*

Examples:

kēlā pule aku nei 'last week'
kēia pule aku nei ā ia pule aku nei 'week before last'
Ua hele a'e nei no Maui. '[He] has just gone to Maui.'
i kēia mau lā iho nei 'these past few days'
ia lā a'e ia lā a'e 'from day to day'
ko'u mua a'e 'the [one born] just before me'
i kēia mau lā iho 'the coming days'
'apōpō ā ia lā aku 'day after tomorrow'
I hea aku nei 'oe (Kelekona 130)? 'Where have you been?'

The use of directionals with verbs of saying (*'ī, pane, nīnau, kāhea, 'ōlelo*) has not been sufficiently studied. *Aku, mai,* and *a'e* seem to be the most common, perhaps in that order. They are sometimes followed by the ∅-demonstrative *lā* 'there (far)' or by *-la* as an enclitic (see Glossary). In English one may say 'John said', but in Hawaiian the relative positions of speaker and addressee may be shown by the directionals. Compare:

'ī maila 'oia 'he said to me'
'ī a'ela 'oia 'he said to someone nearby'
'ī akula 'oia 'he said to someone else'

TABLE 12
Spatio-Temporal Proximity Chart

	Speaker or Near Speaker	Indefinite	Addressee or Near Addressee	Far
Singular pronouns	*au, a'u*		*'oe*	*ia*
Singular possessives				
Classifying	*ka'u, ko'u*		*kāu, kou*	*kāna, kona*
Affectionate	*ku'u*†		*kō*†	
Demonstratives				
ke-class	*kēia*		*kēna*†	*kēla*
ø-class	*neia, nei*†	*ia, ua*	*nā*†	*ala, la/-la, ana*
Directionals	*mai, iho*		*a'e*‡	*aku*
Locatives	*'ane'i, 'one'i*	*laila*	*'ō*	*'ō*

† Sometimes indicates emotion: *ku'u* and *kō* affectionate, *kēna* and *nā* sometimes derisive, *nei* sometimes affectionate.

‡ Less precisely indicative of relative position than the other directionals; visible.

In the discussion of *wahi* 'say' in section 8.1 is the following example (X represents a direct quotation):

'Ī aku ke kaikamahine: "X." 'The daughter said: "X." '
'Ī mai ka makua kāne: "X." 'The father replied: "X." '

Here *'ī aku* means 'say to someone else'; *'ī mai* seems to mean 'say back to the first speaker'. The two directionals here can be equated with 'thither' and 'hither'.

The combinations *mái-la, ihó-la, a'é-la,* and *akú-la* are usually written as single words because they take the stress of single words, as shown above. (In fast speech the *a-* in *akula* may be lost: *hele akúla* may become *hele kula*.)

Examples of *a'e* meaning visible space:

'O wai hou a'e? 'Who will be next?'
Eia a'e 'o Pua. 'Here comes Pua.'
ma'ō a'e nei nō 'just over there / not far'

A'e also expresses the comparative degree: *maika'i a'e* 'better'. It frequently follows *'ē* 'different': *'A'ole anei o'u makuakāne 'ē a'e* (FS 119)? 'Haven't I a different father?' This common usage seems vaguely related to the idea of "adjoining."

The directionals have other syntactic and semantic roles. *Mai* occurs as a verblike idiom without any verb markers: *Mai! Mai e 'ai!* 'Come! Come and eat!' Other meanings include 'give' and 'say':

Mai naʻu! 'Give to me! Give [it] to me!'
"E ō," maila ʻo Ka-welo (FS 39). ' "Yes," said Ka-welo.'

Mai is also used at times after the indefinite article *he: He mai! E kipa i kauhale. Mai i kauhale nei* (Kelekona 19)! 'Come! Visit the house! Come to this house!'

Iho occurs as an intransitive verb and may be preceded and followed by particles:

Ua iho maila ke aliʻi. 'The chief has come down.'
Ua iho ʻia ke ala. 'Someone has gone down the path' (lit., the path has been gone down on).

Iho also denotes bodily processes and frequently follows such verbs as *ʻai* 'eat', *aloha* 'love', *inu* 'drink', *makaʻu* 'fear', and *manaʻo* and *noʻonoʻo* 'think': *ʻAi ihola ʻoia i ka puaʻa.* 'He ate the pork.'

As a noun and after pronouns and locatives, *iho* may mean 'self':

paʻakikī me kāna iho (Kep. 103) 'stubborn with his own [things]'
Ke nānā nei au iaʻu iho. 'I'm looking now at myself.'
noʻu iho 'as for me'
i loko iho o kou noʻonoʻo 'within your thoughts'

These examples indicate that *iho*, like *mai*, commonly refers to self. For a love song in which *iho* equates with self, and *aʻe* with a nearby sweetheart, see the poem at the end of section 8.3.6. And for another song with contrasting directionals, see at the end of section 5.3.

Iho and *aʻe* sometimes qualify *luna* and *lalo: maluna iho* seems less high than *maluna. Maluna aʻe* is sometimes 'still higher', and *malalo iho* 'still lower'.

In sentences the directionals follow *ʻia* and precede the anaphoric *ai* (section 7.3) and the *ɸ*-demonstratives (see table 7): *I aha ʻia aku nei?* 'What happened a while ago?' In noun phrases the directionals may follow the nominalizer *ʻana: kona hele ʻana mai* 'his coming'.

The directionals frequently occur in noun phrases after place names and locatives, as *mai Honolulu mai* 'from Honolulu this way', *mai Honolulu aku* 'away from Honolulu', *malaila aku* 'away from there'.

Directionals are most commonly used with five types of verbs (page references to FS are given for rare usages):

(1) Intransitive verbs of motion: *ea, hāʻule, hele, hiki, hoʻi, holo, iho, kū, noho* 'to sit', *puka*. Also, rarely, *ʻaʻā* (91), *newa* (89).

(2) Deliberate transitive verbs of saying: *ʻae, haʻi, hea, ʻī, kāhea, mele, ʻōlelo, paha*.

(3) Deliberate transitive verbs of motion: *hopu, kākiʻi, luku, nānā, pakele*. Also, rarely, *ʻapo* (93), *hahau* (89), *hoʻolale* (91), *kau* (91), *kīkoʻu* (91), *moe* 'to marry', *pāpale* (91), *waiho* (91).

(4) Spontaneous transitives indicating bodily processes, as previously indicated, with *iho: aloha iho, makaʻu iho, manaʻo iho, noʻonoʻo iho*.

(5) *Loaʻa*-statives:

Aloha mai! 'May you be welcome here! Greetings!'
ʻimi i wahi e lilo mai ai ʻoia ma ke mele 'seeking a way that he might escape by singing'
Nahā akula ka hale (89). 'The house is broken.'
Peʻa aʻela nā lima. 'The hands are crossed.'
Also: *loaʻa, make, nalowale.*

Directionals are used in verbless sentences or noun phrases with meaning of coming or going.

I Maui aku nei au. 'I was on Maui. / I went to Maui.'
Eia mai au. 'Here I am. / Here I come.'
Eia aʻe ʻo Kimo. 'Here comes James.'

Kona	hele	ʻana	aku	nei	nō	ia.
his	go	(nominalizer)	away	(past)	(intensifier)	it

'He's just gone. / He just went.'

Lākou	mā	wale	mai	nei	nō.
they	and others	only	come	(past)	(intensifier)

'Only those people came.'

A very rare use of directionals is as nouns preceded by *nā*, presumably the plural article:

he mea ʻai i nā aku 'food for the future'
I nā iho ke ala. 'Here is the road.'
I nā aʻe nā makamaka. 'There the friends are coming.'

In conclusion: It is difficult or impossible to fashion hard and fast rules for the use of directionals. The safest course is simply to follow examples slavishly.

AI

7.3   This common particle, found in nearly all Polynesian languages, was called a relative particle by such mid-nineteenth-century writers as Hale (1968, first published in 1846), Pratt (1960, first published in 1862, Samoan), and Alexander (1968, first published in 1864, Hawaiian). The name "relative" was given by Hale (1968:276-277) because *ai* "in many cases supplies the place of the relative pronoun in English, though frequently it cannot well be translated. It usually refers to some word in the first part of the sentence, expressive of time, place, cause, means, manner, etc." Today, items in a given language are named for their role *in that language*, not for their translation into another language.)

Alexander (1968:22) gives numerous examples in which, he believes, *ai* corresponds to English "by which," "when," or "where," as *Eia ka mea i make ai nā kānaka.* 'Here is the cause from which the people died.' But no English relative is involved in such sentences as *Āhea 'oe e hele mai ai?* 'When are you coming?' If a locative phrase comes first, it corresponds to a final (but frowned on) "at": *Mahea 'oe e noho ai?* 'Where do you live at?' The *ai* in this case seems to replace postverbal *ana*, as in the following sentence, with the same meaning but with less focus on the where: *E noho ana 'oe i hea?* (Note that the pronoun subject precedes the verb after a sentence-opening locative.)

The use of *ai* after preverbal noun phrases is clearly shown in table 9. *I* (verb) *ai* and *e* (verb) *ai* replace *ua* (verb) and *e* (verb) if a noun phrase precedes the verb phrase as in the sentence in section 5.2: *i ka manawa i hele mai ai ke kanaka* 'at the time at which *(ai)* the man came'.

In the Dictionary the term "linking particle" is used as a name for *ai*; in the Pocket Dictionary *ai* is defined as a "linking or anaphoric particle." The term **anaphoric** was apparently first used with reference to a Polynesian language by Milner (1966). Bloomfield (1933:249) characterizes anaphoric substitutes as replacing forms that have occurred in recent speech. Every *ai* in Hawaiian has an antecedent, usually expressed, but sometimes understood.

Examples follow of sentences (a) without and (b) with *ai*. The orders are:

(a) verb phrase + subject + noun phrase

(b) noun phrase (antecedent of *ai*) + pronoun subj. + verb phrase + *ai*

or

noun phrase (antecedent of *ai*) + verb phrase + *ai* + noun subject

The fronted noun phrases (the antecedents of *ai*) are in focus. They may express time, place, cause, means or manner, and goal. These headings correspond roughly to Alexander's "by which," "when," "where," previously listed.

Time

(a) *Ua hele ʻoe ināhea?* 'When did you go?'

(b) *Ināhea ʻoe i hele ai?* 'When did you go?'

(a) *Ua hānai ʻia lākou ʻakolu i ka wā hoʻokahi.* 'The three were raised at the same time.'

(b) *I ka wā hoʻokahi lākou ʻakolu i hānai ʻia ai.* 'The three of them were raised at the same time.'

Another example: *I ka wā e holo ai i ka luʻu heʻe . . .* (FS 19) 'at the time [he] sailed to dive for octopus . . .'

Place

(a) *Ua holo mākou i laila.* 'We rode there.'

(b) *I laila kahi a mākou i holo ai. I laila mākou i holo ai.* (Insertion of *kahi a* is optional.) 'There was the place we rode to.'

(a) *Ua noho ʻo Punia i ka ʻāina o Kohala.* 'Punia lived at the land of Kohala.'

(b) *ʻO ka ʻāina i noho ai ʻo Punia, ʻo Kohala* (FS 9). 'The land where Punia lived at was Kohala.'

Another example: *Maʻaneʻi ʻoe e lana ai ā loaʻa mai iaʻu.* 'Here you will float until I find you. / You'll float here until I find you.'

Cause

No ka hewa ʻana o Kumu-honua mā, papapau ai kānaka i ka make (Kep. 49). 'Because of the sin of Kumu-honua and companion, all the people died from it.'

ʻO Koʻolau ka lēpela nāna i kīpū pōwā maila iā Lui H. Stoltz ā make ai (Kelekona 93). 'Koʻolau was the leper who shot Louis H. Stoltz who died from it.'

Means or manner

(a) *Ua kope hele lāua me ka lima a me ka wāwae.* 'They raked on with hands and feet.'

(b) *Me ka lima ame ka wāwae, lāua i kope hele ai.* 'They raked on with hands and feet.'

Other examples: *Pēlā i loaʻa ai ka iʻa.* 'That's how fish were gotten.' *E ʻimi ana au i kanaka ʻaihue, e loaʻa ai aʻu leho* (FS 21). 'By my looking for a thief by whom my cowries will be gotten. / I'm looking for a thief who'll get my cowries.'

Goal

If a direct object is fronted, the pronoun subject is replaced by an *a*-possessive (never *o*-), and the verb is preceded by *i* (replacing *ua*) and is followed by the anaphoric *ai.* (The possessive following a preposed noun object is neutralized.)

(a) *Ua makemake au i ka hale.* 'I liked the house.'
(b) *Ka hale aʻu i makemake ai.* 'The house I liked.'

(a) *Ua kamaʻāina i kēia leo ā i aloha nui au i kēia leo.* 'I am used to this voice and greatly love this voice.'
(b) *Kēia leo aʻu i kamaʻāina ā i aloha nui ai* (Kelekona 99). 'This voice I'm used to and greatly love.'

The words *hale* and *leo* in the last four examples ordinarily take the *o* possessive, but take *a* after a fronted direct object. Kelekona 136 provides an instance of the same noun, *hoʻoilina,* taking both *o*- and *a*- possessives: *kō lākou mau hoʻoilina a lākou i aloha nui ai* 'their heritage they greatly loved'.

E (verb) *ana* versus *e* (verb) *ai:* In table 9, *e* (verb) *ana* occurs initially, and *e* (verb) *ai* medially. An example of this contrast:

E lana mai ana nō ʻo ʻUmi makai o lāua nei. ʻĪ aku ʻo ʻIwa iā Keaʻau . . . "Ē Keaʻau, maʻaneʻi ʻoe e lana ai ā loaʻa mai iaʻu (FS 25)."

'Umi was floating on the sea side of the two here. 'Iwa said to Keaʻau . . . "O Keaʻau, here you must float so that I [can] get [the cowry]." '

In the following, *e* seems to indicate purpose rather than mere intention, evidence of the wide semantic range of what has been called imperative/intentive:

Haʻalele ʻo Keaʻau iā Hawaiʻi, holo i Maui e kaʻapuni ai. . . . Holo i Lānaʻi e huli ai . . . holo i Molokaʻi . . . , i laila, loaʻa he kamaʻāina e lawaiʻa ana (FS 19).

'Keaʻau left Hawaiʻi, sailed to Maui in order to go around it. . . . Sailed to Lānaʻi to search there . . . sailed to Molokaʻi . . . , there [he] found a native fishing.'

Ai following a verb ending in -*a* coalesces with the -*a* in fast speech; thus *hana ai* becomes *hanāi, aloha ai* becomes *alohāi* written in the Bible, but not in the Dictionary, *aloha'i*). *Ai* is commonly pronounced *ei*, or the first vowel suggests the *a* in English *fat*.

(This discussion of *ai* has benefited by reference to Chapin, 1974, and to an unpublished paper by John Dupont, 1973.)

ø-DEMONSTRATIVES *ala, lā/-la, ana*

7.4   *Lā/-la* is much more common than *ala* or *ana*. *Ala* has the same meaning as *lā/-la*, but *ana* (see below) is rather different. They are listed in table 12 (section 7.2). In that section numerous examples are given of *-la* preceded by directionals. In section 8.3.4 the demonstrative *ua* + *noun* + ø-demonstratives is explained and illustrated. *Lā* and *ala* may also replace "X" in the present tense in the sequence *ke* (verb) *X* depicted in table 9 (section 5.1).

Makanani Lee (1973) studied the occurrence of *lā/-la* in fourteen tapes of native speakers, in twenty chapters of Malo's *Hawaiian Antiquities*, in Beckwith's *Kepelino's Traditions of Hawaii*, (pages 75–113 and 123–147), and in Nakuina's *Moolelo Hawaii* . . . (pages 1–8). The tapes were conversational, Malo and Kepelino factual, and Nakuina narrative. She found *lā/-la* rarely used in the conversational and factual categories, but fairly common in indirect discourse in narratives. She concluded that use of this demonstrative is a narrative device, otherwise infrequently used.

An idiom is *'oia lā ho'i* 'for that reason': *Inā e hānau mai ke keiki, a laila, 'oia lā ho'i ka mea e nā ai ka huhū o nā mākua ona* (Nakuina 6). 'If a child should be born, that would be the thing to pacify the anger of her parents.'

Lā is common as a meaningless refrain in songs, as *Hanohano Hawai'i lā, lei ka lehua lā*. 'Glorious is Hawai'i, *lehua* is the lei.' *Lā* here may serve to separate and emphasize the preceding phrase from what follows, and of course repetition is a favorite device in Hawaiian poetry.

Postposed *ana* most commonly forms a discontinuous item in the sequence *e* (verb) *ana* discussed in section 5.2. *Ana* also occurs without *e* after the verb, and seems to indicate a single event, whether a command or a statement, whether completed or incomplete:

Ō hele ana 'oe, ē ka noe (Emerson 1915:65). 'Go then, O mists.'
Ha'ina 'ia mai ana ka puana. 'Tell the refrain.'

Pau ana ka 'ai i ke poho (FS 81). 'The food will be consumed in the hollow of the hand.'

Iāia nō a hele, kū ana ke ka'a. 'As soon as he had gone, the car came.'
'Oia ana nō. 'It's the same result./Regardless.'

The demonstrative *lā/-la* occurs earlier in the phrase than the dubitative *lā* described in section 7.5.

PARTICLES FOLLOWING THE ϕ-DEMONSTRATIVES

7.5   These particles fall into semantic categories. They come in a fixed order, indicated in the following list. Certain incompatible items in the list are bracketed; they cannot occur in the same phrase.

⎧ *nō*	intensifying
⎨ *nona'e*	conditional
⎩ *noho'i*	intensifying
kā	intensifying
lā	dubitative
auane'i 'probably'	dubitative
na'e	conditional
⎰ *ho'i*	intensifying
⎱ *ho'ihā*	intensifying
'ānō	temporal
anei	interrogative
paha	dubitative
auane'i 'soon'	temporal
kau	intensifying

These particles are discussed in the order of their occurrence after the nucleus, and not according to semantic features.

The intensifier *nō* is not to be confused with *no*, the benefactive/causative/locative preposition that introduces noun phrases (section 9.11). The intensifier most commonly comes in verb phrases, but it occurs also in other environments, as illustrated below. Note the following contrasts:

Ua maika'i nō ke ali'i. 'The chief is quite well (now).'
Ua maika'i no ke ali'i. '[It's] good (now) for the chief.'

Nō is an extremely common particle; context determines

which of the many meanings is appropriate. The common environments follow:

(1) After verbs: *E hana mua 'ia ana nō ke alanui.* 'The road will actually be made first.' *Pehea 'oe? Maika'i nō.* 'How are you? Oh, all right.' (*Maika'i nō* is less emphatic than *maika'i loa* 'very good'.)

(2) After nouns and pronouns: *Ke aloha nō!* 'Much love!' *'O au nō.* 'Just me.'

(3) *Nō* frequently follows *wale* (see section 7.1) and may occur between a numeral and a noun: *'elua wale nō mea* 'only two things'.

(4) *Nō* follows conjunctions: *inā nō au i make nou* 'if only I had died for you'. *A'ole nō au e 'ae.* 'I won't agree.'

(5) *Nō* combines with *na'e* 'yet, but' and *ho'i*, a common intensifier, but the vowel is shortened: *no-na'e, no-ho'i.* Before *kā*, an exclamation of surprise, the vowel remains long. The three terms share the distribution of *nō* and may replace *nō* in any of the above sentences, but with slight changes in meaning.

Nona'e and *na'e* have the meaning 'still, yet, however': *Ua koe nona'e ke ola.* 'Yet life remains.' *Noho'i* is a strong intensifier, as in the common exclamation *Auē noho'i ē!* 'My! Oh my!' *Nō kā* expresses astonishment: *Eia a'e nō kā!* 'So here [he] is!'

Nō, nona'e, and *noho'i* are mutually exclusive.

Kā is most commonly heard alone as an exclamation of scorn, and is pronounced frequently with extra-systematic sounds: *chā! sā! kē!* Within utterances, it more frequently follows nouns than verbs:

'O	*ke*	*kua*	*kā*	*ko'u*	*hoa*	*'ōlelo* (FS 243)!
(subj.)	the	back	so	my	companion	speak

'So the back is my speaking companion!'

'O	*ka*	*pua'a*	*kā*	*lā* (FS 217)!
(subj.)	the	pig	so	there

'So it's the pig there!'

'O	*'oe*	*kā!*
(subj.)	you	so

'So it's you!'

Ā	*hina*	*kā*	*ho'i*	*māua* (FS 37).
and	fall	so	indeed	we-two

'And so we two really fell.'

'Ōlelo aku 'o Kama-pua'a me ka huhū: " *'A'ole nō kā e no'ono'o iho kou 'ōpū* (FS 239)?"

'Kama-pua'a said in anger: "So your stomach doesn't think?" (Haven't you any brains?)'

Lā, dubitative, is commonly heard in answers to questions one cannot, or doesn't choose to, answer, with the question word repeated in the answer followed by dubitative *lā:*

Question: *'O wai kona inoa?* 'What's his name?'
Answer: *'O wai lā.* 'I don't know (or care).' (Lit., who so.)

Question: *He aha kēlā mea?* 'What's that thing?'
Answer: *He aha lā.* 'I don't know (or care).' (Lit., a what so.)

Lā also occurs in long sentences, and may even be preceded by the homophonous *ø*-demonstrative *lā:*

(Agentive phrase)
I	*'ai*	*'ia*	*nō*	*lā*	*e*	*aha?*
(purpose)	eat	(pas./imp.)	indeed	doubt	by	what

'To be eaten for what reason?'

Pehea iho-la	*lā*	*kona*	*mana'o?*
what (reflexive-there)	doubt	his	opinion

'What then may be his opinion?'

Auane'i and its variants *'ane'i* and *uane'i*, infrequent dubitatives, usually follow nouns and are translatable as 'probably, merely, just'. In the Dictionary examples, *auane'i* follows a noun and the interrogative *pehea*. Other examples:

He aha auane'i ho'i (Nakuina 103)? 'So what of it?'
'o ka nīnau mai auane'i kāu (Kelekona 116) 'probably your question'
He pa'akai ane'i e hehe'e ai? 'Maybe you are salt and therefore melt?' (Said to one who hesitates to go out into the rain.)

Uane'i usually follows words ending in -*a*; see the Dictionary for an example. The more common *auane'i* 'soon' occurs in the next-to-the-last position in the phrase, and is discussed near the end of this section.

Na'e, already introduced, precedes *ho'i: Aloha maila na'e ho'i kō ipo.* 'But your sweetheart did indeed send greetings.' *Na'e* also follows initial *'a'ole: 'A'ole na'e ia i hiki mai.* 'He hasn't come yet.' *Na'e* seems not to occur in noun phrases.

Ho'i: This common particle is not to be confused with the equally common homophonous intransitive verb *ho'i* 'to go back, return, leave'. The verb may follow verb markers and may come initially in affirmative sentences. The particle follows verbs in affirmative sentences and follows 'a'ole in negative transformations. The particle also follows nouns, pronouns, and conjunctions.

The somewhat disparate meanings of the particle are (1) general intensifier, and (2) 'also', or, after a negative, 'either'. Context determines the translation. '*Elua ho'i* may mean 'also two' or 'two then'. After *no-* the meaning is that of intensifier (see *noho'i*). Doubt may be emphasized after interrogatives in such exclamations as *pehea ho'i* 'how indeed' or *he mea aha ho'i* 'what in the world for'.

In chants, the intensifier *ho'i* may for aesthetic reasons contrast with the verb *ho'i:*

Ku'u	*wahine*	*ho'i*	*ē,*	*ho'i*	*mai* (FS 277).
my	wife	(intensifier)	(vocative)	come-back	here

'O my dear wife, come back.'

Ho'ihā is an intensifier indicative of slight anger or annoyance. *I Hawai'i ho'ihā me Pele e noho ai* (FS 239). 'Then stay at Hawai'i with Pele.' *Kāhea 'ia ho'ihā* (FS 265). 'Then summon [her].' (See the Dictionary for the idiom '*oia ho'ihā*.)

'*Ānō* 'now': *Hele mai nei nō 'ānō*. 'Come here now.' *Hele mai ke ali'i 'ānō*. 'The chief is coming now.' The temporal particles '*ānō* and *auane'i* seem to be the only postnuclear particles that are sometimes used as sentence words. An idiomatic use of '*ānō* is illustrated in section 4.6.

Anei is an optional particle indicating that the sentence in which it occurs is a question that can be answered by yes or no. *Maika'i nō anei kēia kula?* 'Is this school really good?' *He kāne anei kāu?* 'Have you a husband?' (See also examples in the Dictionary.)

Paha: This extremely common particle occurs before, but never after, a pause of some kind, and may usually be glossed 'perhaps, maybe, probably, approximately'. *Maika'i anei paha?* 'Perhaps good?' *Pēlā paha!* 'Maybe so!' Preceded by a verb, *paha, 'a'ole paha* is a common idiom. *Maika'i paha, 'a'ole paha.* 'Maybe good, maybe not.' (This is a modest way of speaking that is perhaps equivalent to "Well, maybe it's okay." *Ā . . . paha* is a way to say 'or': '*Elua ā 'ekolu paha* 'two or three'. *Paha* is often used to make speech more polite and conciliatory, and in some ways corresponds to such English mildly deprecatory words as "should" and "might," terms not found in Hawaiian.

Auane'i 'by and by, soon': *E noho mai paha auane'i ā kipi mai iā'oe.* 'Perhaps [they] will wait and later revolt against you.' *He lohe mai auane'i i ka makua.* 'Later there will be obedience to the parent.' *He ali'i waiwai auane'i ia* (FS 137). 'Soon he will be a rich chief.' Compare the less common dubitative *auane'i* discussed earlier in this section. Variants are *uane'i* and *'ane'i*.

Kau, a superlative, usually but not always follows *ho'i*. *He nani mai ho'i kau!* 'Oh, so beautiful!' *E lohe mai auane'i kau i ka leo o ka makua!* 'Soon [you] will listen to the parent's request!'

8 Nouns and Substitutes, Locative Nouns, Compounds, Qualifiers

Table 7 in chapter 3 shows that noun phrases differ from verb phrases principally in the prenuclear elements. These are discussed in chapters 9 and 10.

The largest part of this chapter is concerned with substitutes for nouns: pronouns, demonstratives, possessives, and interrogatives. They are called substitutes because they occupy many of the slots of ordinary nouns. (*Ua 'ike ke ali'i.* 'The chief knows.' *Ua 'ike 'oe.* 'You know.') Substitutes differ radically from nouns and verbs in that most of them (pronouns, demonstratives, and possessives) are not bases and do not contain bases; they are composed of small, easily recognized elements that cannot stand alone. Finally in this chapter are discussions of locative nouns, compounds, and qualifiers.

NOUNS

8.1 Nouns, as contrasted with noun-verbs, are limited largely to material objects, plants and animals, and names of persons and places. Most affixes in the language occur with noun-verbs. About the only prefixes to nouns are *Hono-* and *Hana-*, that occur in place names, and *kai* 'related person'.

Hana- and *Hono-* are not translated into English because they form the initial part of many place names. Most of such names are near the sea, although a few are inland. They are discussed in some detail in Pukui, Elbert, and Mookini (1974:245–247). *Hana-* is listed in section 2.11 as a shift from *faCa-* and is termed "vestigial" because it is the ancestral form and is less common than *Hono-*. A table in Pukui, Elbert, and Mookini shows that *Hana-* is most common on the Northwestern Hawaiian Islands, Ni'ihau, and especially Kaua'i; O'ahu has both forms, and on the other islands to the east and south *Hono-* is the most common. Examples are *Hono-lulu* 'fair harbor' and *Hono-uliuli* 'dark bay' on O'ahu, and *Hono-ke-ana* 'the cave bay' on West Maui. On Kaua'i are *Hana-lei* 'lei bay' and *Hana-pēpē* 'crushed bay'; *Hana-uma* 'curved bay' is on O'ahu. Retention of the older form is in keeping with the Ni'ihau retention of vestigial *t*, also mentioned in section 2.11.

Hana- and *Hono-* are prefixes because they occur only as parts of place names. **Hele i ka hana* 'go to the bay' is impossible. *Hono* is known to occur as a noun in only a single poetic phrase: *nā Hono a Pi'i-lani* (Elbert and Mahoe 63) 'the *Hono*-bays of [chief] Pi'i-lani', that is, Honokahua, Honokeana, Honokohau, Honokowai, Honolua, Hononana.

Six kinship terms listed and defined in section 9.6.1 begin with *kai-* (*kai-kaina, kai-ko'eke, kai-kua'ana, kai-kunāne, kai-kuahine, kai-kamahine*). Without initial *kai-*, the terms are vocative. With *kai-* they are reference terms. One might define *kai-* as "classificatory kin reference prefix": *kaina* 'younger classificatory sibling of ego's sex' is the vocative; *kai-kaina*, the usual term of reference. (For a definition of "classificatory," see 9.6.1.)

Ten nouns designating kinds of people, some of them kinship terms, form the plural by lengthening the third from the last vowel:

'aumākua 'family gods'	*kānaka* 'people'
'elemākule 'old men'	*kūpuna* 'grandparents'
kāhiko 'old persons'	*luāhine* 'old women'
kāhuna 'priests'	*mākua* 'parents'
kaikamāhine 'girls'	*wāhine* 'women'

Plurality may be indicated redundantly: *kekahi mau kānaka* 'a few people', *he mau po'e wāhine* 'several women'. The added vowel length in these words may be called an infix since it is affixed within a base.

A noun with limited distribution is *wahi*, usually translated 'to say'. It has, however, no verb characteristics at all and is invariably followed by the possessive preposition *a* or by an *a*-class ∅-possessive:

" 'Ae," *wahi a Laenihi* (FS 253). ' "Yes," said Laenihi.'
Wahi a wai? 'Who said so?/According to whom?'

" 'Ae, ua pono!" *wahi āna* (Green and Pukui 40). ' "Yes, [that's] right!" he said.'

106

"E hele holoholo wale aku ana au," wahi aʻu i pane aku ai (Kelekona 100). ' "I'm just going for a walk," I said in answer.'

"Ma ka hale," wahi a kāna pane (Kelekona 109). ' "At the house," was his answer.'

Wahi a Ka-haka-loa: "Ināhea kā Ka-welo aʻo ʻana i ke koa (FS 89)?" 'Ka-haka-loa said: "When did Ka-welo learn warfare?" '

In all but the last example, *wahi* follows the direct quotation.

In contrast to *wahi*, which most commonly follows direct quotations, verbs of saying generally *precede* direct quotations. A single paragraph in FS 59 has the following (X represents the quotations): *ʻĪaku ke kaikamahine: "X." ʻĪ mai ka makua kāne: "X." Nīnau hou mai ka makua kāne, ʻo ke kolu ia: "X." ʻĪaku ke kaikamahine: "X." Ia wā oli mai ka makua kāne pēnei: "X."* The daughter said: "X." The father replied: "X." The father asked again, this was the third time: "X." The daughter said: "X." Then the father chanted, thus: "X." (See section 7.2.)

PRONOUNS

8.2   Hawaiian pronouns are tabulated in table 13.

Wau is a rare variant of *au*; both are nominative. *Aʻu* is non-nominative and follows the agentive preposition *e*, or coalesces with the objective/locative preposition *iā (i-aʻu)*. Third person singular *ia* is 'he, she' or rarely 'it'. The clitic subject marker *ʻo* is commonly written joined to *ia (oia;* in the Dictionary *ʻoia)*. Similarly the nonsubject marker *iā* is written joined to the pronouns *ʻoe* and *ia: iāʻoe, iāia*.

In the dual and plural, certain morphemes are readily recognizable:

kā-, inclusive
mā-, exclusive
-ua, -lua, dual (probably related historically to *lua* 'two'); some persons substitute *-ʻua* for *-ua*

TABLE 13
Hawaiian Pronouns

Person	Singular	Dual	Plural
1 inclusive	au/wau, aʻu	kā-ua	kā-kou
exclusive		mā-ua	mā-kou
2	ʻoe	ʻo-lua	ʻou-kou
3	ia	lā-ua	lā-kou

107

-kou, plural (more than two, related historically to *kolu* 'three')
lā-, third person

Some examples:

Subject	Object	Agent
'Ike au.	*'Ike ke ali'i ia'u.*	*'Ai 'ia e a'u.*
'I know.'	'The chief sees me.'	'Eaten by me.'
'Ike 'oia.	*'Ike ke ali'i iāia.*	*'Ai 'ia e ia.*
'He/she knows.'	'The chief sees him/her.' *	'Eaten by him/her.'
'Ike lāua.	*'Ike ke ali'i ia lāua.*	*'Ike 'ia au e lāua.*
'They two know.'	'The chief sees them.'	'I am seen by them.'
'Ike kāua.	*'Ike ke ali'i ia kāua.*	*'Ike 'ia 'oia e kāua.*
'We (you and I) know.'	'The chief sees us (you and me).'	'He was seen by us (you and me).'
'Ike māua.	*'Ike ke ali'i iā māua.*	*'Ike 'ia 'oia e māua.*
'We (he and I) know.'	'The chief sees us (him and me).'	'He was seen by us (someone else and me).'

Pronouns are frequently omitted unless there is ambiguity. In answer to the question *Ua 'ike?* or *Ua 'ike 'oe?* 'Know? Do you know?' the answer may be merely *'Ike.* 'Know.' In the imperative, however, the subject is most commonly expressed: *E hele 'oe.* 'You go away.'

Another difference from English is that a pronoun subject of successive verbs may follow the last verb rather than the first one:

'Imi   i   wahi   e   lilo   mai   'oia.
look (obj.) way (intentive) escape hither he
'He looked for a way to escape.'

Dual and plural pronouns are sometimes followed by partially appositional *'o*-phrases (nominative) or *me*-phrases (comitative) in which are named specifically one of the referents.

Hele   mai   lāua   'o   Pua.
come hither they-two (subj.) Pua
'He/she and Pua came.'

```
māua      me     ku'u   makuahine
we-two   with   my     mother
(exclusive)
'my mother and I'
```

The pronouns usually have reference to animate antecedents. These examples have been noted of third person *'oia* with reference to inanimate antecedents:

```
'Oia       kāna  i       mea mai   ai             ka    malihini.
(subj.)-it  his   (perf.)  say hither (anaphoric)  the   stranger
'It's what the stranger said to me.'
```

(Object phrase)
```
'Oia       ka    mea    a'u   e  hā'awi aku   ai             iā   'oe.
(subj.)-it  the   thing  my   give  away (anaphoric)  to   you
                                     (imperfective)
'It's the thing I'll give you./It's what I'll give you.'
```

Both these sentences are complex; each consists of a verbless sentence followed by a simple sentence. The steps taken in combining two simple sentences to get these two complex sentences are described in section 11.3.

For distinction of the pronoun *ia* and the demonstrative *ia*, see section 8.3.3.

A completely unrelated pronoun of limited distribution is *ha'i* 'someone else'. Its distribution is shown below:

Hā'awi iā ha'i. 'Give to someone else.'
nā keiki a ha'i 'someone else's children'
nā hale o ha'i 'someone else's houses'
Hana 'ia e ha'i. '[It was] done by someone else.'
Na ha'i kēlā. 'That was done by someone else./That belongs to someone else.'
No ha'i kēlā. 'That was done for someone else./That belongs to someone else.'
kō ha'i waiwai 'someone else's wealth'
'auikōha'i 'possessive case' (lit., case belonging to someone else, a term invented by Andrews).

In section 7.3 are numerous examples showing that pronoun subjects *precede* the verb phrase after a nonsubject noun phrase. This occurs also after initial *'a'ole: Hele mai lāua.* 'They came.' *'A'ole lāua i hele mai.* 'They did not come.'

Pronouns may be followed by a noun in apposition: *Hāʻawi mai iā mākou kamaliʻi.* 'Give [it] to us children.'

For the inclusive/exclusive distinction, see section 8.4.1. For use of demonstratives as pronouns, see section 8.3.1.

It is a commonplace in language study that very common forms are sometimes quite irregular, as the verb "to be" in various European languages; their high frequency of use prevents them from being regularized. An example of this in Hawaiian is the frame *ē*, vocative + third person pronoun + *nei* or *ala (e* replaces *ē):*

> *E ia nei. E ia ala* (Fornander 5:715). *E i nei.* 'O you.'(sg.)
> *E lauala.* 'O you.'(dual; from *lāua ala*)
> *E lākou ala.* 'O you.'(pl.)

These expressions are quite polite in Hawaiian, more so than "O," "Say," or "Hey" in English. The affectionate phrase *e ia nei* is discussed in section 8.3.2. It is often used between husband and wife, and is frequently shortened to *e i nei.* "*Ē lākou nei e peʻe hoʻopue nei, ʻaʻole o ʻoukou lohe i ke kani o nā pū . . . ?*" (Kelekona 81). ' "O you who are hiding crouched over here, don't you hear the sound of the guns?" '

DEMONSTRATIVES

8.3

kē-DEMONSTRATIVES

8.3.1   The demonstratives (see table 12) are *kēia* and *nei* (near speaker), *ia* and *ua* (indefinite location), *kēnā* and *nā* (near addressee), *kēlā, ala, lā,* and *ana* (far), and an aberrant *neia*. Those beginning with *kē-* may be called *kē*-demonstratives. *Neia* is the only *n*-demonstrative. The others are *ø*-demonstratives.

The *kē*-demonstratives occur in the following environments:

(1) Preceding nouns as determiners: *i kēia kanaka* 'to this person'. *He aha kāu, e kēnā moʻo!* 'What's that to you, you reptile!' (*Kēnā* is starred in table 12 because it may indicate emotion, perhaps always pejorative.) *Maikaʻi ia mea.* 'This thing is good.'

(2) As substitutes for noun phrases: *Ua maikaʻi kēia.* 'This is good.' *ʻAʻole kēnā ʻo ke kolopā.* 'That (near you) is not the crowbar.' (This is a quotation from a risqué but sweet song. The Hawaiian is amused by the fact that the female speaker is comparing the addressee's penis to a crowbar.) *ʻAʻole nā he wahine*

'ē. 'That (near you) is not a strange woman.' *Ua maikaʻi ia.* 'This is good.'

(3) As substitutes for pronouns: *E hele ana* $\begin{Bmatrix} k\bar{e}ia \\ au \end{Bmatrix}$ *i ka hana.* 'I'm going to work.' *Ua hele aku* $\begin{Bmatrix} k\bar{e}l\bar{a} \\ ia \end{Bmatrix}$ *i ka hana.* 'He has gone to work.'

Kēlā precedes *kēia* if the two are juxtaposed (see section 11.2). In fast speech *kēia* is frequently *keia*.

φ-DEMONSTRATIVES *nei* AND *nā*

8.3.2　　*Nei* has many uses and environments, some of which have been described. In the sequence *ke* verb *nei* (section 5.3) it indicates present time (*ke kali nei au* 'I'm waiting'). After directionals and some nouns it indicates past time (section 7.2). Following nouns and pronouns it means 'this'; the common phrase *Hawaiʻi nei* 'this [beloved] Hawaiʻi' carries affection, as does *e i(a) nei* 'you', as used between husband and wife (section 8.2). Preposed *nei* is not common and seems to have emotional undertones, good and bad:

Good connotations:

> *Ua noho ā kupa i nei ʻāina.* 'Stayed until well acquainted in this (fine) land.'

> *Kuhi nō paha ʻoe no Hōpoe nei lehua āu i ka hana ʻohi ai* (Emerson 1965:115). '[You] probably thought that these (fine) *lehua* blossoms you were picking were for Hōpoe.'

Bad connotations:

> *Haʻina mai ka puana no nei maʻi ʻo ka lēpela* (Pukui and Korn 127). 'Tell the refrain about this (terrible) disease, leprosy.'

> *He mea ʻē nei wai nui o uka* (FS 87). 'This great (and terrible) water of the uplands is extraordinary.'

Nei was noted as the object of the preposition *me* in Green and Pukui 1936:56: *Me nei ke ʻano o ka ʻuwē ʻana.* 'Such was the nature of the weeping.'

Nā, also, has both favorable and unfavorable connotations, but the latter are more common.

Good connotations:

> *Aloha i ka hoʻi wale, ē nā pōkiʻi ē; nele ē nā pōkiʻi i ka ʻāina ʻole lā* (FS 83). 'Pitiful to return with nothing and landless, O younger brother.' (In this legend, the younger brother is usually addressed as *kuʻu pōkiʻi* 'my beloved younger brother'.)

Bad connotations:

Ē nā luahine maka piapia mākole. 'O you old woman there with en-
crusted secretions in the eyes, red-eyed one.' (The reference is to
Pele, whose eyes are red from her volcanic fires.)

Ē nā wahi keiki hoʻopunipuni (Nakuina 42). 'O you little lying kid
there.' *(Ē kēnā wahi keiki hoʻopunipuni* is also acceptable, equally
pejorative, and more common.)

Postposed *nā* is probably obsolete.

ia

8.3.3   *Ia* either is preposed or functions as the second noun phrase of a
verbless sentence, or, more rarely, as the one-word subject of a
verb phrase. It is translated 'this, that' or sometimes 'it', but
seems to mean 'aforementioned':

ʻO ia kai kapu lā, ua noa (Pukui and Korn 160). 'This tabooed sea is
now free.'

ʻO ka piʻo mau o ke ānuenue i luna o ia wahi (FS 127). 'The continued
arching of the rainbow over this place.'

The phrases *ia wā* and *ia manawa* 'at this or that time, then'
are very common:

Nānā aku i ka pali e halehale mai ana, he luna ia (FS 21). 'Look at
the cliff towering here, it is above.'

ʻO ka waiwai o kuʻu waʻa, nāu ia (FS 21). 'The property in my
canoe, it's for you.'

Ma kēia mau ʻōlelo a Kaʻōleiokū, ua ʻoluʻolu ia i kō ke aliʻi mau maka
(FS 133). 'As for these words of Kaʻōleiokū, they were pleasing in
the chief's eyes.'

Table 12 illustrates the need for distinguishing the
demonstrative *ia* from the pronoun *ia*. The demonstrative *ia*
gives no indication of proximity; use of the pronoun, in the ex-
treme right column of the table, indicates far distance.

In most texts, all the following are written *ia:* *ia* 'he, she, it';
ia, ∅-demonstrative; *ʻia*, passive/imperative; *iā*, preposition.

For use of ∅-demonstratives with pronouns and possessives see
sections 8.2 and 8.4. The two parts of the sequence *ʻO ia*, subject
marker + ∅-demonstrative, are frequently separated by a noun
phrase; this common construction is discussed in section 9.2.

ua

8.3.4   The following construction is quite common in the literature:

$$ua + \text{noun} + \begin{cases} nei \\ n\bar{a} \\ l\bar{a} \\ ala \end{cases}$$

Ua here refers to a previously mentioned noun. Examples:

> *ua kanaka nei* 'this person (just mentioned)'
> *ua hale lā* 'that house (just spoken of)'
> *ua po'e kānaka mākua nei* (Nakuina 13) 'these old people'
> *ua mau 'enemi nei ou* (Nakuina 37) 'these aforementioned enemies of yours'
> *ma kēia lohe 'ana o ua wahi kanaka kama'āina nei* (FS 153) 'in this hearing of this unimportant native person'

In the last three noun phrases, *ua* is followed directly by the plural markers *po'e, mau, wahi* (section 10.4) + a noun. If the noun is *mea*, the meaning may be cause: . . . *'ano 'ē ke kūlana i ka ua mea a ka make wai* (Kelekona 107). '. . . the situation was uncomfortable because of thirst.' More frequently, however, the preposition *o* occurs:

> *Nui kō mākou holo i ka ua mea o ka maka'u.* 'We ran fast because of fear.'
> '*A'ohe nō kā ho'i   i   ka'e   mai   ua mea he i'a āu*
> not   (intensifiers) (perf.) limit   hither   because a fish your
> 'There's absolutely no limit whatsoever to your fish.'

The noun after *ua* may be deleted (cf. section 11.3): *Holo a'e nei na'e 'o ua o Wānu'a!* (Nakuina 42) 'Now Wānu'a's [canoe] has just sailed on!' It seems almost impossible to translate *ua* as 'aforesaid' or 'cause' in this excited exclamation about canoes at sea.

Ua o, o ua o, and *ua ona o* idiomatically precede nouns, with reference to previously mentioned things:

> *Mehameha nā hale ua o Ka'ōleiokū* (FS 133). 'The previously mentioned houses of Ka'ōleiokū are lonely.'
> *ka 'ōlelo 'ana a ua o Maui nei* (Alexander 1968:17) 'the speech of the person from Maui here just mentioned'

Ua can also be used in the vocative, as when a woman says to her husband (Kelekona 117): *'Auhea 'oe ē ua kāne nei.* 'Listen, O husband here.'

neia

8.3.5   *Neia,* is a rare demonstrative defined in the Dictionary as equivalent to *kēia.* Haunani Apoliona (1973) has made a study of its use. In tapes made by four present-day Hawaiian speakers, she found not one use of *neia.* Also she reported no examples at all in Malo's *Hawaiian Antiquities* or in Emerson's *Unwritten Literature.* Three examples were found in Elbert and Mahoe's song book. The most common uses were found to be Biblical, in phrases such as *me neia* 'like this', *i neia mau mea* 'these things', *o neia manawa* 'of this time', *i neia pō* 'this night', *me neia hope aku* 'from henceforth', *o neia wā* 'of this time'. (See FS 133 for an example of use of *me neia.*)

The following was found by the present authors in FS 59: *'O neia mau 'olelo āu, ua lohe akula nō ku'u kāne.* 'These words of yours have indeed been heard by my husband.'

A time schedule taped by a native Hawaiian speaker for a Honolulu radio station begins: *'O neia ka hola* . . . 'This is the time. . . '

pē-DEMONSTRATIVES

8.3.6   The Hawaiian *pē*-words have not previously been called demonstratives, but a precedent for Polynesian languages has been set by Churchward in chapter 23 of his *Tongan Grammar* (1953). The five *pē*-words in Hawaiian are *pē-nei* 'like this' (definite), *pē-ia* 'like that' (indefinite), *pē-nā* 'like that' (near the addressee), *pē-lā* 'like that' (far), and *pe-hea* 'how'. Arguments supporting such a class follow:

(1) The term "demonstrative" is vague. Bloomfield (1933:258) says, "Demonstrative or deictic substitution-types are based on relative nearness to the speaker or hearer." Lyons (1969:278) says that demonstratives "are to be distinguished in terms of a category of 'proximity.' "

(2) The initial element occurs elsewhere. *Pē* is a preposition (section 9.12) indicating similitude. Similarly, the first element in *kē*-demonstratives occurs in other forms.

(3) Of the three environments listed near the head of section

8.3.1 for occurrence of *kē-* and *ϕ-*demonstratives, the *pē-*forms occupy the second—as substitutes for noun phrases:

Kēlā ka pane. 'That's the answer.'
Pēlā ka pane. 'The answer is like that.'
'A'ole kēlā ka pololei. 'That's not the truth.'
'A'ole pēlā ka pololei. 'The truth is not like that.'

The following points argue against positing such a set of *pē-*demonstratives:

(a) *Pē-* precedes *nei;* the *kē-*demonstratives do not (they do in other Polynesian languages).

(b) *Pē-*words do not precede nouns as determiners.

(c) *Pē-* precedes the interrogative *hea;* the *kē-*demonstratives do not.

(d) *Pē-*words precede directionals; *k-*words do not.

(e) The *pē-*words (and not the *kē-*demonstratives) function idiomatically as verbs but are not preceded by verb markers. *Pēlā mai ke ali'i.* 'The chief spoke thus.'

(f) The term *pēnā* is obsolete, but *kēnā* is not.

In conclusion, the parallelism of the *pē-*set and the *kē-*set and the florescence of the *pē-*set, justify its inclusion among the demonstratives.

This section concludes with a song that answers a universal problem:

Pehea ke ki'ina a ka ipo?
Pēnei iho, pēnei a'e, pēnei nō.

'How to get a sweetheart?
Thus, thus, and thus.'

(*Iho* here refers to self, *a'e* to one close at hand, but how can this be shown in a translation that carries the impact of the succinct Hawaiian? See section 7.2.)

POSSESSIVES

8.4   Possessives are of three types: *k-*possessives (those beginning with *k-*), *ϕ-*possessives (without *k-*), and *n-*possessives (those beginning with *n-*).

115

k-POSSESSIVES

8.4.1   The *k*-possessives are listed in table 14. (The table will seem less
        formidable when it is noted that the dual and plural forms con-
        sist of *k-ā* or *k-ō* plus the pronoun forms tabulated in section
        8.2.)
            The English glosses in the table do not indicate that the
        possessives are translated by English possessive pronouns as well
        as by English possessive adjectives: *k-o-'u hale* 'my house' and *k-
        o-'u kēlā* 'that is mine'.
            The *a-* (or *ā-*) in the possessives is equatable with the possessive
        preposition *a*; similarly *-o* (or *-ō*) is equatable with the preposi-
        tion *o*. Both are treated in section 9.6.
            The two forms in the table without *a-* (or *ā-*) or *o-* (or *ō-*), *(k-u-
        'u* and *k-ō)*, are neutral and may be used with any possessed ob-
        ject. Their use seems to have changed. In the ancient Fornander
        chants *ku'u* is a term of affection usually reserved for kinfolk
        and names of people. In modern songs *ku'u* is also used affec-
        tionately, but much more generally.
            In the Fornander chants, *ku'u* was noted before the following
        (numbers in parentheses refer to FS pages): *ali'i* (67) 'chief', *haku*
        (39) 'lord', *hoa* (275) 'companion', *hō'ike* and *hō'ike'ike* (273)
        'guide', *kaikaina* (87) 'younger brother', *kaikamahine* (59)
        'daughter', *kaikuahine* (87) 'sister', *kaikunāne* (273) 'brother',
        kāne (247) 'husband', *lawai'a ali'i* (39) 'chiefly fisherman',
        makamaka (273) 'friend', *pōki'i* (81) 'younger brother', *wahine*
        (277) 'wife'.
            Frequently the terms were repeated, sometimes with embel-
        lishments or changes:

    ku'u haku, ku'u lawai'a ali'i 'my lord, my chiefly fisherman'
    'o ku'u maka, 'o ku'u aloha 'my beloved one, my love'
    ku'u kaikunāne, ku'u kaikunāne o ka wao nāhelehele 'my brother,
      my brother of the forest dells'

            Only one inanimate head word was noted: *nani ku'u noho
        'ana* (243), 'how pleasant my way of life'.
            In the post-missionary songs in Elbert and Mahoe's *Nā Mele o
        Hawai'i*, however, *ku'u* is used before the following, including
        two English words (numbers refer to pages): *belle* (28), *dear love*
        (87), *hoaloha* (99) 'friend', *home* (30) 'home', *'īlio* (70) 'dog', *ipo*
        (70) 'sweetheart', *lei* (71), *lima* (199) 'hand', *one hānau* (42)

TABLE 14
k-Possessives

Person		Singular	Dual	Plural
1	inclusive		k-$\frac{a}{o}$kā-ua 'our'	k-$\frac{a}{o}$kā-kou 'our'
	exclusive	k-$\frac{a}{o}$-ʻu 'my'	k-$\frac{a}{o}$mā-ua 'our'	k-$\frac{a}{o}$mā-kou 'our'
		k-u-ʻu 'my'		
2		k-$\frac{a}{o}$-u 'your'	k-$\frac{a}{o}$ʻo-lua 'your'	k-$\frac{a}{o}$ʻoukou 'your'
		kō- 'your'		
3		k-$\frac{a}{o}$-na 'his' her, its'	k-$\frac{a}{o}$lā-ua 'their'	k-$\frac{a}{o}$lā-kou 'their'

'birth sands', *poli* (54) 'bosom', *pua* (73) 'flower', *puʻuwai* (41) 'heart', *wahi kupuna wahine* (93) 'little grandmother'. Some of these sequences occur frequently.

Kō is used less frequently but with more general application in the Fornander chants (numbers refer to FS pages): *inaina* (247) 'anger', *kaikuahine* (265) 'sister', *kāne* (57) 'husband', *pīkoi* (95) 'sling'. In Pukui and Korn's *Echo of Our Song*, *kō* appears before *waʻa* (p. 53) 'canoe', *inoa* (p. 75) 'name chant', and *nuʻa hulu* (p. 159) 'pile of feathers'.

Particularly interesting is a chanter's ridicule of Ka-welo, his son-in-law; he is addressing his daughter, and one can only conclude that he is being sarcastic: *'Eʻoe kū ka hauna lāʻau a kāua i kō kāne, he kōlea kō kāne, he wāwae liʻiliʻi, he ʻūlili kō kāne, he holoholo kahakai* (FS 57). 'Our war strokes are not suitable for your (fine) husband, your (fine) husband is a plover, a small-legged [one]; your (fine) husband is a tattler, running along the beach.'

Also interesting is the name song for Kīnaʻu (Elbert and Mahoe 45), in which *kō* appears before *kino* 'body', *maka* 'eye', *papālina* 'cheek', *ihu* 'nose', *waha* 'mouth', *poʻohiwi* 'shoulder', *lima* 'hand', *poli* 'bosom', *ʻōpū* 'stomach', *kuli* 'knees', *wāwae* 'legs'.

Kuʻu and *kō* are in juxtaposition in Nakuina 43: " 'O kuʻu haku aʻe paha kēia?" " 'Aʻole ia 'o kō haku." ' "Maybe this person coming is my lord?" "He's not your lord." '

Vestigial third person singular possessives corresponding to *kāna* and *kona* are *kā ia* and *kō ia* (they occur in the Marquesas as *ta ia* and *to ia*; length is not shown in the Marquesan dictionary). They are usually followed by *nei* or *ala*:

He wahine kā ia ala (Beckwith 1919:485). 'That one has a wife.'

'Ae mai i kā ia nei 'ōlelo. 'Agreed to his word.'

'A'ole i pau . . . kō ia nei hale (FS 31). 'This [man]'s house is not finished.'

A hō'aikāne me kō ia nei makuahine (Nakuina 29). 'And make friends with his mother.'

Kā ia and *kō ia* are formed exactly as the dual and plural possessives are formed: *kā* and *kō* plus pronouns.

A saying quoted by Kelekona (p. 135) has second person singular forms similar to *kā ia* and *kō ia* for *kāu*, but this use apparently is confined to the single saying: *Ua pau kā 'oe hana, ua pio kā 'oe ahi.* 'Your work is finished, your fire is out.'

Inclusive and exclusive possessives occur in the first person dual and plural forms. *Kō kāua hale* is 'our (including the addressee) house', such as a husband might say to his wife, and *kō māua hale* is 'our (excluding the addressee) house', as a man might say of his house to an outsider.

Possessives are not commonly used with body parts. 'Headache' is *'eha ke po'o* 'the head hurts'. (Compare the French *mal à la tête.*) However, *ku'u po'o* 'my head' has been noted in the 23rd Psalm, and is occasionally used by elderly people.

φ- AND *n*-POSSESSIVES

8.4.2   Two other sets, called *φ*-possessives and *n*-possessives, correspond exactly to the inventory of *k*-possessives at the beginning of section 8.4.1, except that neither of them has forms corresponding to *k-u-'u* and *k-ō*. The *φ*-possessives substitute *φ* for every initial *k-*; the *n*-possessives substitute *n-*. The former are discussed in section 9.6.3, the *n*-forms (including *naia*), in 9.11.

Both *n*-possessives and *k*-possessives are used in verbless sentences to indicate ownership (no verb 'to have' occurs in Hawaiian).

(a) *Ka'u   ka   mea   li'ili'i.*
    my   the   thing   little
    'The little thing is mine.'

(b) *Na'u   ka   mea   li'ili'i.*
    for-me   the   thing   little
    'Give me the little thing.'

(c) *He   keiki   ka'u.*
    a   child   mine
    'I have a child.'

(d) *He   keiki   na'u.*
    a   child   for-me
    'A child for me. / Let me have a child.'

(e) *He   ka'a   kona.*
    a   car   his
    'He has a car.'

(f) *He ka'a n-o-na.*
    a   car   for-him
    'There's a car for him.'

A student thinking of English might suggest that 'me' in the translations of sentences (b) and (d) is an indirect object, but the parallelism of *n*-forms and *k*-forms is too similar for such an interpretation, and indirect objects ordinarily occur with transitive verbs (see section 9.3.1).

INTERROGATIVES

8.5   The common interrogatives are *aha* 'what?', *hea* 'where, which?', *wai* 'who?', and *hia-*, a numeral interrogative. Derivatives of *hea* are the conjunctions *āhea* and *ināhea* (section 11.1), and the demonstrative *pehea* (section 8.3.6).
    Aha, *hea*, and *wai* substitute for nouns:

He   puke   kēlā.
a   book   that
'That's a book.'

He   aha   kēlā?
a   what   that
'What's that?'

Aia   ke   kumu   ma   Maui.
there is   the   teacher   on   Maui
'The teacher's on Maui.'

Aia   ke   kumu   ma   hea?
there is   the   teacher   at   where
'Where [in the world] is the teacher?'

'O   Kimo   ke   kumu.
(subj.) Jim   the   teacher
'Jim is the teacher.'

'O   wai   ke   kumu?
(subj.) who   the   teacher
'Who's the teacher?'

'O   Kimo   ko'u inoa.
(subj.) Jim   my   name
'Jim is my name.'

'O   wai   kou   inoa?
(subj.) who   your name
'What's your name?'

Aha occurs also as an intransitive verb (section 4.2) but commonly follows the indefinite *he*, as illustrated above. The common idioms *no ke aha? i ke aha?*, translated 'why?' are illustrated in the Dictionary.

Hea frequently follows the locative prepositions *i* 'to, at' (definite), *ma* 'at', *mai* 'from', and *no*, locative. (*Mai* and *no* + *hea* contrast: *Mai hea mai 'oia?* 'Where is he from?' *No hea mai 'oia?* 'Where is he a native of?'). With the temporal prefixes *ā-*, future, and *inā-*, past, *hea* functions as a conjunction meaning 'when?' (see section 11.1). *'Au-hea* means 'where?'; however, in commands, as in *'au-hea wale ana 'oe*, the meaning is 'listen, pay attention'; both are common in songs. *Hea* also follows nouns as a qualifier meaning 'which?': *ka manawa hea?* 'which time?'

Wai is glossed 'what?' in the question *'O wai kou inoa?* 'What is your name?' Otherwise the glosses are 'who?' or 'whom?' *'O wai?* 'Who?' *Na wai?* 'By whom? For whom?' *Iā wai?* 'To whom?'

-Hia most commonly follows the numeral-classifying prefix *'e* (section 10.3): *'Ehia kālā?* 'How much money?' *'Ehia po'e?* 'How many people?' It also occurs as a suffix to *koko'o: Koko-ohia?* 'How many associates?'

LOCATIVE NOUNS

8.6   Both place and time words are included in this term.

Both place and time words are included in this term.

The place locatives are of two kinds: (a) those used both with and without the preceding articles *ka* and *ke*, usually with resulting differences in meanings; and (b) those used only without articles.

(a) The ten words in the first class are shown in table 15. Only a few of the meanings are given; for others, see the Dictionary.

In Hawaiian one says *i luna o ka waʻa* and *i luna o ke kaʻa* for 'in the canoe' and 'in the car'; this idiom is carried over in Island pidgin English.

The locative *muli* occurs in the idiom *mamuli o* 'because of, due to, by means of'. This is apparently shortened to *ma o*, with the same meanings: *kona make ʻana ma o Ka-welo ala* (FS 84) 'his death because of Ka-welo'. *Ua hele mai au ma ona ala.* 'I came for his sake.' *Ma o wai ʻoukou i pili ai?* 'Through whom are you all related?' In these idioms *muli* seems to have the meaning 'reason'. *Hope* seems to have similar glosses.

(b) Members of the second class are place names and the following:

> *ʻaneʻi, ʻoneʻi* 'here' (*Ma* 'at' + *ʻaneʻi* is written *maʻaneʻi*.)
>
> *haʻi* 'edge'
>
> *hiʻialo* 'carried in front' ⎱ See section 11.2 for use of
> *hiʻikua* 'carried in back' ⎰ these poetic idioms
>
> *kaha* 'place'
>
> *kahakai, kahaone* 'beach, seashore'
>
> *kahi* 'the place' *(ka + wahi)*. Note in section 7.3 the insertion of *kahi* after a fronted locative *(I laila kahi a mākou i holo ai)*. A similar example from Kelekona 94: *ka lapa kahi i peʻe ai ʻo Koʻolau ma lalo iho* 'the ridge where Koʻolau hid beneath'. The underlying sentence with the locative at the end would be *Ua peʻe ʻo Koʻolau malalo iho o ka lapa.* 'Koʻolau hid under the ridge.' The fronted position plus *kahi* is in focus.

TABLE 15
Locative Nouns without and with Articles

Without Article/Meaning	With Article/Meaning
luna 'up'	*ka luna* 'the top, the foreman'
lalo 'down'	*ka lalo* 'the bottom, the depths'
mua 'before, first'	*ka mua* 'the first'
waena 'middle, center'	*ka waena* 'the middle, center'
hope 'after, last, because'	*ka hope* 'the last-born'
muli 'after, last, because'	*ka muli* 'the last-born'
loko 'in, mainland'	*ka loko* 'the inside, the lake, the inner organs'
waho 'out'	*ka waho* 'the outside'
kai 'seaward'	*ke kai* 'the sea'
uka 'inland'	*ka uka* 'the inland area'
(muamua, rare variant of *mua)*	

kapa, kakapa 'edge, boundary'
kauhale 'household, home'
kulakula 'fields'
laila (usually pronounced leila and often lila; see section 2.7) 'there'
   (indefinite and used idiomatically)
makālae 'beach'
na'e 'windward, easterly'
ne'i 'here'
'ō 'there'

If 'ō 'there' and 'ane'i 'here' are juxtaposed, 'ō precedes: ma'ō ā ma'ane'i 'from there to here' (English demands 'from here to there'; see section 11.2).

Rare locatives used without a preceding article include kua nalu 'wave crest' (Green and Pukui 8) and kaupoku 'ridgepole' (Fornander 5:713).

Time words commonly used without determiners (section 10.1) include nehinei 'yesterday', kinohi 'beginning', and 'ānō 'now'. The time word 'apōpō 'tomorrow' sometimes follows kēlā 'that'.

The locatives of both types (a) and (b) commonly follow the locative prepositions discussed in sections 9.3.2 and 9.4: i 'to, at' (definite) and ma 'at'. Examples:

Hele i loko. 'Go to the mainland.'
Noho i waho. 'Stay outside.'
Aia mauka. 'There in the uplands.'
Hele i laila. 'Go there.'

They also follow mai, ablative; 'o, subject; o, possessive; no, locative, and kō, locative possessive:

Mai laila mai 'oia. 'He's from there.'
Ā laila, puni 'o waho i nā akua (FS 207). 'And then the outside was filled with gods.'
'A'ohe mea o loko. 'Nothing inside.'
No loko mai 'oia. 'He's from the mainland.'
kō kauhale po'e (Kelekona 100) 'the people of the homestead'

Locatives other than time words are rather commonly used in a metonymical sense (the container for the thing contained). Loko 'inside' may actually mean 'people inside' and wa'a 'canoe', may mean 'crewmen'.

Inā	*lāua*	*e*	*kāhea*	*i*	*Wai-kīkī,*	*ua*
if	they (dual)	(int.)	call	at	Wai-kīkī	(perf.)

lohe	*ʻo*	*ʻEwa,*	*ā*	*inā*	*i*	*ʻEwa,*	*e*
hear	(subj.)	ʻEwa	and	if	at	ʻEwa	(int.)

hea	*ai,*	*ua*	*lohe*	*ʻo*	*Wai-ʻanae* (FS 49)
call	(anaphoric)	(perf.)	hear	(subj.)	Wai-ʻanae

'If they should call at Wai-kīkī, the people of ʻEwa would hear, and if the calling were at ʻEwa, the people of Wai-ʻanae would hear.'

Such usages might be termed **personalized** or **metonymical locatives.**

Locative names are continually being created. Inventions of place names by Mary Kawena Pukui include *Ulu-mau* 'ever growing', the name for a Hawaiian village, and *Pōhai-nani* 'beautiful circle', the name for a retirement home. A new park on Kauaʻi was named *ʻOlu-pua* 'flower coolness' by Dorothy M. Kahananui.

COMPOUNDS AND QUALIFIERS

8.7

Noun Compounds

8.7.1   Most compounds are nouns. The most numerous are probably names of plants, people, and places; others are of fish, birds, rocks, stars, winds, rains, diseases, *lua* fighting holds, and tapa, plaiting, or quilt designs. Such compounds are mostly of ancient vintage, but those listed below are highly imaginative postcontact coinages describing foreign objects:

Compound	Gloss	Literal Meaning
huaʻōlelo	'word'	'verbal fruit'
ʻilipuakea	'white person'	'white flower skin'
kūkaehao	'rust'	'iron dung'
kūkaeloli	'mildew'	'sea cucumber dung'
kūkaenalo	'beeswax, unbleached muslin'	'fly dung'
kūkaepele	'match'	'volcanic dung'
laholio	'rubber'	'horse scrotum'
palemaʻi	'underpants'	'genital protector'
ulepuaʻa	'corkscrew'	'pig penis'
waiūpaka	'butter'	'butter (English) milk'

All of these are compounds: it would be hard to guess their meanings from the literal meanings. This is the main criterion for distinguishing compounds and noun + qualifier sequences. (In Hawaiian, pronunciation provides no clue, as it does sometimes in English, for example, rèd bírd versus rédbird). A second criterion is that of indivisibility. If insertion of particles or words changes the meaning or makes the sequence ungrammatical, it is not a compound. Some examples:

Compound: *pa'a   kai* 'salt'
           solid   sea
With insertions and different meaning:
pa'a   i   ke   kai
solid   in   the   sea

Compound: *na'au   ao* 'wise'
           intestines   daylight
With insertions, ungrammatical
*Ua ao ka na'au

Compound: *wai   ū   paka   pa'a* 'cheese'
           liquid   breast   butter   hard
With insertions and different meaning:
Ua pa'a ka waiūpaka. 'The butter is hard.'

Compound: *wili   kī* 'engineer'
           turn   key
With insertions and different meaning:
Wili   i   ke   kī.
turn   (obj.)   the   key
'Turn the key.'

Spelling rules for writing compounds are formulated in section 2.12.

VERB AND NOUN-VERB COMPOUNDS

8.7.2   The most common verb compound consists of verb + *ā* + noun. This *ā*, contrasting semantically with *a* 'of', *ā* 'to', and *ā* 'and', is commonly translated 'like, similar to'. Such compounds are much favored by Kelekona. They are considered compounds because the total meaning is usually somewhat different from the meaning of the parts, and because they are indivisible. If an article is inserted before the noun, the result is a possessive or is

124

ungrammatical. *'Ai-ā-pua'a* is 'eat like [a] pig', but *'ai a ka pua'a* is 'the pig's food'. Examples:

Inu 'oe ā holoāi'a (Kelekona 138). 'Drink until [you] swim like [a] fish.'

i ka holopapa holoāwai a ka nonoho mai o nā helehelena malihini (Kelekona 135) 'as the settlements of foreign faces spread everywhere like flood waters'

kekahi kuāua kaheāwai (Kelekona 107) 'a shower flowing like water'

Kūākanaka a'ela ua mo'o nei. 'The supernatural turned into a human. / The reptile looked like a man.'

I waiho kūāma'i maoli 'oia. 'He lay down really sick.'

Nā 'ano lapa'au Hawai'i, ua pūlumi ā ua 'umiāpua'a 'ia (Kelekona 144). 'The kinds of Hawaiian medicine were swept away and strangled like pigs.'

'ai-ā-manō 'eat like a shark'; i.e., to have a prodigious appetite

hanu-ā-pua'a 'to breathe like a pig'; i.e., to gasp for breath

huli-ā-mahi 'turn like a strong [cock]'; i.e., cooperation, strength

moku-ā-wai 'to burst, as flood waters'; i.e., to rush, as a crowd

pa'i-ā-uma 'beat chest' (as in lamentation)

puka-ā-maka 'to appear to the eyes'; i.e., to seal a relationship of two families by intermarriage

Less common is verb + *ā* + verb, as *uhai-ā-holo* 'chase like running': *nā lima uhaiāholo kā'ilikū me nā pōkā pū raipela* (Kelekona 6) 'the violent pursuing hands with the rifle shots'.

Some verb + noun sequences are not compounds because the meaning becomes obvious on examination of the parts. Common verb-object sequences include *hoe wa'a* 'paddle [a] canoe', *kalaiwa ka'a* 'drive [a] car', and *'ai kanaka* 'to eat human beings'. Some of these sequences may be followed by a qualifier, as *hoe wa'a mālie* 'paddle [a]canoe carefully'.

Verb-subject sequences that are compounds are not very common. An example is *'āha'i-ka-pupuhi* 'the blowing runs away' (i.e., 'to disappear, vanish'): *Ua 'āha'ikapupuhi mua akula ka 'eu'eu Ko'olau* (Kelekona 55). 'The clever Ko'olau first disappeared completely.'

A verb-subject sequence that seems to be used both as an ordinary sentence and as a compound is *kau-ka-weli:*

ua kia ho'omana'o nei e kūha'o kūkila kaukaweli (Kelekona 107) 'this commemorative monument standing alone, majestic, awe-inspiring'

Ā no laila, kau ka weli (FS 93). 'And therefore [he] was afraid.'

125

The compound *kū-ka-liki* 'boasting appears' (i.e., 'to boast') is used as both noun and verb:

> *He maika'i wale nō kāu mau kūkaliki i painu'u mai nei* (Kelekona 135). 'Your boasting and bragging were quite fine.'
>
> *kēia mau nani e kūkaliki ai* (Kelekona 136) 'these pretty things [you] are boasting about'

Holo-ā-i'a 'to swim like a fish' is also used as a noun meaning 'the bends, caisson disease'.

COMPOUND PROPER NAMES

8.7.3   In this Grammar, the parts of divisible proper nouns are set off by hyphens (*Ka-wena* 'the glow') unless the proper noun itself occurs as part of a larger noun (*Nā-maka-uahoa-o-Kawena* 'the haughty eyes of Ka-wena'). The meaning of *Kawena* in the long Hawaiian name is 'person's name'—not 'the glow'. A Kī-lau-ea cliff is written *Pali-kapu-o-Kamohoali'i* 'sacred cliff of Ka-moho-ali'i' (lit., the chiefly representative).

Common qualifiers to place names are the following:

> *uka* 'mountainward'   *poko* 'short'   *nui* 'big'   *wai* 'wet'
> *waena* 'central'   *loa* 'long'   *iki* 'small'   *malo'o* 'dry'
> *kai* 'seaward'

Such words are qualifiers rather than compound members and are therefore capitalized and written as separate words, as *Ka-lihi Uka*, *Ka-lihi Waena*, and *Ka-lihi Kai*. Another example is *Wai-lua Nui* and *Wai-lua Iki* on Maui. But what of places that have only one qualifier, as *Lahaina* and *Lahaina Luna* on Maui, or *Niu* and *Niu Iki* in Honolulu? Again, *Luna* and *Iki* seem to be qualifiers. *Niu Iki* does not mean 'small coconut' but rather, 'small Niu' with reference to the place Niu.

For a structural analysis of Hawaiian place names, see Pukui, Elbert, and Mookini 1974:243–253.

OTHER COMPOUNDS

8.7.4   Many names of winds, tapa and mat designs, *lua* fighting holds, and stars are composed of analyzable words or words and particles with total meanings not ascertainable from the meanings of the parts. They may be considered compounds. The compounds are written as single words (with components hyphenated) unless they are followed by qualifiers, as the *Kona* (leeward) winds *Kona Hea, Kona Hili Mai'a, Kona Kū, Kona Lani, Kona Mae*; or the *Ka-maile* stars *Ka-maile Hope* and *Ka-maile Mua*.

Note the many qualifiers for *hōkū* in the Dictionary. Names that are long, cumbersome, and poetic are written with hyphens between components, as the long *lua* hold *'Ōnohi-ka'i-'ole-pōhihihi-ka-lawai'a-a-ka-lā-'ino*, 'Rainbow patch that does not move, puzzling the fisherman on a stormy day.' And the name of Pele's favorite younger sister is *Hi'iaka-i-ka-poli-o-Pele*, 'Hi'iaka in the bosom of Pele.'

NOUN + QUALIFIER SEQUENCES

8.7.5   Many nouns followed by qualifiers are Dictionary entries, as types of buildings *(hale)*, machines *(mīkini)*, or seas *(kai)*. In the Dictionary, *mea* 'thing, person' has many qualifiers.

Word order in noun + qualifier sequences is important, and change of order often changes meaning; for example: *kino maika'i* 'fine physique' and *maika'i kino* 'physical attractiveness', *kāne 'ōpiopio* 'young man' and *'ōpiopio kāne* 'male youth', *kāna wahine maika'i* 'his beautiful wife' and *kona maika'i wahine* 'her feminine attractiveness', *manu nui* 'large bird' and *nui manu* 'gathering of birds'. In this last example, the English translation is clearer with a possessive or other insertion; similarly with *ka li'ili'i keiki* 'the smallness of children', or *ha'aheo Kaimana Hila* 'pride in Diamond Head'.

In the above examples, *maika'i* 'fine, attractiveness' would be considered a single dictionary entry which either follows the noun *kino* or precedes it, and similarly for *'ōpiopio* 'young, youth'. The common word *pono* usually follows nouns, with the gloss 'righteous, correct': *he kanaka pono* 'a righteous man'. Preceding nouns, *pono* has two glosses, 'any kind' and 'equipment': *he pono hale* 'any kind of house, house furniture'.

In naming a place or object in honor of a chief, the chief's name was combined with the type of named object. A ship was named *Kīna'u Moku* in honor of Kīna'u, and a horse was named *Kīna'u Lio*. Princess Ruth's Honolulu mansion was *Keōua Hale*. King Ka-lā-kaua, wishing to honor himself, called his summer palace at Kai-lua, Hawai'i, *Hiku-lani Hale* 'seventh royal chief house', for he was the seventh monarch. (The palace had been, and is now, called Huli-he'e.)

This reversal of order also occurs as a means of showing affection. A famous example is the beloved song *Hawai'i Aloha* (Elbert and Mahoe 42). In Emerson (1965) is this poetic line: *Kūpiliki'i Hanalei lehua lā*, 'the (beautiful) *lehua* of Hanalei are storm-buffeted'. The following is acceptable to Mrs. Pukui: *Aloha nō 'o Hawai'i lāhui!* 'Alas for the Hawaiian people!' Is Honolulu Hale, the name of the city hall in Honolulu, a tribute to Honolulu, or is it a means of distinguishing this particular house from others? Hawaiian speakers seem uncertain.

The reversal of the usual order (noun + qualifier) is perhaps comparable to such English phrases as *house beautiful, court martial, attorney general, life everlasting*, in which adjective follows noun. This practice may have been thought to give a certain cachet to the nouns.

Nouns plus two or more qualifiers are rather rare:

He po'e   li'ili'i, nāwaliwali na'aupō mākou   (Alexander 1864:30).
a   people   small   weak   ignorant we
'We are a small, weak, and ignorant people.'

i   ka   wā   'ilihune 'āina 'ole
at   the time poor   land   none
'at the poverty-stricken landless time'

ka   ho'onaue   ōla'i   ikaika 'ana
the   cause-shake earthquake strong (nominalizer)
'the strongly shaking earthquake'

An English sequence of noun preceded by two adjectives such as a 'fine new house' might in Hawaiian be:

hale   maika'i   ā   hou
house   good   and new

As pointed out, compounds also may be followed by qualifiers:

he   mea   hou   maika'i
a   thing new   good
'some good news / a good new thing'

limu   kala   lau   li'i
seaweed rough leaf   small
'small-leafed *Sargassum* sp.'

nā kāhuna ho'omeamea me ho'opunipuni ho'omanamana mā
(Kelekona 149) 'the false, lying and superstitious sorcerers and
associates'

The final word in the last example, *mā*, is a common qualifying particle usually translated 'and friends, and others, and
wife, and folks, and Company (in business)'. This has been carried over into pidgin English as 'John folks' or 'John them'.
Other examples:

Lākou mā wale mai nei nō. 'Just they and the others here.'
Eia a'e 'o 'Ole-wale mā! 'So here are Mr. and Mrs. No-good!'

Nui and *loa* are adjectival stative verbs that commonly follow
both nouns and verbs. *Nui* follows both deliberate and spontaneous transitive verbs as intensifier *('ai nui, aloha nui)*; *loa*
follows both adjectival and *loa'a*-statives *(maika'i loa, make
loa)*; neither follows intransitives as *intensifier* (see table 8). Examples of various meanings, including that of intensifier,
follow.

After nouns: *ali'i nui* 'high chief, great chief', *hale nui* 'large
house', *kanaka nui* 'important person', *mauna loa* 'long mountain', *mea nui* 'beloved person, important thing'
After intransitive verbs: *hele loa* 'go far, go permanently'
After deliberate transitive verbs: *kōkua nui* 'big help, to help
a lot', *'imi loa* 'to look far', *leo nui* 'to talk loudly'
After spontaneous transitive verbs: *aloha nui* 'much *aloha*',
mahalo nui 'much thanks, many thanks'
After adjectival stative verbs: *anuanu loa* 'very cold', *mahalo
nui loa* 'thanks very much', *maika'i loa* 'very good', *māmā loa*
'very fast', *wela loa* 'very hot'
After *loa'a*-stative verbs: *make loa* 'dead, completely dead',
pohō loa 'completely out of luck'
Loa may indicate the superlative degree: *'O wai ka mea
lapuwale loa?* 'Who is the most worthless?'

The converse of *nui* is *iki* 'small, little', used as an intensifier
after negative + noun or verb, perhaps as a form of understate-
ment:

'A'ohe he hana iki 'not a small task' (said of giant undertakings)

'A'ole au i hele iki i laila. 'I've never been there.'

'A'ole kohu iki 'not [even] a little suitable' (said of things most inappropriate)

Iki occurs in the common idiom, he mea iki 'just a trifle', used today as a translation of 'you are welcome'.

A common adjectival stative verb occurring most frequently as a qualifier is 'ē. It was termed pluperfect by Andrews, and has been discussed in section 1.4. It serves as a verbal base in such sentences as ua 'ē loa 'very odd'.

Sex qualifiers are kāne 'male' and wahine or -hine 'female', applicable to both humans and nonhumans: kupuna kāne 'grandfather' and kupuna wahine 'grandmother', moa kāne 'rooster' and moa wahine 'hen'.

9   Prepositions

INVENTORY OF PREPOSITIONS

9.1   The prepositions are initiators of noun phrases (see table 7). They may be listed as follows:

  'o/ø: subject (9.2)
  i/iā: direct and indirect object marking/agentive/source/instrumental/causative (9.3.1)
  i/iā/iō: definite locative (9.3.2)
  ma: locative/instrumental/manner marking (9.4)
  ā: place to (emphatic) (9.5)
  a: possessive (9.6)
  o: possessive (9.6)
  me: comitative/instrumental/simulative (9.7)
  mai: ablative (9.8)
  e: agentive (9.9)
  ē/ø: vocative (9.10)
  na: benefactive/agentive (9.11)
  no: benefactive/causative/locative (9.11)
  pe: simulative (9.12)

Appositional noun phrases (9.13) are introduced by the subject marker 'o/ø or by the same preposition as the referent.

SUBJECT MARKER: 'o/ø

9.2   The nominative function of 'o in simple sentences with verbs is shown by its complementary distribution with two other case-marking prepositions:

  Ua   'ike   'o-ia.
  (perf.) see   (subj.)-he
  'He saw.'

Ua   'ike   iā-ia.
(perf.) see   (obj.)-him
'[He] saw him.'

'Ike 'ia   e   ia.
see (pas/imp.) by him
'[He] was seen by him.'

Alexander (1968:28) followed Andrews' lead (1838:403) in calling this particle the "*o* emphatic." He buttressed his argument by giving a number of translations of the English sentence 'I give this to you' with shift of emphasis shown by placing various '*o*-phrases at the beginning. Alexander's sentences are rewritten here to conform with the style used in this Grammar.

(a) *Ke hā'awi aku nei au i   kēia iā'oe.*
        give   away   I (obj.) this to you
        (present)
     'I *give* this to you.'

(b) *'O wau ke hā'awi aku nei i kēia iā'oe.*
     '*I* give this to you.'

(c) *'O 'oe ka mea a'u e hā'awi aku nei i kēia.*
     'I give this to *you*.'

(d) *'O kēia ka'u e hā'awi aku nei iā'oe.*
     'I give *this* to you.'

The last two sentences are complex; they are analyzed in section 11.3. Italic type in the English indicates emphasis, according to Alexander.

The emphasis could have been shown, probably more accurately, by fronting the emphatic words in the English translations, as (b) 'I'm the one giving this to you.' (c) 'You're the one I'm giving this to.' (d) 'This is what I'm giving you.'

In verbless sentences emphasis may be shown by a transformation:

'Oia ke ali'i. 'He is the chief.'
'O ke ali'i nō ia. 'He's the chief.'

Alexander (1968:29) called this construction the "nominative absolute" and gave three examples, the first of which is: *'O ka honua nei, he mea poepoe nō ia.* 'The earth here, it [is] a round thing.' To emphasize "roundness" one would say: *He mea poepoe ka honua nei.* The final *ia* in the transformation cannot be replaced by *'oia* (**O ke ali'i nō 'oia*).

Actually, Alexander's *'o*-phrases are "emphatic" because they come at the beginning of the sentences, not because they begin with *'o.* The most common use of *'o* is before the third person singular pronoun *ia* after verbs, and in this position it might well be called the *'o*-unemphatic. In the first noun phrases in verbless sentences (*'O-ia ke ali'i.* 'He's the chief.'), the emphasis, if present at all, is slight, as in the common question and answer: *'O wai kou inoa? 'O Pua.* 'What's your name? Pua.' Further, the complementation of the prepositions *'o, ia,* and *e* shown earlier, is clear evidence that the primary function of *'o* is to introduce the subject, or the first noun phrase in equational sentences.

Alexander's theory of important things coming first, however, is strongly endorsed and is strengthened, although he doesn't say so, by other arguments, summarized in section 11.5.

For use of *'o* in appositional phrases, see section 9.13.

'O as a subject marker occurs most commonly before the third person singular pronoun *ia,* but even there the *ø*-alternant may occur, as in sentence (3) in section 9.3.1. *'O* is commonly used also in the sentences *'O wai kou inoa?* 'What's your name?' and *'O Pua ko'u inoa,* 'Pua's my name.' Note in section 9.3.1 the *ø*-alternant before nouns in sentences (2), (6), (7), and (8). *'O wau* and *'o 'oe,* as in initial position in sentences (b) and (c) above, are less than common.

MULTIFUNCTIONAL *i/iā,* AND *iō*

9.3

i/iā

9.3.1   *I/iā* marks direct and indirect objects, agent, source, instrument, cause. *Iā* as an alternant of *i* occurs before all the pronouns, the interrogative *wai,* and names of people and places. *Iā* is written joined to the singular pronouns as *ia'u (iā + a'u), iāia,* and (less consistently) *iā'oe.* (Historically *iā* derives from *i + a,* personal particle; this *a* does not exist otherwise in Hawaiian and hence *iā* is considered a single entity.) The following sentences illustrate the various functions of *i/iā:*

> (1) *Nānā iā Pua. Nānā ia'u. 'Ike iā Maui.* 'Look at Pua. Look at me. See Maui.'

133

A direct object usually precedes an indirect object:

(2) *Hā'awi ke kanaka i ka makana iā Pua.* 'The man gives the present to Pua.'

The object marker is sometimes omitted before or after *i:*

(3) *Ha'alele akula ia (i) ia aku* (FS 127). 'He rejected this bonito.'

The object marker is usually also omitted in sentences beginning with the agentive *na* (section 9.11):

(4) *Na Pua i 'ike ka hale.* 'Pua saw the house.'

In songs *i* as object marker is sometimes replaced by *a'i:*

(5) *malihini ka 'ikena a'i nā Kona* 'seeing the Kona [districts] for the first time'

In Nakuina 63, *iā* introduces an agentive phrase followed by a source phrase:

(6) *Ē ke keiki, i loa'a nā hana iā'oe iā wai?* 'Boy, who did you get such activities from?' (Sentence [5] in section 3.1 contains an agentive phrase introduced by *i* after the stative verb *loa'a.*)

I as an instrumental marker:

(7) *I ka 'ōlelo ke ola, i ka 'ōlelo ka make.* 'Life is in the word, death is in the word.'

I/iā as causatives:

(8) *Kaulana 'o Maui iā Hale-a-ka-lā.* 'Maui is famous because of Hale-a-ka-lā.' *Maika'i ka wahine i kāna mau hana pono.* 'The woman is good because of her righteous deeds.'

i/iā/iō: DEFINITE LOCATIVE

9.3.2   *Iā* and sometimes *iō* occur before pronouns and proper names. In Biblical usage *iō* and *a'u* contract to *io'u* 'to me' (*Ka Baibala,* Luka 23.14). *Iō* occurs in the name *Lele-iō-Hoku,* King Ka-lā-kaua's younger brother; as a locative it indicates time: 'flight-on-full-moon-night' *(Hoku),* and refers to the death of Ka-mehameha III on the day of Lele-iō-Hoku's birth (Elbert and Mahoe 9).

If *i* and *ma,* both locatives, contrast, *i* is more definite and precise than *ma: ā noho i Wai-kīkī ma O'ahu* (FS 35) 'living at Wai-kīkī on O'ahu'.

Hawkins (1975, section 2.2.4) explained the difference in the two prepositions by suggesting that when *i* and *ma* are spoken together, the larger area is marked by *ma* and the smaller, or more specific one, by *i*. She also suggested that "stationary" descriptions are marked by *ma*, and nonstationary ones by *i:* *Ola nā mākua ma Puna.* 'The parents survive/live in Puna.' *Pā'ani nā mākua i Puna.* 'The parents play at Puna.' *Pā'ani*, a deliberate transitive verb, might be considered here a single definite act, and *ola*, a *loa'a*-stative verb, an indefinite state.

In ordinary discourse, one hears both *ma* and *i*.

I/iā/iō are frequently followed by noun + *nei, lā, ala:*

hiki iō Kea'au lā (FS 25) 'go as far as Kea'au [a place]',
ho'i akula iō 'Umi lā (FS 29) 'go back to 'Umi [a person]'.

In section 9.2, examples were given of fronting *'o*-phrases for emphasis. Locative phrases also may be moved to the front for emphasis, in which case the noun may be qualified by *kahi* 'the place' (*ka* 'the' + *wahi* 'place'), and the verb is preceded by noninitial verb markers and followed by the anaphoric *ai*.

Ua	*noho*	*ke*	*kanaka*	*i*	*Hilo.*
(perf.)	stay	the	man	at	Hilo

'The man stayed at Hilo.'

i	*Hilo*	*kahi*	*i*	*noho*	*ai*	*ke*	*kanaka*
at	Hilo	the place	(perf.)	stay	(anaphoric)	the	man

'at *Hilo* where the man stayed'

In Proto Polynesian the object marker is **i*, and the locative marker is **ki*. These two forms have coalesced in Hawaiian. *I* and *iā* have so many functions that Hawkins (1975, section 2.2.8) has called them "a neutralization of all case markers."

LOCATIVE/INSTRUMENTAL/MANNER: *ma*

9.4 *Ma* is conventionally written joined to locative nouns, but elsewhere it appears as a separate entity: *mahope* 'after', *ma Honolulu* 'at Honolulu'. *Mā* (with a long *ā*) occurs before syllables containing long vowels or diphthongs; elsewhere, *ma* is used: *mā Kīlauea, mālaila* 'there', but *mauka* 'inland'. Since length here is predictable, it need not be written.

The term "locative" is considered to mean time as well as place: *Ma kēia 'ōlelo a 'Iwa i ka 'elele, lawe 'ia akula ā mua o 'Umi* (FS 23). 'Upon this speech of 'Iwa to the messenger, [he] was taken to the presence of 'Umi.'

Ma marks cause, especially when preceding *muli* 'after' (section 8.6). *Mamuli* is followed by the possessive preposition *o* and the *ɸ*-possessive: *mamuli o kona akamai* 'because of his cleverness'. *Ua hele aku mamuli ona.* '[He] went because of (or after) him.' The *muli* in some contexts may be deleted: *kona make 'ana ma o Ka-welo ala* (FS 89) 'his death at Ka-welo's [hands]'.

   Ma also marks instrument and manner:

>   *Kāhea akula 'o Ka-welo iā Ka-malama ma ka paha* (FS 51). 'Ka-welo called to Ka-malama in a *paha* chant.'

>   *'Imi i wahi e lilo mai ai 'oia ma ke mele.* 'He looked for a way he might escape by singing.'

>   *'A'ole au i hele mai ma ke 'ano ikaika, i hele mai au ma ka māka'ika'i.* 'I did not come in a forceful way, I came to sightsee.'

ā: PLACE TO (EMPHATIC)

9.5   The locative *ā* is used to stress the distance traveled:

>   *hele i Maui* 'going to Maui'
>   *hele ā Maui* 'going as far as Maui'
>   *hele ā ke kuahiwi* 'going to the mountain'
>   *Lele ka manu ā luna.* 'The bird flies way up.'

   For *ā* as a conjunction see section 11.1.

POSSESSIVES

9.6

a- AND *o*-POSSESSIVES

9.6.1   The possessive prepositions are *a* (or *ā*) and *o* (or *ō*), and *kā* and *kō*. Long *ā* and *ō* precede syllables containing long vowels and diphthongs, short *a* and *o* occur elsewhere (see section 2.5). Only *a* and *o* are written; their lengthening is predictable. *Kā* and *kō* are discussed in section 9.6.4. The possessives listed in table 14 contain the same *a* and *o* (exceptions are *ku'u* and *kō*). The same *o* occurs in the prepositional phrase *ka hale o ke ali'i* 'the house of the chief' as in *kona hale* 'his house'.

   Use of *a* and *o* is one of the most discussed, and most intriguing, of Polynesian problems. The following dichotomies have been proposed for distinguishing their usages.

a	*o*
active	passive
alienable	inalienable
inherited	acquired
subordinate	dominant
agentive	benefactive

No terminology is completely logical; there are always some usages that don't seem to fit any scheme.

One of the more logical categories is in the domain of kinship, and here the labels "inherited" and "acquired" seem the most appropriate. Ego's affinal generation and all later generations are acquired and take *a*. Ego's consanguineal generation and all earlier generations are inherited and take *o*. The terms in the following list are classificatory (the same terms are used for collateral relatives in the same generation, as father and uncle). Possession is shown by the use of the possessive pronouns. Equate *koʻu kupuna* with *ke kupuna o ke keiki* 'the grandparent of the child'. Both have the *o*-possession.

> *koʻu kupuna* 'my grandparent'
> *koʻu makua kāne* 'my father'
> *koʻu makuahūnōwai* 'my father-in-law'
> *koʻu kaikuaʻana* 'my older sibling of same sex'
> *koʻu kaikaina* 'my younger sibling of same sex'
> *koʻu kaikuahine* 'my sister (male speaking)'
> *koʻu kaikunāne* 'my brother (female speaking)'
> *koʻu pōkiʻi* 'my younger sibling'
> *koʻu hoahānau* 'my cousin'
> *koʻu hanauna* 'my generation'
> *koʻu kaikoʻeke* 'my sibling-in-law'
> *koʻu puluna* 'parent of my child-in-law'
> *kāna keiki* 'his child'
> *kāna kaikamahine* 'his daughter'
> *kāna hiapo* 'his first-born'
> *kāna muli loa* 'his last-born'
> *kāna kāne* 'her husband'
> *kāna wahine* 'his wife'
> *kāna hūnōna* 'his child-in-law'
> *kāna ipo* 'his sweetheart'

This may be stated in another way. The possessive indicates the *nature of the relationship* of the possessed and the possessor.

The *a*-forms, as just illustrated, show that the possessor ('his' or 'her') *caused* the ownership. The *o*-forms show that the possessor ('my' in each case) had nothing to do with the cause.

Today some of these terms (all of them classificatory and applying to one generation) are replaced with English loans: *'anakala* 'uncle', *'anakē* 'aunt', *kika* (or *tita*) 'sister', *māmā* 'mama', *pāpā* 'father'. In an Americanized culture, it seems clearest to distinguish collateral and lineal kinsmen; it is easier to say *'anakē* rather than *lūau'i kaikua'ana o ko'u lūau'i makuahine* 'true older sister of my true mother', and it now seems unnecessary to state whether mother's sister is senior or junior to mother. *Māmā* and *pāpā* are said to have been introduced by missionaries in the vain hope that this would discourage children from calling their parents by their first names. A fairly recent slang introduction is *palā* (or more commonly *balā*) for 'brother' and as an easy label for any young Hawaiian male who adheres to stereotyped Hawaiian ways.

Another dichotomy proposed is subordinate versus dominant, and this extends to the social and religious systems. Subordinate chiefs take *a*, but dominant inherited ones take *o*. Gods take *o*; they are dominant. *Kāna ali'i* 'his chief' is said if the antecedent has initiated the relationship between antecedent and chief. More usual *kona ali'i* indicates that the antecedent did not initiate the relationship; at birth he had a superior chief.

With an apparent lack of logic 'his teacher' *(kāna kumu)* and 'his student' *(kāna haumāna)* use *a*. According to our rules this would indicate that the antecedent initiates the relationship with both teacher and student. When Elbert was beginning his Hawaiian studies he once said *"ko'u kumu"*—to be scornfully corrected by an old lady who said in English of Elbert's teacher: "She's not *that* important." Would this indicate that to some native speakers *a*-objects are less "important" or are inferior to *o*-objects?

Of the three words for 'friend', *hoa* and *makamaka* take *o*, and *'aikāne* takes *a*. Perhaps *hoa* is associated with *hoahānau* 'cousin'. And is *makamaka* associated with *maka* 'eye', which like other body parts takes *o*?

Words known to nearly all tourists are *kama'āina* 'native-born person' and *malihini* 'visitor'. Preceded by possessives, the meanings change. *Ko'u kama'āina* becomes 'my host'. *Ka'u malihini* is 'my guest'.

Most material objects take *a*. Only a few take *o*: house, canoe, land, and sometimes adzes. These were highly important in the old culture and were inherited; the owner did not, in theory, initiate the ownership nor might he unilaterally dispose of them. Similarly, some post-contact introductions (horse, automobile) take *o*, perhaps because of analogy with canoe. Body parts also take *o*: one does not originate his own body parts. A similar feeling seems to extend to clothing, since it is in intimate contact with the sacred body.

Many possessed objects may take either *a* or *o*, usually but not always with different meanings. *A* and *o* in the following examples may be translated 'of' and ' 's'. *A* is sometimes translated 'by'.

> *ke ali'i a Ka-lani* 'the chief [appointed] by Ka-lani'
> *ke ali'i o ka 'āina* 'the [hereditary] chief'

> *Hale-a-ka-lā,* name of a Maui mountain, 'house [acquired or used] by the sun', a term probably referring to the legend in which the demigod Māui lassoed the sun there in order to stop its course and lengthen the day so that his mother, Hina, could dry her tapa.
> *ka hale o ke ali'i* 'the house [owned] by the chief' (Cf. *Ka-lua-o-Pele* 'the pit of Pele', an O'ahu crater to which Pele fell heir.)

> *ka heana a ke ali'i* 'the chief's victim'
> *ka heana o ke ali'i* 'the chief's corpse'

> *ka i'a a kākou* 'our fish'
> *ka i'a o kēia wahi* (FS 17) 'the fish of this place'

> *nā iwi a Pua* 'Pua's bones' (as the chicken bones she is eating)
> *nā iwi o Pua* 'Pua's [own] bones'

> *kahi a nā ali'i e he'e nalu ai* 'place where the chiefs surf' (not belonging to them)
> *kahi o nā ali'i* 'place of the chiefs' (belonging to them)

> *ke kanaka a ke ali'i* 'the subject [controlled or appointed] by the chief'
> *ke kanaka o ke ali'i* 'the [hereditary] subject of the chief'

> *ke keiki a Pua* 'Pua's child'
> *ke keiki o ka 'āina* 'the child of the land'

> *ke ki'i a Pua* 'the picture [taken or painted] by Pua'
> *ke ki'i o Pua* 'the picture of Pua' (as her photograph)

> *ka lei a Pua* 'Pua's lei' (to sell)
> *ka lei o Pua* 'Pua's lei' (to wear)

ka leo a Pua 'the tune [composed] by Pua, Pua's command'
ka leo o Pua 'Pua's voice'

ka make a ke ali'i 'the killing (or murder) by the chief'
ka make o ke ali'i 'the chief's [own] death'

ka mele a Pua 'the song by Pua'
ka mele o Pua 'the song [honoring] Pua'

ka'u nani 'my pretty one'
ko'u nani 'my fine looks'

ka wahine a ke ali'i 'the chief's wife'
ka wahine o ka lua 'the woman of the pit' (Pele)

A few words that usually take *o* may take *a* if the possessor causes the state of being:

ka melemele a ka 'ōlena (Green and Pukui 16) 'the yellow [stain] of the *'ōlena*'

ka 'ona a ka 'awa (Green and Pukui 20) 'the intoxication [caused] by the kava'

The Fijian possessive system has been called a gender system in that every noun belongs to one or another class. The same is not true of Hawaiian because so many words take both *a* and *o*. Hockett's second rule (1958:268) to qualify as a gender system is that extensive intersection does not exist; that is, a word belongs to one and only one class (French *soeur* 'sister' is always feminine).

VERBS WITH *a* AND *o*

9.6.2   As shown in table 8, all types of verbs may take *o*. Only deliberate transitives ordinarily take *a*. Some examples:

vi + *o*
'*O kō lāua hele akula nō ia* (Nakuina 85). 'The two then went.'
ka ho'i 'ana o kākou 'our going'
ma kēia pae 'ana o 'Umi (FS 153) 'on this landing of 'Umi'
ma kēia pi'i 'ana o Ka-'ehu-iki-'awakea (FS 83) 'on this going up by Ka-'ehu-iki-'awakea'
i ka pō 'ana o ka lā (FS 167) 'at nightfall'

vi + *a* (less common than *o*)
ka holona a ku'u 'īlio 'the running of my dog'
ka heihei a kākou (Nakuina 13) 'our race'

140

ka'u hele 'ana (Nakuina 2) 'my going' (but *kona hele 'ana* in Naku-ina 4)

vtsp + *o*

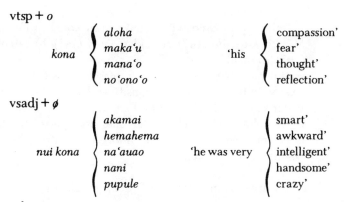

kona	aloha	'his	compassion'
	maka'u		fear'
	mana'o		thought'
	no'ono'o		reflection'

vsadj + *ø*

nui kona	akamai	'he was very	smart'
	hemahema		awkward'
	na'auao		intelligent'
	nani		handsome'
	pupule		crazy'

vsl + *o*

ka 'eha 'ana o ko'u lima 'the hurting in my arm'

kēia eo 'ana o Pai'ea iā 'Umi (FS 153) 'this defeating of Pai'ea by 'Umi'

ka hina 'ana o ke kanaka ikaika i kō lāua kaikaina (FS 37) 'the throwing of the strong man by their younger brother'

kēia ili 'ana o kāna i'a (FS 51), 'this going aground of his fish'

ka lilo 'ana o ka wa'a i ke kai 'the taking of the canoe by the sea'

ka nalowale 'ana o nā leho (FS 19), 'the losing of the cowries'

kēia puni 'ana o Kaua'i iā Ka-welo (FS 103) 'this conquering of Kaua'i by Ka-welo'

vtd + *a* with such words as (numbers refer to pages in FS): *āha'i* (45) 'to tow', *hahai* (51) 'to follow', *ha'i* (99) 'to say', *kākau* 'to write', *ō* (51) 'to pierce', *'ōlelo* (51) 'to say', *paha* (65) 'to chant', *peku* (63) 'to kick'.

vtd + *o* is less common than vtd + *a*, but it is not difficult to find examples in the literature, for example this description by Pi'ilani of the solitary burial of her leper husband (Kele-kona 7):

ko'u 'eli ho'okahi 'ana i kona home e ho'omaha hope loa ai; ko'u ho'omoe maika'i 'ana iāia e hiamoe me kāna pū . . . me ko'u ha'alele 'ana aku iāia me ka lei 'my digging out by myself his home of everlasting rest, my placing him carefully down to sleep with his gun . . . my leaving him with a lei'.

The following inconsistent sequence (FS 47) is difficult to explain: *'O ke pa'i 'ana o 'Ai-kanaka i nā mākua. . . . Ma kēia pa'i 'ana a 'Ai-kanaka i nā mākua* 'the eviction by 'Ai-kanaka of the parents. . . . Upon this eviction by 'Ai-kanaka of the parents'.

Perhaps *a* here indicates greater deliberateness and control; it makes the eviction more forceful. The preceding *kēia* 'this' makes the act more specific and less general.

Other verbs used with *o* have been noted in Fornander: *'ai* (47) 'to eat', *'alo* (147) 'to dodge', *'apo* (147) 'to catch', *ha'iha'i* (165) 'to break'.

Wilson (1976:73) gives examples contrasting use of possessives with the two types of transitives: *ka wela 'ana o ka wai* 'the water's getting hot' (vtsp) and *ka 'ai 'ana a ke keiki* 'the eating by the child' (vtd). The water does not control the heating or begin or terminate it. The child *does* control the eating; he begins and terminates it.

Locative nouns (section 8.6) are preceded by *o* or *i:*

Ua nani nā mea o waho. 'The things of the outside are pretty.'
Ua nani o waho. 'The outside is pretty.'
'A'ohe mea o loko. 'Nothing inside.'
He 'elua o laila mau hale. 'There are two houses there.'

The preposition *i* 'at' may replace *o* in any of these sentences; older people may prefer *o*.

The *o*-possessive preposition is frequently replaced by *a'o* in songs: *nā pali a'o Ko'olau Loa* 'the cliffs of Ko'olau Loa'.

For a neutralized use of *a*-possessive after all fronted nouns with a following *ai* anaphoric, see section 7.3.

φ-POSSESSIVES

9.6.3   The φ-possessives are

a'u, o'u 'my, mine'
āu, ou 'your, yours'
āna, ona 'his, her, hers'
a, o, prepositions

Initial *k* in the *k*-possessives (table 14) is a variant of the singular definite articles *ka* and *ke*. Thus the φ-possessives do not have the features singular definite, as in the following examples:

(1) After numbers: *a'u mau keiki* 'my children'. *'Elua a'u keiki.* 'I have two children.'

(2) After negatives: *'A'ohe a'u keiki.* 'I have no children.' *'A'ohe mea o loko.* 'There's nothing inside.' A similar idiomatic use is: *'A'ole o kana mai ka u'i!* 'How perfectly beautiful!'

(3) After locative nouns: *i mua ona* 'in front of him'. The *mua* is sometimes dropped: *Kauoha aku nei 'oia i kona mau kāhuna e hele mai i ona lā* (Green and Pukui 128). 'He called to his priests to come to him.' *Hele mai i o'u nei.* 'Come to me here./Come unto me.'

(4) After nouns if a *k*-word (section 10.1), *nā*, or *he* precedes the noun: *kēia keiki āna* 'this child of his'.

(5) After the prepositions *ma, me, mai,* and *e* 'by':

Ua hele aku au ma ona ala. 'I went because of him.'
Ua noho 'oia me a'u. 'He stayed with me.'
Ho'onoho akula 'o Saula iāia mai ona akula (*Ka Baibala*, Samuela I, 18.13). 'Saul placed him in his presence.'
hana 'ia e a'u 'done by me'

FRONTED POSSESSIVES

9.6.4   In section 9.2 Alexander's theory of emphasis by fronting was introduced. In the sentence *ke keiki a Pua* 'the child of Pua' the emphasis is on *ke keiki* 'the child'. It is easy and commonplace to emphasize Pua: Pua's child. This is done by (1) inserting the phrase *a Pua* between *ke* and *keiki,* (2) dropping the *-e* of *ke* (or *-a* of *ka*), and (3) lengthening the *a-* (or *o-*) possessives. The steps performed are depicted below for *ke keiki a Pua* and *ka hale o ke ali'i:*

Possessed Object: Possessor:
ke keiki   *a Pua*
the child   of Pua

   Steps:
   (1) **ke a Pua keiki*
   (2) **k- a Pua keiki*
   (3) *k-ā Pua keiki*

Possessed Object: Possessor:
ka hale   *o ke ali'i*
the house   of the chief

   Steps:
   (1) **ka o ke ali'i hale*
   (2) **k- o ke ali'i hale*
   (3) *k-ō ke ali'i hale*

The resulting phrases focus on the possessor rather than on the possessed object. (1) and (2) are starred because they are ungrammatical.

An optional step (4) is to delete the final possessed object *(k-ā Pua, k-ō ke ali'i),* sometimes with resulting ambiguity. Common ways to speak of upland and coastal peoples are *kō uka* and *kō kai,* the longer phrases being *kō uka po'e* 'people of the uplands' and *kō kai po'e* 'people of the coast'. (For other variants, see section 11.1.)

Another way to refer to people, with the final possessed object omitted, is *kā* or *kō* plus a place name: *Māmā kō Hilo.* 'The Hiloites are fast.' *Māmā kā Hilo* (FS 139). 'Those [who went to] Hilo are fast.' (Land-belonging-to-a-person takes *o,* land-visited-by-a-person takes *a.* Hilo in these sentences is a personalized locative; see section 8.6.)

The following idiomatic sequence may be analysed in similar fashion: *ka mea a kō iwi* 'the things of your bones/your own things'.

(1) **ka a kō iwi mea*
(2) **k- a kō iwi mea*
(3) *k-ā kō iwi mea*
(4) *k-ā kō iwi*

The final sequence occurs in the sentence

Ki'i	nō	'oe	i	k-ā	kō	iwi
fetch	indeed	you	(obj.)	the-belonging-to	your	person

'Fetch your own things.'

(Iwi is literally 'bone' but here means 'person'. The deleted *mea* 'thing' takes *a* because it is acquired.)

Kehau Lee (1973) attempted to explain the difference between *kō* + locative and *o* + locative. Her numerous examples seem to indicate that *kō* + locative is more definite (see *ka* and *ke,* the definite articles) and permanent than *o* + locative. Two of her examples follow:

(1) *Maluna o ia pu'u, 'a'ohe pōhaku, 'a'ohe lā'au, he mau'u a me ka lepo kō luna, akā, ma ka 'ōlelo a Kūmaikeau a me Kūmakaia, he pōhaku kō luna* (FS 189). 'On this hill were no stones, no trees, grass and dirt were above, but in what Kūmaikeau and Kūmakaia had said, stones were above.'

(2) *'I aku 'o Kea'au: "E 'imi ana au i kanaka 'aihue e loa'a ai a'u leho iā 'Umi, a 'oia kēia waiwai o luna o ka wa'a, he makana*

i ka 'aihue e loa'a ai 'o a'u leho" (FS 19–21). 'Kea'au said: "I'm looking for a thief to get my cowries for 'Umi, and this is the wealth on the canoe, a gift for the thief who gets my cowries." '

In (1) *maluna*, as usual, takes *o*, but repeated *kō luna* indicates a permanent condition; however, the wealth in (2) is temporarily on the canoe. Lee concluded that *o* + locative is more common than *kō* + locative.

Wilson (1975) posited that after a fronted locative, either *a* or *o* may be used: *kahi a nā ali'i e noho ana* (Nakuina 3) 'place where the chiefs were staying', *kahi ona e noho nei* (Nakuina 38) 'place where he stays now'. (The specialist is referred to Wilson's thesis, certainly the most detailed study ever made of *a* and *o*.)

COMITATIVE/INSTRUMENTAL/SIMILITUDE: *me*

9.7   The term "comitative" indicates accompaniment (cf. Latin *cum* 'with'). The disparate functions of Hawaiian *me*, indicated by the title of this section, are commonly glossed 'with' or 'like':

Noho 'o Pua me kāna keiki. 'Pua stayed with her child.'
Kākau 'oe me kēia penikala. 'Write with this pen.'
Noho ihola me ka 'olu'olu (FS 159). '[He] lived then in comfort.'
inā me neia ka hānai (FS 133) 'if the adopted child were like this'
Me nei 'oe i hana ai. 'Do it this way.'
Ua holo ia me he lio lā. 'He ran like a horse.' (*Me he* is often written as a single word.)

A noun phrase is frequently connected with a *me*-phrase by the conjunction *ā* 'and': *Hā'awi maila ia i kona malo ā me kona niho palaoa* (FS 117). 'He then gave his loincloth and his whale-tooth pendant.'

For use of *me*-phrases after dual and plural pronouns, see section 8.2.

ABLATIVE: *mai*

9.8   "Ablative," a term from Latin grammar, expresses relations of removal or direction away.

mai Honolulu 'from Honolulu'
mai Honolulu mai 'here from Honolulu'

(The second *mai* is the directional 'hither' rather than the homophonous preposition; one can also say *mai Honolulu aku* 'away from Honolulu'. For the directionals *mai* and *aku* see section 7.2.) Before names of people and pronouns the definite locative preposition *iā* or (rarely) the possessive preposition *o* may follow *mai* (*mai iā* may be pronounced in fast speech *maiā*):

> *mai iā Pua, mai Pua mai* 'from Pua'
> *mai ia'u, mai a'u* 'from me'
> *mai iāia* 'from him'
> *Hele mai mai o Hilo.* '[He] came *(hele mai)* from *(mai o)* Hilo.'

AGENTIVE: *e*

9.9   The agentive has these features:

(1) It occurs only after a verb followed by the passive/imperative *'ia* or an alternate and an optional subject. It rarely occurs with either type of stative verb.

(2) It never occurs in a clause containing an object marker.

Examples:

> *'Ai   'ia   ka   poi   e   ia.*
> eat (pas.) the   poi   by   him
> 'The poi was eaten by him.'

> *Ke   'aina   maila   e   ka   manu* (FS 79).
> (pres.) eat (pas.) hither-then by   the   bird
> '[It is being] eaten then by the bird.' (Poetic for 'destroyed by the enemy'.)
> (The suffix *-na* is a variant of *'ia*; see section 6.6.3.)

> *O   ha'i   'ia   e   ke   kaiko'eke* (FS 177).
> lest   tell   (pas.) by   the   brother-in-law
> 'Lest [it] be told by the brother-in-law.'

> *Ua   hō'ala   'ia   ka   lumi   e   ka   pīkake.*
> (perf.) perfume (pas.) the   room   by   the   *pīkake*
> 'The room was perfumed by the *pīkake* flower.'

VOCATIVE: *ē/ø*

9.10   The vocatives precede names of people and classes of people addressed, and for emphasis may also follow a person's name. *Ē*

146

Pua, hele mai! 'Pua, come here!' *Ē Pua ē, hele mai!* 'Pua, come here!' Or a phrase may be embedded between the head noun and *ē: Ē ke aliʻi o Hawaiʻi ē.* 'O chief of Hawaiʻi.' In this sentence, *ē ke aliʻi . . . ē* is a discontinuous phrase in which the possessive phrase *o Hawaiʻi* is embedded.

In vocative phrases with classes of people, a *k*-word commonly precedes the noun: *Ē ke kumu, hele mai.* 'O (the) teacher, come here.' *Ē kuʻu aliʻi maikaʻi, hele mai.* 'O my good chief, come here.'

The vocative *ē* is used only with third person pronouns. To express a second person, one uses the third person plus a demonstrative, as described in section 8.2. *Ē lākou lā* 'say, all of you' (lit., vocative they there). In the singular the form is contracted to *e i nei*, in slow speech *ē ia nei*, vocative he here.

na AND *no*

9.11   These common prepositions consist of *n-* and the possessive prepositions *a* and *o*. *Na* and *no* are predictably long before primary stress and before syllables containing long vowels or diphthongs, and hence the macron need not be written. (Further study may indicate that *na* is always long, just as the *a* possessive is long in *kāu* 'your' and *kāna* 'his, hers'.) The preposition *no* is not to be confused with the intensifier *nō*. Like the agentive *e*, previously described, *na* and *no* do not occur with either type of stative verb.

An *n*-phrase at the beginning of a sentence is in focus, as in sentence (3) below.

(1) *Ua   kākau Pua i   ka   leka.*
     (perf.)   write Pua (obj.) the ˉletter
     'Pua wrote the letter.'

(2) *Ua kākau ʻia ka leka e Pua.*
                              by
     'The letter was written by Pua.'

(3) *Na Pua i   kākau ka leka.*
     by   (perf.)
     '*Pua* wrote the letter.'

In sentence (3) *na* has an agentive function; both (2) and (3) seem derived from (1). Note that an object marker does not follow the transitive verb *kākau*. (But compare sentence [14].)

In sentence (4) *no* has benefactive functions, in (5) locative, and in (6) causative:

(4) *No   ka   lani   ka   inoa.*
     for the royal chief the   name-song
     'The name song honors the royal chief.'

If the focus in this sentence is changed to *inoa*, *ka inoa* is replaced by *he inoa: He inoa no ka lani.* 'A name song honors the chief.'

(5) *Ua   hele   a'e nei   no   Maui.*
     (perf.) go   recently   to   Maui
     '[He] has just now gone to Maui.'

(6) *No   laila,   maika'i   'ole.*
     because   there   good   not
     'Therefore [it's] no good.'

In (7) *na* has no passivizing function and the verb *hana* is active. Both versions are encountered in the literature and in conversation. In a single story in the July 1860 issue of the newspaper *Hoku Loa* appeared these two sentences:

(7) *Na   ke   Akua   i   hana   i   nā   mea.*
     by   the   God   (perf.) make   (obj.)   the (pl.)   thing
     'God made the things.'

(8) *Na   wai   ka   mahina   i   kau   malaila?*
     by   whom   the(subj.) moon   (perf.) place   at-there
     'Who placed the *moon* there?'

The position of the subject *after* the verb in sentence (3) is more common than its position before the verb in (8), in which position it is probably more emphatic.

The *a/o* contrast is maintained in the following sentences with benefactive focus phrases. In (9) and (10) the antecedents of *a* are objects that one himself acquires and controls (book, fish), and the antecedents of *o* are objects that, in the old culture, one was born with or had a right to possess (*ka'a* 'car', like *wa'a* 'canoe', takes *o*—see section 9.6.1).

(9) *Na wai ka puke?* 'For whom is the book?'
     No wai ka wa'a? 'For whom is the canoe?'
(10) *Na'u kahi i'a.* 'Give me a fish.'
     No'u kahi ka'a. 'Give me an automobile.'

In (11) a person's son or daughter takes an *a*-possessive, and a land of which one is a native takes *o*:

(11) *Na Lani 'oia.* 'He is [a son] of Lani.'
No Maui 'oia. 'He is from (a native of) Maui.'

Agentive and benefactive contrast in (12) and (13):

(12) *He mo'olelo na 'Umi.* 'A story by 'Umi.'
He mo'olelo no 'Umi. 'A story concerning (or honoring) 'Umi.'

(13) *Nāna ke ki'i.* 'The picture is by him.'
Nona ke ki'i. 'The picture is of (or belongs to) him.'

In sentence (3) *kākau* is translated literally by the passive voice (even though there is no *'ia*) and is followed by a noun phrase with ϕ-preposition serving as marker of the subject of the sentence. A function of *na* in this sentence is to passivize the verb that follows it. The following sentence, however, is also acceptable:

(14) *Na Pua i kākau i ka leka.* 'Pua wrote the letter.'

The *n*-possessives are used in similar constructions:

(15) *Nāna au i ha'i mai nei* (FS 9). '*He* told me [so].'

The *n*-possessives were introduced in section 8.4.2. In sentence (10) above, *na'u* 'for me' (*a*-class object) and *no'u* 'for me' (*o*-class object) appear. In sentences (13) and (15), *nāna* 'by him/belongs to him' appears. In a single paragraph in Nakuina 19 occur *na'u*, *nāna*, and *nāu* 'by you':

(16) . . . *na'u e mālama kona mau iwi ā hiki i ka wā e loa'a ai 'o ka'u pua, a laila, hā'awi aku au nāna e mālama, ā 'oiai, 'o 'oe ho'okahi ka'u pua, no laila, ke hā'awi aku nei au iā'oe nāu e mālama.* 'I was to care for her bones until I had a child, then I would give [the calabash] and he would take care [of the bones], but since you are my only child, therefore I give [the calabash] to you to care for.'

(17) *Na Kimo e holoholo ana 'o Honolulu.* '*Jim* will travel around Honolulu.'

(18) *No wai i 'eha ai ā i make ai 'o Jesu-Kristo?* 'For whom did Jesus Christ suffer and die?'

(19) *Na wai i ho'ohina i ke kanaka mokomoko?* 'Who threw the fighter?'

The use of object markers in sentences (7) and (14) is perhaps aberrant. In sentences (3) and (16), object markers do not occur after transitive verbs. '*Ia* occurs in no *n*-sentence, even though some may be translated by passives. Six of the 19 sentences are verbless.

Comparable to *kā ia* 'his, hers' (section 8.4) is *na ia*; like *kā ia* it is usually followed by φ-demonstratives *nei* or *ala*. *Na ia ala* in fast speech may become *naila*. Such forms as **na 'oe*, **no 'oe*, or **no ia* have not been noted. *Naia ala (naila) i kākau* 'he there wrote [it]' is similar to *nāna i kākau*, but here proximity is indicated. See *kāpe'a* in the Dictionary.

The functions and meanings of the *n*-prepositions may be summarized as follows:

na:	benefactive	'belonging to, for'
	agentive	'by'
no:	benefactive	'belonging to, for, concerning, honoring'
	causative	'because of'
	locative	'originating from, going to'

Three common causative *no*-phrases are *no ka mea* 'because' (lit., because the thing), *no ke aha* 'why' (lit., because the what), and *no laila* 'therefore' (lit., for there).

SIMULATIVE: *pē*

9.12   This rare preposition is encountered in the phrase *pē kēia* 'like this'. It is far more common as the first part of the demonstratives *pēnei, pēnā, pēlā, pēia* (section 8.3.6).

APPOSITIONAL PREPOSITIONS

9.13   A noun in apposition is commonly preceded by the subject marker '*o*, by φ, or by the same preposition that precedes the referent.

(1) *Ā ha'alele   'o   Kama-pua'a   i   nā   wāhine   ā*
and leave   (subj.)   Kama-pua'a   (obj.)   the   women   and
me   kona   makuahūnōai   'o   Kāne-iki (FS 243).
with   his   father-in-law   (app.)   Kāne-iki
'And Kama-pua'a left the women and his father-in-law, Kāne-iki.'

(2) *Ā   hiki   'o   Kama-pua'a   iā   Waili-nu'u,*
    and go   (subj.) Kama-pua'a   to   Waili-nu'u
    ka   lawai'a (FS 243).
    'And Kama-pua'a went to Waili-nu'u, the fisherman.'
    (In this sentence the appositional phrase, *ka lawai'a*, is intro-
       duced by ø.)

(3) *'Auhea   nā   wahi   'elemākule,   'o   Nūnū   ā*
    where the (paucal) old men   (subj.) Nūnū   and
    me   Kākohe (FS 147)?
       Kākohe
    'Where are the unimportant old men, Nūnū and Kākohe?'
    (Both the nominative phrase and the appositional phrase are in-
       troduced by ø.)

(4) *ka   hale   o   ke   ali'i   'o   'Umi*
    the house of the chief (app.) 'Umi
    'the house of the chief, 'Umi'

(5) *ka   huaka'i   ka'apuni   a   ke   ali'i   a   'Umi* (FS 155)
    the trip   circulate of the chief (app.) 'Umi
    'the tour of the chief, 'Umi'

(6) *me   kāna   wahine   me   Kāne-wahine-iki-a-Oha* (FS 101)
    with his wife   (app.) Kāne-wahine-iki-a-Oha
    'with his wife, Kāne-wahine-iki-a-Oha'

(7) *ma   kēia   mau   'ōlelo   hō'olu'olu. . .   i   kāna*
    with this (pl.) word make-pleasant to his
    keiki   iā   Hākau (FS 123)
    child (app.) Hākau
    'with these pleasing words . . . to his son, Hākau'
    (*I* and *iā* are alternants, *i* before the noun *keiki*, and appositional
      iā before the proper noun Hākau.)

(8) *no   ke   ali'i   no   'Umi*
    for the chief (app.) 'Umi
    'for the chief, 'Umi'

(9) *ā   hā'awi   na   kona   akua,   na   Kā'ili*
    and give for his god (app.) Kā'ili
    'and give for his god, Kā'ili'

Nouns in apposition are sometimes preceded by the indefinite
article *he* rather than by a preposition: *ā loa'a nā wa'a, he mau
kaulua* (FS 63) 'after getting the canoes, double outriggers'.

In poetry, an 'o-appositional phrase at the end of a sentence may be emphasized by replacing 'o with a'o: *Lapakū ka wahine a'o Pele.* 'The woman Pele is active.'

PREPOSITIONAL PHRASES IN VERBLESS SENTENCES

9.14   Verbless sentences commonly consist of a prepositional phrase followed by a phrase consisting of article or *k*-word + noun. The prepositions are *'o,* subject; *i,* locative/instrumental; *ma,* locative; *mai,* ablative; *na,* benefactive/agentive; *no,* benefactive/causative. Examples:

'O wai nā wa'a (FS 85)? 'Who are the canoemen?'
I ke ahiahi ka pā'ina. 'The party is in the evening.'
I ka 'ōlelo nō ke ola. 'Life is in the word.'
Ma ka lae kona maka'ani'ani. 'Her glasses were on her forehead.'
Mai loko mai ke kanaka. 'The person is from the mainland.'
Na Pua ka lei. 'The lei was [made] by Pua.'
No ka lani ka inoa. 'The name song honors the chief.'

If the order of these phrases is reversed, the result is ungrammatical or incomplete. All the sentences except the first can be negated by initial *'a'ole.*

Hawkins, who has made a valuable contribution to the study of Hawaiian sentence structure, also gives examples of the *he*-phrase + prepositional phrase (1975, section 3):

he uluna { *mai ka hale* / *i ka noho* / *no ke keiki* / *na ke ali'i* } 'a pillow { from the house' / on the chair' / for the child' / [made] by the chief' }

10   Determiners, Numerals, and Plurals

10.1   Elements occurring between prepositions and noun nuclei are shown in table 7. All of those beginning with k- may be called k-words. The meaning of k- is singular/definite; deletion of k- from a sentence removes the singular/definite meaning:

> *Makemake au i ka wai.* 'I want the water.'
> *Makemake au i wai.* 'I want water.'

Deletion of k- in the k-possessives also removes the singular/definite meaning: *ka'u keiki* 'my child' and *nā keiki a'u* 'my children'. (A common alternant is *ka'u mau keiki* 'my children'. Here the plural marker *mau* nullifies the singularity of k-.)

The article *ka/ke* is discussed in section 10.2.

An extremely common k-word that should probably be considered an article is *kekahi*, with a broad range of meanings: 'a, a certain, some, another, other': *i kekahi lā* 'on another day', *kekahi kanaka* 'a man, a certain man, another man'.

Less common are *kau* and *kauwahi: Ua 'ike anei 'oe i kau pua'a a mākou?* 'Have you seen our pigs?' *Na'u ho'i kauwahi i'a.* 'Give me a few fish.' *Kauwahi* can be considered a diminutive, since it contains the paucal *wahi* discussed in section 10.4. For *kauwahi* as a noun, see the Dictionary. *Kau + hale* is usually written as a single word and has come to mean 'home, household', probably because the old Hawaiian homestead consisted of several buildings. *Kekahi* is sometimes replaced by *kahi: Na'u kahi.* 'Give me some.' *E holoholo mai ana neia wahi keiki . . . e lewalewa ana kahi ma'i* (FS 21). 'The little boy whose genital was dangling was running along.' This *kahi* is not to be confused with the locative noun, *kahi* 'place', the deliberate transitive verb *kahi* 'to cut', or the numeral *kahi* 'one'.

All the words discussed in this section and in 10.2 may be called determiners.

ARTICLES

10.2   The singular definite article is *ka/ke*. Some of its uses differ from English usage:

(1) Before abstract and general terms, as *ke aloha* 'love', *ka hanohano* 'glory', *ke Akua* 'God', *hui o nā wāhine* 'association of women'

(2) Before body parts instead of possessives: *Me ka lima a me ka wāwae lāua i kope hele ai.* 'They raked on with their hands and feet.' (Cf. section 8.4.1.)

(3) As an indication of the plural: see the example under (2) above. The well-known place name, Ke-ala-ke-kua, is literally 'the path the god' but actually means 'the pathway of the gods' and refers to images from Kona carried overland to Puna-luʻu in Kaʻū, Hawaii.

(4) Before collective nouns: *hāʻawi i ka ʻawa* 'gave ʻawa'

Ka/ke is often translated 'the', but this is a convention and is by no means a certain translation into English. Often it need not be translated at all, as indicated in examples under (1) and (4) above. In the following sentence *ka/ke* is translated 'a, a, his, its'. *Inā mahalo ʻia ke kāne i ke kanaka maikaʻi . . . inā mahalo ʻia ke poʻo i ka pālahalaha maikaʻi . . .* (FS 143). 'If *a* man was admired as *a* handsome person . . . if *his* head was admired for *its* handsome flatness . . .' As usual, translation depends on context.

Ke, an alternant of *ka*, occurs before all nouns beginning with *a- (ke aloha), e- (ke ea), o- (ke ola),* and *k- (ke kanaka).* Elsewhere *ka* is used, except that some words beginning with the glottal stop and with *p-* are preceded by *ke*.

ke ʻala 'the fragrance'	*ka ʻaka* 'the laugh'
ke pā 'the dish'	*ka pā* 'the enclosure'
ke poʻo 'the head'	*ka ʻehu* 'the red-head'

In the Fornander legends and in the Biblical "Song of Solomon" *mele* 'song' is usually preceded by *ke: Kau hou ʻo Ka-maunu-a-Niho i ke mele* (FS 201). 'Ka-maunu-a-Niho chanted the song again.' This usage seems to be obsolete. In section 2.12

the alternant *ke* is termed a vestigial form because it occurs as *te* in other Polynesian languages.

In slow speech the definite article is followed by plus juncture, indicated below by a period (see section 2.4), but in fast speech this may be lost:

Slow: *ka.ua* 'the rain', *ke.ehu* 'the spray'
Fast: *kaua* 'the rain, war', *keehu* 'the spray'

The old Hawaiian "feeling" that the article is a "part" of the noun is shown by Andrews' statement (1854:18) that it was very common for Hawaiians to write the article joined to the noun. A great many such combinations slipped into Andrews' dictionary under the *k*'s, as *ka-la-wa-ia* 'fisherman' *(ka lawai'a)* and *ke-a-li-a* 'salt encrustation' *(ke alia)*.

This joining of articles and nouns is apparent in place names and personal names. In Pukui, Elbert, and Mookini's *Place Names of Hawaii* (1974), 555 names are entered that begin with *Ka-* and 159 with *Ke-* (p. 252). In the 1974 Honolulu telephone directory there were 23 pages of names beginning with *Ka-* and five pages of names beginning with *Ke-*. A large percentage of these are Hawaiian.

In at least three circumstances *ka/ke* fuses with other elements:

(1) *Ka* followed by *wahi* 'place' is *kahi*. (This is further evidence of the fleeting, glidelike character of the sound *-w-* that led Hawaiian writers to vacillate in the spellings of such words as *koali* and *kowali* 'morning glory', mentioned in section 2.1.)

(2) Possessive phrases embedded within preceding determiner-plus-noun phrases were described in section 9.6.4: *Ke keiki a Kimo* 'the child of Jim' becomes *k-ā Kimo keiki: ke* plus *a* becomes *k-ā*.

(3) In an idiom common in texts but apparently not in conversation, *ka/ke* fuses with a following imperative/intentive verb marker *e*, as in the sentence *'O wau k-e hele mai.* 'I'm the one who is to come.' This sentence may be interpreted as a combination of an equational sentence and a simple sentence:

'O wau ka mea. 'I'm the person.'
E hele mai ana au. 'I'm coming.'

The combining of the two sentences is effected by the following steps:

(1) The sentences are combined and *ana* is deleted: **'O wau ka mea e hele mai au.*

(2) The final subject is deleted: *'O wau ka mea e hele mai.*

(3) *Mea* is dropped: **'O wau ka e hele mai.*

(4) *Ka* plus *e* becomes *k-e*: *'O wau k-e hele mai.*

Note that sentence (2), as well as (4), is grammatical.

With perfective verb markers, the steps are somewhat different. They are performed here for the sentence *'O wau ka i hele mai ai.* 'I'm the one who came.'

(a) The underlying sentences are combined: **'O wau ka mea ua hele mai au.*

(b) The past perfect *i* replaces *ua* (see table 9): **'O wau ka mea i hele mai au.*

(c) The anaphoric *ai* replaces the final subject: **'O wau ka mea i hele mai ai.*

(d) *Mea* is dropped: *'O wau ka i hele mai ai.* (*Ka i* here is spoken as a single stress group.)

Similarly, *ka mea o* 'the one of' may be replaced by *kā o*: *'O wau kā o kāua ke ha'alele iho ana iā'oe* (Kelekona 60). 'I'm the one of the two of us who is leaving you.' The *o kāua* may be omitted, with the meaning 'I'm the one who is leaving you.'

As shown earlier, *ka/ke* is often used in sentences with a plural meaning, instead of the common plural article *nā (nā lani* 'the chiefs', *nā mele* 'the songs') Like *ka/ke, nā* is common in proper names (70 place names in *Place Names of Hawaii* begin with *nā*). This common *nā* should not be confused with the rare ⌀-demonstrative *nā* illustrated in 8.3.2: *ē nā pōki'i ē* 'O younger brother'. Nor should it be confused with the benefactive/agentive preposition *na* discussed in section 9.11.

A rare plural article is *nāhi*, a contraction of *nā* and the paucal *wahi*: *'Auhea akula nāhi keiki?* 'Where are the boys?'

The indefinite article *he* differs in distribution from the definite article *ka/ke* in that it does not follow prepositions other than *me*, comitative/instrumental/similitude (section 9.7), and commonly occurs as the initial phrase in verbless sentences, such as:

(1) *He kumu 'o Pua.* 'Pua is a teacher.'

The reverse order in this sentence seems ungrammatical (**'O Pua he kumu)* unless one adds the third person singular pronoun:

'O Pua, he kumu ia. He (noun) *ia* as well as the *'o* (noun) *ia* (section 9.2) is common: *He mea maika'i nō ia.* 'It's a very good thing.' *'O ke kaua ihola nō ia* (Alexander 1968:34). 'Then there was war.'

In sentences with verbs, the English indefinite article is usually translated *kekahi:*

(2) *'Ike 'oia i kekahi hale.* 'He saw a house.'

In sentences with verbs, *he*-phrases such as the following occur in the slot occupied by a prepositional phrase in sentence (2):

(3) *'Ike 'oia he mau hale.* 'He saw some houses.'
(4) *'Ike 'oia he wahi hale.* 'He saw a small house.'

If in sentences (3) and (4), *he* is replaced by the preposition *i* in its function as the object marker, the translation of (3) becomes 'He saw houses.' The meaning of (4) seems unchanged.

A *he*-phrase functioning as subject may also follow the verb: *Hele mai he 'elua wāhine.* 'Two women came.'

A noun phrase with *kekahi*, as in sentence (2) above, may be fronted for emphasis. These changes occur:

(a) *I kekahi* is replaced by *he* and *he hale* is fronted: **he hale 'ike 'oia.*
(b)ˡ*'Oia* is replaced by *āna*, a *ø*-possessive after a preposed object (see section 9.6.3): **he hale 'ike āna.*
(c) *Āna* follows *hale*, and *'ike* is preceded by the perfective marker *i* in noninitial position: **he hale āna i 'ike.*
(d) The anaphoric *ai* follows the verb; its antecedent is *hale: he hale āna i 'ike ai* 'a house that he saw'.

Any word after *he* is considered a noun, regardless of English translation.

He   poepoe   ka   honua (Alexander 1968:36).
a   round/globe   the   earth
'The earth is round./The earth is a globe.'

He coalesces with the negative *'a'ole* to *'a'ohe* 'to be none'. A *ø*-possessive (section 9.6.3) may follow: *'A'ohe āna hana.* 'He has no work.' *'A'ohe o'u makemake i poi.* 'I don't want any poi.' *'A'ohe mea i loko./ 'A'ohe mea o loko.* 'Nothing inside.'

The *'a'ohe* form is sometimes followed by the singular definite article. Perhaps a slight nuance distinguishes *'a'ohe kūpuna* 'no grandparents [at all]' and *'a'ohe ke kupuna* 'not [a single] grandparent'. The form without the article is by far the

157

most common. Today *'a'ohe* + X (noun) 'there is no X' is often followed by a gesture, a quick flick of the hand with the palm turned downward and away from the body, originally significant of an empty hand.

NUMERALS

10.3   Numerals in noun clauses (table 7) come between the determiners and before the plural markers. Digits below ten are preceded by a general classifier *'e-* (or rarely *'a-*):

'e-kahi	1	*'e-hā*	4	*'e-hiku*	7
'e-lua	2	*'e-lima*	5	*'e-walu*	8
'e-kolu	3	*'e-ono*	6	*'e-iwa*	9

The classifier *ho'o-* precedes *kahi* 'one' except when counting in sequence, as, one, two, three: *'e-kahi, 'e-lua, 'e-kolu,* or *kahi, lua, kolu.*

The post-missionary names of the days of the week (except Sunday, *Lāpule* 'prayer day') are *Pō* 'night' + *'a-* + digit: *Pō'akahi* 'Monday', *Pō'alua* 'Tuesday', *Pō'akolu* 'Wednesday', *Pō'aha* 'Thursday', *Pō'alima* 'Friday', *Pō'aono* 'Saturday'. (Each "day" was thought to begin at nightfall, hence the use of *pō* for 'day'; the days of the month are called *nā pō o ka mahina,* literally, the nights of the moon. 'Tomorrow' is *'apōpō,* literally, when night darkens.)

A prefix to numerals, in addition to *'e-, 'a-,* and *ho'o-,* is *koko'o-* and its alternant *ko'o-* 'partnership, association', usually only with the numerals *kahi, lua,* or *kolu. Kō māua koko'okolu ia.* 'He is a member of our partnership of three.'

'E- is usually stressed as a separate group (*'e.iwa* 'nine', but sometimes *'eiwa*).

'E- + numeral is very rarely preceded by *ai* or *a,* perhaps short for *aia* 'there are': *ko'u mau lima ai 'elua* (Kelekona 109) 'my two hands'.

'A-: The wonder debater, Kai-palaoa, chants seven uses of the *hau* tree:

'O ke ama hau lā 'akahi
'O ka 'iako hau lā, 'alua,
'O ka 'ili hau lā, 'akolu . . . (Fornander 1917, vol. 4, p. 593)

'The outrigger float is number one
The outrigger boom is number two
Hau bark is number three . . . '

158

The first slot labeled 'particles' in table 7 occurs only after the numerals: *'elua wale no kānaka* 'only two people', *'elua nō kānaka* 'just two people'. Other ways to separate a numeral from its head:

> *'elua i'a* 'two fish'
> *'elua mau i'a* 'two fish'
> *'elua a'u mau i'a* 'my two fish'
> *'elua a'u mau kāuna i'a* 'my two foursomes of fish' (For discussion of *kāuna*, see below.)

Numerical compounds are formed with *hapa* 'portion' (from English 'half'), as *hapa-lua* 'half', *hapa-kolu* 'third', *hapa-hā* 'fourth'. Coins are *hapa-'umi* 'five cents', *hapa-hā* 'twenty-five cents', and *hapa-lua* 'fifty cents'.

Numbers above nine have no classifying prefixes. They are:

'umi	10	*kana-ono*	60
'umi kūmā-kahi	11	*kana-hiku*	70
'umi kūmā-lua	12	*kana-walu*	80
iwakālua	20	*kana-iwa*	90
iwakālua kūmā-kahi	21	*hanele*	hundred
kana-kolu	30	*kaukani*	thousand
kana-hā	40	*miliona*	million
kana-lima	50		

Kana-ono and *kana-iwa* do not diphthongize in ordinary speech.

Kana 'ten' is usually followed by the word for a numeral, as in the decades 30–90 listed above. Occasionally it is used alone, for example (Nakuina 40), *'o ka wa'a kana ko'okahi mai, kana ko'olua mai, kana ko'okolu mai* 'ten one-man canoes, ten two-man canoes, ten three-man canoes'. Andrews (1854:57) and Alexander (1968:13) thought that the numerals above fifty were introduced by the missionaries. The etymologies of *kūmā-* and *iwakālua* are not known. (*Kūmā-* is probably old: in Rennellese *tuma'a* is glossed 'more than'; thus 'eleven' is *angahugu tuma'a tahi*.) In the Bible and in very formal speech *kūmā-* is replaced by *kumamā*. The words for hundred, thousand, and million are English borrowings.

Other prefixes to numeral words are *pā-* and *kua-*:

Pā-, called a "distributive" by Alexander (1968:14), adds the concepts 'at a time, at once, number of times': *miki pā-lua* 'to dip twice' (as to eat poi with two fingers), *hānau pā-lima* 'quintuplet birth'. Four Honolulu streets are named *Pā-kahi* 'First',

Pā-lua 'Second', *Pā-kolu* 'Third', and *Pā-lima* 'Fifth'. In
Nakuina 106 the terms *pā-ka'au* 'forty each' and *pā-kāuna* 'four
each' occur with reference to catching flying fish *(mālolo)*. Rare
forms are *pā-kakahi* 'distribute one at a time' and *pā-kaukani*
'by thousands'. *Pā-* forms are occasionally transitive (*pā lua i ka
i'a* 'divide the fish in two shares'). More commonly they qualify
transitive verbs, as *hā'awi pā-kolu* 'to give to three', *ho'onoho
pā-hā* 'arrange in fours' and *māhele pā-ono* 'distribute in six
shares'. *Pāpā-* also occurs with numerals, apparently with the
same meanings as the *pā-* forms.

Kua-, a rare ordinal-number former, has been noted in three
place names: *Ka-holo-kua-iwa* 'the ninth run' (probably a
reference to an avalanche), a cliff at Wai-pi'o, Hawai'i; *Kua-
hiku-ka-lapa-o-Anahulu* 'seventh of the ridges of Anahulu', the
peak of Anahulu mountain on Hawai'i; *Kua-lua* 'twice', a surf-
ing area at Wai-mea, Kaua'i. *Kua-* also refers to generations
removed, but strangely, *kua-kahi*, usually meaning 'one', means
two generations removed, as a grandchild. *Mo'opuna kua-lua* is
a great-grandchild.

Numerals differ from determiners in two important ways: (1)
They may follow nouns as qualifiers: *Nānā i nā hale 'e-lua.*
'Look at the two houses.' (2) Without classifiers, numerals are
nouns and are translated as ordinals: *ka lua o nā hale* 'the second of the houses'.

The numeral interrogative *-hia* occurs with the prefixes, most
commonly *'e: 'E-hia kānaka? 'E-hia mau kānaka?* 'How many
people?' *'E-hia noho'i kānaka?* 'So how many people?'

Ancient names for large numbers are *lau, mano, kini,* and
lehu, and the reduplicated derivatives *manomano, kinikini,* and
lehulehu. They are used poetically as nouns indicative of great
numbers:

> *He lau ka pu'u, he mano ka ihona.* 'Many are the hills, numerous are
> the descents.'

> *He kini, he lehu kahawai o Hilo ē* (FS 279). 'The streams of the Hilo
> District are countless, endless.'

These two sayings are applicable to deep troubles or unfathom-
able problems of any kind. Note that in both of them the smaller
quantity precedes the larger, an order reversed in the following
saying that shows the great respect and even awe felt toward traditional Hawaiian knowledge: *Kini ā lau ka 'ikena a ka Hawai'i.*
'Multitudinous and endless is the knowledge of Hawaiians.'

Elsewhere these quantities are somewhat fancifully translated 400, 4,000, 40,000, and 400,000. It is doubtful that actual counts of this magnitude were ever made. In a confusing account of the warriors defending Hawai'i against a Maui invader, these numbers of fighters are given (FS 188–191):

'elua lau mano kānaka '32,000 men'
2   400 4,000

'ehiku lau mano kānaka '112,000 men'
7

'umi lau mano kānaka '160,000 men'
10

'eono lau mano kānaka '96,000 men'
6

The editor (presumably Thrum) questioned the arithmetic, and suggested in a footnote that *lau mano* may refer to a wing or body of 400 men.

The addiction to high numbers is shown also in the Kumulipo genealogical chant (Beckwith 1951) describing the goddess Haumea, who had the mysterious power of living to old age, being reborn, and mating with a descendant. This went on for some ten generations. To indicate that vast number of progeny the poet says (p. 232):

'O Hau-mea kino pāha'oha'o, 'o Hau-mea kino pāpāwalu
'O Hau-mea kino pāpālehu, 'o Hau-mea kino pāpāmano
I manomano i ka lehulehu o nā kino

'Hau-mea of mysterious forms, Hau-mea of eightfold forms
Hau-mea of four-hundred-thousand-fold forms, Hau-mea of four-thousand-fold forms
Four thousand, four hundred thousand, on and on the forms'

Of even greater magnitude is *nalowale*, usually translated 'lost' but sometimes considered a number equal to ten *lehu*, which is four million. It is inconceivable that people counted that many. Andrews points out in his Dictionary that *nalowale* merely signifies that the counter can go no farther.

In Hawaiian, four and multiples of four are sacred or formulistic numbers and the basis of the traditional counting system. A unit of four is *kāuna*, a term that perhaps arose, according to Alexander (1968:13), "from the custom of counting fish, coconuts, taro, etc., by taking a couple in each hand, or by

161

tying them in bundles of four." 'Twelve' in the old counting was *'ekolu kāuna* 'three fours', 'eighty' was *'elua kanahā* 'two for-ties'. (As illustrated earlier in this section, *kāuna* may follow the plural marker *mau.*)

Walu 'eight' is sacred when used as a suffix: *kūwaluwalu* 'many', *makawalu* 'numerous', *olowalu* 'simultaneously', *puwalu* 'in unison, cooperative'. A mythical character slain by the pig demigod, Kamapua'a, has eight foreheads (*'ewalu lae*, FS 211); does this really mean 'many foreheads' or 'eight fore-heads'?

Rarely used terms for forty are *'iako*, as in counting tapas and canoes, and *ka'au* in counting fish (Alexander 1968:14). *Ho'okahi a'u ka'au i'a.* 'I have forty fish.'

OTHER PLURAL MARKERS

10.4   The special plurals are *mau, po'e,* and *kau* (for more than two), and *wahi nāhi,* and *ona;* these last may be called paucal since they imply several but not a great many. *Po'e* is most commonly a singular noun meaning 'people, persons', but is occasionally used as a pluralizer before both animate and inanimate nouns, as *ka po'e kānaka* 'the people' and *kēia po'e hale* 'these houses'. *Po'e* is sometimes preceded by the plural article *(nā po'e).*

In Kelekona 92, numerals precede *mau: Ua ho'iho'i mai 'oia ia 15 mau lēpela.* 'She [a ship] returned these 15 lepers.'

The rare plural *kau* probably occurs also in *kauwahi* and *kauhale* (section 10.1); also in *kaukolu* 'triple, trinity'. *Ua 'ike anei 'oe i kau pua'a a mākou?* 'Have you seen our pigs?'

Very rarely the sequence *nā mau* is heard, although it has not been noted in writing: *'Ike au i nā mau lio.* 'I saw the horses.'

The common paucal determiner *wahi* may be glossed 'little, small, some, a few, insignificant, unimportant'; it frequently im-parts modesty, as in a request: *E 'olu'olu 'oe i wahi wai.* 'Please, just a little water.' *Wahi* most commonly occurs as the only plural marker, that is, without *nā* or *mau.* In Nakuina 31, however, *kau* and *mau* precede *wahi: ā kau mau wahi 'āina li'ili'i* 'and those few small lands'. In FS 147, *nā* precedes *wahi: nā wahi 'elemākule* 'the unimportant old men'. Such oc-currences are rare. Most commonly the distributions of *mau* and *wahi* may be summarized thus:

$$\left. \begin{array}{c} \text{demonstrative} \\ \text{and} \\ \text{possessive} \end{array} \right\} + \left\{ \begin{array}{c} mau \\ \\ wahi \end{array} \right\} + \text{noun}$$

kēia mau wāhine 'these women'
kāna mau wāhine 'his wives'
kāna wahi wāhine 'his unimportant wives'
kēia wahi kalo 'this small bit of taro'

Rare *nāhi* is a contraction of the plural article *nā* and *wahi: E pōkaʻakaʻa mai ʻoe i nāhi lau hala.* 'Wind up some pandanus leaves.' *ʻAuhea akula nāhi keiki?* 'Where are the boys?'

An uncommon paucal plural marker is *ona* 'and also', always preceding the last of two or more things (usually goods, not persons), and usually preceding *mau:*

kalakoa me ona mau lipine 'calico and also ribbons'
Lawe mai i ʻai me ona mau iʻa. 'Bring poi and also fish.'
Lawe mai i puke, i pepa, a me ona mau peni. 'Bring books, paper, and also pencils.'

11 Conjunctions and Complex Sentences

CONJUNCTIONS

11.1   Those particles called **conjunctions** sometimes introduce simple sentences or phrases, but more commonly they are used to connect simple sentences, making complex sentences of them, or to connect noun phrases. Simple sentences are called **clauses** when they are combined into complex sentences. There are various ways to combine simple sentences, the simplest being merely the insertion of conjunctions—or, still simpler, making no changes whatsoever. (More complicated operations are discussed in section 11.2.)

     The following conjunctions are briefly described in this section (see also the Dictionary):

ā	'and, until, like' (1)	*i 'ole*	'so that not, (7) in order not'
a i 'ole *ā . . . paha* }	'or' (2)	*i loa*	'no sooner than' (8) 'as soon as'
i 'ole ia *akā* }	'but' (3)	*malia* *māki'a* *malama* }	'perhaps' (9)
emo 'ole	'in no time at all' (4)	*nani*	'since, because' (10)
i/iā *'oiai, 'oi* }	'while' (5)	*o*	'lest' (11)
inā, i *'e'ole* *ke* }	'if' (6)	*āhea* *ināhea* }	'when' (future) 'when' (past) } (12)
		'a'ole	negative (13)

     (1) *Ā* 'and, until, like' is probably the most common conjunction. It introduces both verb phrases and noun phrases, and oc-

curs in the common expressions *aloha ā nui* 'much love' (as in signing a letter) and *mahalo ā nui loa* 'thank you very very much'. See also section 8.7.2. A rare use is *Ā hua, ā pane* (FS 83), 'and [you] speak and [I] answer'. *Ā* is usually long but in fast speech may be short; it is short in *a i 'ole* 'or'.

Some analysts may see a connection between the conjunction *ā* and the locative preposition *ā* (section 9.5); both express distance in time or space:

Distance in Time
Preposition: *Hana ā ka hola 'elua.* 'Work until two o'clock.'
Conjunction: *Hana nō ā pau ka hana.* 'Work until the work is finished.'

Distance in Space
Preposition: *Hele ā uka.* 'Go as far as the uplands.'
Conjunction: *Hele nō ā pau ke alanui.* 'Go until the road is finished./Go until the end of the road.' *Hele nō ā puni ka honua.* 'Go until the world is circled./Go around the world.'

Similitude
Conjunction: *ua hele ā huhū* 'in a state of anger'

The conjunction *ā* connects noun phrases:

ma'ō   ā   ma'ane'i
at there   and   at here
'here to there'

Ua   hele   i   Maui   ā   i   Moloka'i.
(perf.) go   to Maui   and to Moloka'i
'[He] went to Maui and Moloka'i.'

i   kēlā   manawa   ā   i   kēia   manawa
at that   time   and at this   time
'now and then, from time to time'

An unusual construction is insertion of the conjunction *ā* in the possessive phrase *kō uka po'e* 'the upland people': *kō ā uka po'e* 'the far upland people'. Such an idiom may be generated by sequences somewhat as follows:

ka po'e o uka loa   underlying sentence
kō uka loa po'e   change of emphasis to the possessor *uka loa* (see section 9.6.4)

165

kō ā uka loa poʻe	further emphasis on *uka loa*
kō ā uka poʻe	deletion of *loa*
kō ā uka	deletion of *poʻe*

(2) *A i ʻole* 'or': *Ua makemake anei ʻoe i kēlā pālule a i ʻole i kēia?* 'Do you want that shirt or this [one]?' *E hele aku ana ʻoe a i ʻole e noho ana?* 'Are you going or staying?'

The verb phrase *i ʻole ia* 'if not that' may also be translated 'or': *Hele ʻoe i kahi o Pele, i ʻole ia, ʻi kō Ka-lama wahi.* 'Go to Pele's place, or if not that, to Ka-lama's place.'

Ā . . . paha is a common way to say 'or': *ʻelua ā ʻekolu paha* 'two or three'.

(3) *akā* 'but, nevertheless' is a common conjunction usually with rising pitch on *-ā* and followed by a slight pause. *Ua makemake au, akā, he hana nui.* 'I like [it], but [it] is difficult.'

(4) *ʻemo ʻole* 'immediately': *ʻEmo ʻole ā hele maila ke aliʻi.* 'In no time at all, the chief came.'

(5) *i/iā* 'when, at the time that, while, no sooner than' is homophonous with the object-marking preposition *i/iā* described in 9.3, with *iā* before pronouns and proper names and *i* elsewhere:

iā Ka-welo mā e noho ana me ʻAi-kanaka (FS 35) 'at the time that Ka-welo and the others were staying with ʻAi-kanaka'
iā lāua e kāhea ana (FS 133) 'while they were calling'
iaʻu e noho ana me ʻoukou 'while I was staying with you'
I ka makua kāne nō ā make, pau ke kālā. 'No sooner had the father died, [than] the money was gone.'

In the last sentence the noun phrase introduced by *i* is followed by the conjunction *ā*, just described. This also occurs in *iāia nō ā hiki i laila* 'when he arrived there'. The same *ā* follows the rare word *hākālia: Hākālia nō ā ao, ʻo kō mākou hele nō ia.* 'As soon as [it] was daylight, we went.'

ʻoiai, ʻoi 'while, at the time that, during': *ʻoiai lākou e hīmeni ana* 'while they were singing', *ʻoiai koʻu mau lā* (Kelekona 122) 'during my days'.

(6) *Inā* 'if' and less commonly *i* introduce conditional clauses. The sequence of verb markers in the conditional clause, and a subsequent resultative clause, has been noted as follows (the absence of a verb marker is shown by *∅*):

166

'if' Clause	Resultative Clause	Example in Sentence
inā i . . .	*inā ua* . . .	(a)
inā ∅ . . .	*a laila* . . .	(b)
inā . . . *e* . . .	*ua* . . .	(c)
inā e . . .	*he* . . .	(d)
i ∅ . . .	*inā ∅* . . .	(e)
i ∅ . . .	*inā lā* . . .	(f)
a i ∅ . . .	*∅* . . .	(g)
'e'ole . . .	*inā ua* . . .	(h)
ke . . .	*∅* . . .	(i)

(a) *Inā i hele mai nei 'oe, inā ua 'ike* (Alexander 1968:50). 'If you had come, then [you] would have known.'

(b) *Inā mahalo 'ia ke po'o . . . ā laila* . . . (FS 143). 'If the head is admired . . . then . . . '

(c) *Inā lāua e kāhea i Wai-kīkī, ua lohe 'o 'Ewa* (FS 49). 'If they called at Wai-kīkī, the people of 'Ewa heard.' (The pronoun is moved up before the verb in this sentence.)

(d) *Inā e hou mai 'o Ka-malama . . . he 'umi kānaka e kū* (FS 85). 'If Ka-malama hurls [his spear] . . . then ten men are hit.'

(e) *I a'o maika'i 'ia e kāua, inā holomua nō ka hana.* 'If [they] had been taught well by us, then the work would really have progressed.'

(f) *I hākālia ihola au, inā lā 'o wau ke make mua i ka haole* (Kelekona 35). 'If I wait, the white man will kill me first.'

(g) *Ā i 'ino mai ke koko, pau pū ka hale i ka 'ino.* 'And if the blood is bad, the house is bad at the same time.'

Two conditional clauses can be followed by a resultative clause: *Inā i hō'ea mai nā wahi 'elemākule . . . , i nīnau mai ia'u, ā laila e mana'o 'oe 'o lāua ia* (FS 133). 'If the two little old men had come and had asked for me . . . , then you might think that the two are the ones.'

(h) *'E'ole au e 'ike aku nei iā'oe, inā ua make 'oe* (FS 101). 'If I hadn't seen you, you would have been killed.' (Some persons prefer the construction *'e'ole au i 'ike . . .*)

(i) In both initial and noninitial positions, *ke* plus verb without a following ∅-demonstrative, is a marker of futurity, usually with conditional connotations: *Ke hele 'oe, hele au.* 'If you go, I go.' *E maluhia lākou ke hiki mai* (Alexander 1968:51). 'They shall be at peace when/if [they] come.'

(7) *I'ole* 'so that not, in order not'. See the Dictionary for examples.

(8) *I loa* at the beginning of an utterance may be translated 'as soon as'. See *loa 3* in the Dictionary for an example.

(9) The most common word for 'maybe, perhaps' is *malia* (*mālia* and *mali'a* are variants); *māki'a* is less common and *malama* is rare. Each may be followed by the particle *o*, probably the imperative/intentive (section 5.4):

Malia paha o hele au. 'Perhaps I'll go.'
Malama o ulu mai ka 'ano'ano. 'Maybe the seeds will grow.'
Māki'a o uhaele aku kāua. 'We'll probably go.'
Māki'a paha e kāhea aku au iā'oe. 'Maybe I should call you.'

This *o* is not to be confused with the conjunction *o* 'if, lest' see (11) below.

(10) For *nani* 'since, because', see the Dictionary.

(11) *O* 'if, lest': *Malama o hina.* 'Be careful lest [you] fall.' *Mai pi'i a'e i ka lālā . . . o 'ike 'ia kou wahi hilahila.* 'Don't climb up the branches . . . lest your private parts be seen.'

(12) The interrogative *hea* was introduced in section 8.5 as a substitute filling noun slots. Derived forms with *hea* function as conjunctions introducing clauses and sentences:

Āhea 'oe e hele mai ai? 'When will you come?'
Ināhea 'oe i hele mai ai? 'When did you come?'
Pehea 'oe i hele mai ai? 'How did you come?'

Hea words also introduce noun phrases:

'Auhea ke ali'i? 'Where is the chief?'
Pehea ke ali'i? 'How is the chief?'
Pehea ho'i ke ali'i? 'So how is the chief?'

(13) The negative *'a'ole* was introduced in section 5.2 as both a conjunction and an interjection. With the conjunctions it shares the following characteristics: (1) It introduces and connects clauses and sentences. (2) It may be followed by the verb-marking particles used after conjunctions, as illustrated in 5.2. (See 10.2 for contraction of *'a'ole + he.*)

COMBINING PHRASES: ORDER

11.2 Many examples have been given of phrases combined with intervening prepositions or conjunctions. In this section we discuss order of phrases that show direction from self. This order is fixed and irreversible. In English one says "this-and-that, here-and-there, to-and-fro": the order of the contrasting poles is irreversible. One cannot say "that-and-this, there-and-here, fro-and-to." This is, however, what one does say in Hawaiian. In English direction is *away* from self; in Hawaiian, *toward* self. Some common Hawaiian expressions follow which illustrate motion toward self in place and time, with literal translations and, in brackets, free or figurative translations.

> *kēlā mea kēia mea* 'that thing this thing [this and that, everything]'
> *ma'ō ā ma'ane'i* 'from there to here [from here to there, to and fro]'
> *ka pua i hi'ikua ā hi'ialo 'ia* 'the beloved child carried on the back and in front [the beloved child carried at the bosom and on the shoulders]'
> *mai ka wā kahiko . . . ā hiki wale mai nō i kēia ao* (Nakuina 28) 'from ancient times until coming right up to this era'
> *hui aku, hui mai, hui kalo me nāwao* 'mix there, mix here, mix tame taro with wild taro [here and there mix tame and wild taro and you get utter confusion]'

COMBINING SENTENCES

11.3   In some instances two simple sentences are combined to form a complex sentence consisting of a simple sentence containing a final noun phrase. The following steps may be involved:

(1) The sentences are combined.

(2) The verb marker in the second sentence is replaced by a definite article.

(3) The subject of the second sentence is deleted if it is the same as the subject of the first sentence. If it is different, it is introduced by the possessive preposition *o*.

(4) The verb that was changed to a noun by step (2) is preceded by *ā 'o* 'and' plus subject marker.

The four steps will be shown on the following four pairs of sentences.

Pair one:

Nānā akula i ka wahine. '[He] looked at the woman.'

Ua noho mai ka wahine. 'The woman is sitting nearby.'

Steps:

(1) *Nānā akula i ka wahine ua noho mai ka wahine.

(2) *Nānā akula i ka wahine ka noho mai ka wahine.

(3) *Nānā akula i ka wahine ka noho mai.

(4) *Nānā akula i ka wahine ā ʻo ka noho mai* (FS 277). '[He] looked a the woman sitting nearby.'

Pair two:

Nānā aku i ka wahine. '[He] looked at the woman.'

Ua hālokoloko mai nā waimaka. 'Tears are flowing.'

Steps:

(1) **Nānā aku i ka wahine ua hālokoloko mai nā waimaka.*

(2) **Nānā aku i ka wahine ka hālokoloko mai,nā waimaka.*

(3) **Nānā aku i ka wahine ka hālokoloko mai o nā waimaka.*

(4) *Nānā aku i ka wahine ā ʻo ka hālokoloko mai o nā waimaka* (FS 279). '[He] looked at the woman, whose tears were flowing.'

A simple sentence may be joined to a preceding equational sentence by replacing the verb marker by the utterance-medial marker; the anaphoric *ai* is inserted at the end of the verb phrase.

Pair three:

ʻOia kāna mea. 'It's his thing.'

Ua mea mai ka malihini. 'The stranger spoke to me.'

ʻOia kāna mea i mea mai ai ka malihini. 'That's what the stranger said to me.'

The second *mea* in the combined sentence is a verb 'to say'. This sentence may be further simplified by deleting the first *mea*. The rather free English translation remains the same.

Another example of a deleted *mea* is seen in section 10.2, in which two sentences were combined to get *ʻO wau ke hele mai* and *ʻO wau ka i hele mai ai.*

Still another example: *He aha kāu mea?* 'What's your thing?' *He aha kāu?* 'What's [that] to you?' Both sentences may be translated 'What's the matter with you?' or 'None of your business.'

Another more complicated procedure involves three steps: (1) replace the verb marker by an utterance-medial verb marker (table 9); (2) replace the subject of the second sentence by a corresponding neutralized *a*-class *φ*-possessive (as explained in section 7.3) and place it before the verb marker; and (3) delete the direct object phrase. Example:

Pair four:

ʻOia ka mea. 'It's the thing.'

Ua hāʻawi aku au i kekahi mea iāʻoe. 'I gave you something.'

Steps:

(1) *'*Oia ka mea i hā'awi aku ai au i kekahi mea iā'oe.*

(2) *'*Oia ka mea a'u i hā'awi aku ai i kekahi mea iā'oe.*

(3) *'Oia ka mea a'u i hā'awi aku ai iā'oe.* 'It's the thing I gave you./It's what I gave you.'

Complex sentences (c) and (d) in section 9.2 are analyzed by similar procedures:

Sentence (c): *'O 'oe ka mea a'u e hā'awi aku nei i kēia.* 'I gave this to *you.*'

The underlying simple sentences:

'O 'oe ka mea.

Ke hā'awi aku nei au i kēia.

Steps (1) and (2) as applied to pair four are followed here:

(1) *'*O 'oe ka mea ke hā'awi aku nei au i kēia.*

(2) *'O 'oe ka mea a'u e hā'awi aku nei i kēia.*

Sentence (d): *'O kēia ka'u e hā'awi aku nei iā'oe.* 'I gave *this* to you.'

The underlying sentences:

'O kēia ka mea.

Ke hā'awi aku nei au iā'oe.

Steps (1) and (2):

(1) *'*O kēia ka mea ke hā'awi aku nei au iā'oe.*

(2) *'O kēia ka mea a'u e hā'awi aku nei iā'oe.*

In sentence (c) *a'u* is without initial *k-* since it follows a *k-*word noun *(ka mea)*. *Mea*, as has been seen, can frequently be deleted: *'*O kēia ka a'u e hā'awi aku nei iā'oe.* Finally, *ka a'u* contracts to *ka'u.*

The discussion in this section is merely an introduction to a complicated subject that future students will study in depth.

A COMPLEX SENTENCE ANALYZED

11.4   The following is a long complex sentence, divided into numbered clauses. All meaningful units of words are separated by hyphens. VP stands for verb phrase and NP for noun phrase.

(1) Ā   loa'a   nā   wa'a,   he   mau   kaulua,
    when   get   the   canoe   a   (pl.) double-outrigger
       (VP)   (NP subj.)   (NP app.)

171

(2) *ho'i   mai-la   lā-kou* (3) *ā   pae   mā   Wai-kīkī,*
    return hither-then   they   and land   at   Wai-kīkī
    (VP)   (NP subj.)   (VP)   (NP locative)

(4) *ho'o-mā-kau-kau   ka   holo,* (5) *ā   holo nō   ia   lā;*
    prepare   the   sailing   and sail indeed this   day
    (VP)   (NP subj.)   (VP)   (NP temporal)

(6) *ia   wā,   ho'o-lā'au mai   'o   Kou,   ke-kahi   wahine*
    this time   urge   hither (subj.) Kou   another   wife
    (NP temporal)   (VP)   (NP subj.)   (NP app.)
    a   Ka-welo, (7) *e   holo   pū   i   Kaua'i,*
    of   Ka-welo   (imp.) sail   together to Kaua'i
    (NP poss.)   (VP)   (NP definite locative)

(8) *hō-'ole aku-la   'o   Ka-welo* (FS 63).
    refuse thither-then   (subj.) Ka-welo
    (VP)   (NP subj.)

'When [they] had gotten the canoes, double outriggers, they returned and landed at Wai-kīkī, made preparations for sailing, and sailed on this day; at this time Kou, another wife of Ka-welo, urged that [she] sail also to Kaua'i; Ka-welo refused.'

Clauses (1), (3), and (5) in this sentence are introduced by the conjunction *ā*. Clauses (2) and (4) are without verb markers or introductory conjunctions. Appositional phrases follow nouns in (1) and (6). Clause (6) is introduced by a temporal noun phrase.

THE ROLE OF FRONTING: A SUMMARY

11.5   In section 9.2, examples were given, taken from Alexander, of various ways to translate 'I give this to you', that will put the emphasis on any word in this sentence (except 'to'). This is achieved by placing the word to be emphasized first, preceded by what Alexander terms the "*o* emphatic." The purpose of the demonstration was to defend the use of this label—and, indeed, each phrase beginning with '*o* is emphatic.

The illustrative sentences in section 9.2 may be considered as being derived in part from underlying sentences which contain an initial verb phrase, and it seems that in underlying sentences the verb phrase is first. (Alexander [p. 28] states as a rule, "The Subject must follow its Predicate.") Does this mean that Hawaiian is a verb-oriented language? The fact that subjects and objects are omitted with impunity would point to the preeminence of the verb in Hawaiian. All of the following sentences are grammatical:

Ua 'ai 'o-ia i ka poi. 'He ate the poi.'
Ua 'ai 'o-ia. 'He ate.'
Ua 'ai. 'Ate.'

Three general rules, summarized here, favor the hypothesis that elements in focus precede elements not in focus:

1. A base precedes its qualifiers, except that a chief's name may precede the object named for him.

2. A possessed object in underlying structure precedes the possessor, but the latter may be emphasized by reversing this order.

3. Verb phrases in underlying structure precede noun phrases, but noun phrases may be fronted for emphasis.

12 Interjections

Interjections, like idioms, are short expressions that for the most part do not fit into the normal patterns of the language. Unlike idioms, they often end with rising pitch level followed by pauses, and are usually spoken with voice modifications reflecting the mood of the speaker. Also unlike idioms, they express feelings and emotions, as joy, sorrow, anger, fear, surprise, disgust, disbelief, shock, pity, pain, relief, affection, affirmation, negation. Some are commands (*Alia, Kulikuli*), taunts (*Ahahana, ʻAikola*), or greetings (*Aloha, Aloha ahiahi, Aloha kakahiaka, Hūi, Pehea ʻoe, Pehea kou piko*). (See following list for glosses.)

In Hawaiian, interjections contain few particles (exceptions: *Auē nohoʻi ē, ʻoia hoʻihā, ʻoia paha, pēlā paha*). A few are used also in ordinary discourse (*aloha, hānau, mahalo*). Some might be called sentence words (*ʻaikola*), phrases (*aloha ʻino*), or sentences (*Wela ka hao*). Some contain sounds not in the ordinary language, as *He aha sananā, Wēsenanā* (both of unknown origin) and the commonly heard variants of *kā*. Some are calls used as a part of the old religious ceremonies and are no longer used (*Kāina, Kapuō, Makani, Nauane*). A good number are missionary introductions (*Aloha ahiahi, Aloha kakahiaka, ʻĀmene, Haleluia, Hōkana*). A great many are from English or translations from English (*Hauʻoli Makahiki Hou, ʻŌkole maluna, Wela ka hao*).

A surprising feature of the inventory that follows is the lack of swear words, other than a few from English that are no longer used (*Kamipulu, Kanapapiki, Kokami*). No four-letter English words were needed in listing glosses for interjections, because no words in Hawaiian were considered obscene by the Hawaiians. Only *ʻŌkole maluna* is considered vulgar by some persons. Some common English interjections have no counterparts (Good night, Sleep well, Sweet dreams, Please [*'Olu'olu* 'kind' is now used to fill the English need]).

Endearments also are in short supply. Instead of loving terms such as are found in many languages, affection may be shown by the choice of grammatical forms, such as the possessives *ku'u* 'my' and *kō* 'your' (section 8.4.1), by the inclusive first person pronouns *kāua* and *kākou* (section 8.2), and by the demonstrative *nei* (section 8.3.2). Flowery poetic terms of endearment abound in songs (numbers in parentheses in these examples refer to page numbers in Elbert and Mahoe's *Nā Mele O Hawai'i*):

> *ka belle o ka noe līhau* (28) 'belle of the cool mist'
> *ke onaona noho i ka lipo* (36) 'fragrance in the blue depths'
> *kahi one o pua rose* (41) 'sand and rose flower'
> *i'a maka onaona* (49) 'sweet-eyed fish'
> *ku'u lei kau i ka wēkiu* (58) 'my lei placed supreme'

It is doubtful, perhaps, that even the most ardent lovers commonly used such phrases in the vocative, but then they may have. Who can tell?

Nonverbal interjections (giggles, laughs, whistles, sobs, wails, clucks) also express feelings; some of them are similar in different languages and are not culture-bound (Hawaiian exception: the *kanikau* that combine wails and words). Refrains in songs, such as *tra la la* in English, can also be called interjections, as can words for nonhuman sounds, mostly onomatopeic, as *kūpākūpā* 'boom boom' and *lawekeō*, the cry of the stilt bird.

Some of the Hawaiian interjections are listed below. Glosses for interjections are particularly tenuous, idiosyncratic, and subject to style: who says "goodness gracious" and "fiddlesticks"? The Dictionary glosses and examples provide more context, but they too should be considered incomplete.

'Ā! 'Ah!'
'A'aea! sound made by infants
'Ae. 'Yes.'
āēīē, chant refrain
āēī eia, chant ending
'Āhā! 'Aha!'
Ahahana! 'Oh! Shame on you!'
Āhē! 'So! Well!'
Aī! 'Oh!'
Ai'a! 'Here! Here it is!'

Aia hoʻi! 'See! Behold!'

Aia kā! 'So there!'

Aia lā! 'There, I told you so!'

ʻAikola! 'Serves you right!'

ʻAiō. 'Heigh-ho!' *(Eng.)*

Ā laʻa lā. 'Serves you right.'

Alia! 'Wait a minute!'

Aloha! 'Greetings!'

Aloha ahiahi. 'Good evening.'

Aloha ʻino! 'What a shame! Too bad!'

Aloha kakahiaka. 'Good morning.'

ʻĀmene. 'Amen.'

ʻĀ ʻoia. 'That's right.'

ʻAʻole. 'No.' (Usually pronounced *ʻaʻale*)

Auē! Auwē! Auwī! 'Oh! Oh boy! Ouch!'

Auē nohoʻi ē! 'What a shame! How terrible!'

Ē! 'Alas!' (Commonly follows nouns or verb phrases and used as a refrain in poetry. *Ua lilo ke koʻi a ke aliʻi ē!. Make māua ē* [FS 31]! 'Alas, the chief's adze is gone! Alas, the two of us will be killed! *ʻAʻohe ou hōʻike mai ē, ua maʻi ke keiki!* 'Alas, you didn't tell me the child was sick!' *Aloha ka leo o ka ʻūlili i ka ʻī mai ē, "ua make ʻoe!"* 'Pity the voice of the tattler saying, "You die!" ')

ʻĒ. 'Yes.'

ʻEa. 'Say! Listen!'

ʻEā! 'Isn't that so!'

ʻeāʻeā, song refrain (Elbert and Mahoe 81)

ēhā, ēhē, song refrain

ehehene, song refrain

E ō. 'Yes.' (in answer to a call)

e ue, chant ending

haikūamuamu, a call to lift a canoe or rally to work

Haleluia. 'Hallelujah.'

Hapenūia! 'Happy New Year!' *(Eng.)*

Hānau! 'Happy birthday!'

haʻuhaʻu ē, song refrain

Hauʻoli Makahiki Hou! 'Happy New Year!'

Hawahawa, a children's taunt

He aha sananā! 'What use is it' (See *Wēsenanā*)

Hele pēlā! 'Get out!'

Hemū! 'Be off! Scat!'

Hiki nō. 'Okay, certainly.'

Hipahipa! 'Hip, hip, hurrah!' *(Eng.)*

Hōkana! 'Hosanna!'

Hōlina! 'Haul in!' *(Eng.)*

Hū! 'Huh!'

Hūi, Ūi! 'Halloo!' (as when knocking at a door)

Hulō! 'Hurrah!' *(Eng.)*

'Ī, rare interjection of scorn. *I ka 'ī!* 'What does [he, she] know about it?'

'ike, interjection of scorn in the phrase *I ka 'ike!* 'What does [he, she] know!'

Inane! 'Show me! Let me see!'

Kā! Kē! Chā! Sā! 'Oh dear! Ridiculous!' (See section 7.5)

Kahāhā! Kahōhō! Kahūhū! 'Amazing!'

Kāhīhī! 'Horrors!'

Kai! 'My! Goodness!' (See Dictionary)

Kaī, Kaū, exclamations of annoyance or displeasure: *Kaī! Chā!* '*Ino maoli kāna hana!* 'Oh! Oh! His work is downright wicked!'

Kāina! 'Strike!' (said by a *kahuna* invoking eternal destruction)

Kāmau! 'Drink!' (a toast)

Kamipulu! 'Damn fool!' *(Eng.)*

Kanapapiki! 'Son of a bitch!' *(Eng.)*

Kao! 'Oh!'

Kapuō! 'Taboo!' (cry announcing a taboo)

Kēlō! 'Sail ho!' *(Eng.)*

Keu, same as *Kai*

Kī! 'Gee!' *(Eng.)*

Kō kō kō, Kolo kolo kolo, call to pigs and chickens

Kokami! 'God damn!'

Kuailo! 'I can't guess!' (See Dictionary)

Kulikuli! 'Keep still! Shut up!'

Kupaianaha! Kupanaha! 'Astonishing! Amazing!'

Kūpākūpā! 'Boom! Boom!'

lā, common song refrain (Elbert and Mahoe 90)

la'ehana, song refrain

lae la lae, song refrain

Lanahō! 'Land ho!' *(Eng.)*

Lawekeō! cry of the stilt bird

Leikō! 'Let go!' (as of an anchor) *(Eng.)*

Mahalo. 'Thank you.'

Makani, call of a sentinel, as 'All's well!'

Mele Kalikimaka! 'Merry Christmas!' *(Eng.)*

Nani . . . 'How much . . . How . . .' (followed by a noun phrase; see Dictionary)

nao, interjection following *'a'ole* expressing damage, havoc, pain, distress; see Dictionary

Nauane! 'Move along!' (said by priests as they carried images)

Niu kūlolo! 'Oily *kūlolo* pudding!/Don't talk so much!'

'Oia ho'ihā! 'Oi ho'ihā! 'That's right! That's so! Then do it!'

'Oia kā! 'You don't say!'

'Oia noho'i! 'That's for sure!'

'Oia paha! 'Maybe so!'

'Okole maluna! 'Bottoms up!' (vulgar)

Oliana! 'Let me see! Show me!'

'Ololaiki. 'All right!' *(Eng.)*

Pehea 'oe! 'How are you!'

Pehea kou piko? 'How's your navel?' (a facetious greeting avoided by some because *piko* also means 'genital')

Pēlā paha! 'Maybe so!'

'Ū! 'Yes!'

uhē, uhē'uhene, song refrain (Elbert and Mahoe 58)

'Ūhū! 'Huh!'

Ūi! same as *Hūi!*

'Ukā, a call to pigs

Uoki! 'Stop it!'

Wela ka hao! 'The iron's hot!/Now's the time for fun, hurray!' (Considered old-fashioned in 1976. Perhaps from English 'strike while the iron's hot!')

Wēsenanā! Same as *He aha sananā,* and also usually followed by *He mau'u Hilo* 'just Hilo grass'

Wō! 'Whoa!' *(Eng.)*

Glossary

Numbers refer to sections in the Grammar where the term is discussed.

ABLATIVE PREPOSITION. A preposition expressing direction away (*mai* 'from'; 9.8).

AFFIX. A general term for prefixes (preceding a BASE), suffixes (following a base), and infixes (inserted within a base) (3.5).

ALTERNANT. Sound and particle variants, technically known as allophones and allomorphs; some, but not all, are predictable (2.1). Alternants are frequently written with intervening slashes (*ka/ke, ʻo/ø*).

ANAPHORIC PARTICLE. A particle referring to a previous word, its antecedent (*ai*, 7.3).

ARTICLE. *See* DEFINITE ARTICLE; INDEFINITE ARTICLE; PAUCAL ARTICLE; PLURAL ARTICLE.

ASPECT MARKER. A particle that indicates whether action is completed (perfective) or still going on (imperfective). These particles do *not* indicate tense—the time may be past, present, or future (5.2).

ASPIRATION. An audible puff of air accompanying English *p*, *t*, and *k* in some environments; Hawaiian *p* and *k* have less aspiration than English *p* and *k* (2.1).

ASSIMILATION. The process by which one sound becomes the same as or similar to a neighboring sound, as *ʻaʻole* 'not' to *ʻaʻale* in Hawaiian, or as the prefix *in-* 'not' in "intolerable" became *im-* in "impossible" in the history of English (Table 2).

BASE. A word without affixes that carries lexical rather than grammatical meaning (3.5; 6.1).

BILABIAL. A consonant produced by closure or constriction of the lips; *p*, *m*, and sometimes *w* in Hawaiian (2.1).

CLASSIFICATORY KINSHIP. A system in which the same terms are used for collateral relatives in the same generation; e.g., *makua kāne* is both 'father' and 'uncle' (9.6.1).

179

CLAUSE. A sequence containing a verb and a noun that forms a part of a complex sentence (11.1).

CLITIC. A grammatical element that forms a single stress group with either preceding or following elements. The former is also called an enclitic, as -*la* after directionals (pronounced *máila*) (7.2). The locative preposition *i* may form a stress group with elements either preceding (*'áu-i ke kai* 'swim in the sea') or following (*hele í-ke kai* 'go to the sea') (2.5).

CLUSTER. Adjacent vowels with stress on either vowel, depending on their positions in a word. *Cf.* DIPHTHONG.

COMITATIVE PREPOSITION. A preposition denoting accompaniment (*me* 'with'; 9.7).

COMPLEX SENTENCE. A sentence consisting of two or more verb phrases, or of a verbless sentence combined with a verb-plus-subject sentence (3.1).

COMPOUND. A word consisting of two or more bases with meanings not deducible from the meanings of the parts (8.7).

CONJUNCTION. A particle connecting sentences, prepositional phrases, or words (11.1).

DEFINITE ARTICLE. A particle that precedes nouns and indicates that the noun is singular and definite (*ka/ke* 10.2).

DENTAL ALVEOLAR. A consonant (*n* in Hawaiian) involving the teeth and the gum (alveolar) ridge (2.1).

DERIVATIVE. Base plus affix (3.5).

DETERMINER. A word following a preposition and preceding a numeral (table 7 and section 10.1); *k*-words, among others, are determiners.

DIPHTHONG. Adjacent vowels always pronounced with the stress on the first one; they are in the same syllable (2.2).

DIRECTIONAL. A particle indicating movement in relation to the speaker (7.2).

DRIFT. The direction in which the changes in the language seem to be going (2.11).

ENCLITIC. *See* CLITIC.

ENVIRONMENT. Adjacent sounds, particles, and words.

FOCUS (IN FOCUS). The portion of a sentence to which the addressee's attention is directed, usually the first part of a sentence (3.1).

FRONTING. The shifting of a grammatical form to the beginning of a sentence, in Hawaiian often to bring it in focus.

GLIDE. A sound characterized by a gliding movement of the tongue toward a high front position (*y*-glide) or high back position (*w*-glide); *w*-glides are frequently not "significant" in Hawaiian (2.1).

GLOTTAL STOP. A common Hawaiian consonant caused by closing the vocal cords; symbolized by a reversed apostrophe or by an ordinary apostrophe (2.1).

IDIOM. A short expression that does not fit into the normal patterns of the language, and with meaning not deducible from the meanings of the parts (4.6).

INCEPTIVE. A grammatical form denoting the beginning of an action or a state, as *ua* (5.2).

INDEFINITE ARTICLE. A particle that precedes nouns and indicates that the noun is singular and indefinite; *he* in Hawaiian (10.2). (In the sequence *he mau* + noun, the singularity of *he* is neutralized.)

INFIX. *See* AFFIX and 8.1.

INFLECTION. A grammatical process in which bases take closely bound affixes but in which the part of speech of the resultant form is the same as that of the base (in English the base "fine" and the derivatives "finer" and "finest" all are adjectives). Hawaiian has no inflections (1.1).

INTENTIVE PARTICLE. A mood marker that indicates a vague desire, need, purpose, or probability; *e* in Hawaiian (5.4).

INTERJECTIONS. Short expressions that do not fit into the normal patterns of the language, often expressing emotion but also including salutations, taunts, song refrains, religious terms both pre-contact and post-contact, calls to animals, and onomatopoeic sounds made by animals (12).

INTRANSITIVE VERBS. A class of verbs that do not take direct objects but that may take markers of the imperative and passive/imperative, and commonly take *o*-class possessives (4.2).

JUNCTURE. Any of four types of pauses in sentences (2.4).

k-WORDS. Articles, demonstratives, and possessives beginning with *k*, with meaning 'singular definite' (10.1).

LOAN WORD. A word taken from one language into another (2.9).

LOCATIVE. A noun denoting place or time (8.6).

METONOMY. Naming the thing contained for the container, as *wa'a* meaning both 'canoe' and 'canoe crew' (8.6).

NOMINALIZER. A suffix or particle converting a verb-like word to a noun, *'ana* being the most common (6.6.2).

NONPRODUCTIVE. *See* PRODUCTIVE.

NOUN. A base that may be preceded by articles (especially *ka/ke*) or prepositions (3.3).

NOUN-VERB. A verb commonly used as a noun without the nominalizer *'ana* (3.3).

NUCLEUS. The base and its modifiers in a verb phrase or noun phrase (3.2).

OFF-GLIDE. An audible glide following a vowel, as in English pronunciation of *e* and *o*; Hawaiian *e* and *o* have no off-glides (they are not diphthongized) (2.2).

PARTICLES. Small items that are not intelligible if used alone and that occur before and after nouns and verbs, usually with grammatical rather than lexical meaning. They differ from affixes in that they need not be closely bound to bases (elements may separate them) (3.4).

PAUCAL ARTICLE. A particle that precedes nouns that are few in number, as *wahi* in Hawaiian, usually translated 'few' or 'some' (10.4).

PHRASE. Sequence consisting of a nucleus (noun, substitute, or verb) with or without modifying particles or bases (3.2).

PHONEME. A "significant" sound that distinguishes meaning in a language, usually called "sound" in this Grammar.

PLURAL ARTICLE. A particle indicating that following nouns have plural meanings (*nā*, 10.2).

PLUS JUNCTURE. The shortest type of juncture; it separates stress groups (2.3).

PREDICTABLE. A term describing a sound or particle variant that may be predicted on the basis of the environment, as *ia* in Hawaiian, a variant of the preposition *i* (9.3.1).

PREFIX. *See* AFFIX.

PREPOSITION. A particle introducing a noun phrase (9).

PRODUCTIVE. A term used to describe a grammatical form used in the formation of new words, as "burger" in English (hamburger, cheeseburger) or *hoʻo-* in Hawaiian (*hoʻokeonimana* 'to behave like a gentleman'; *keonimana* is from English 'gentleman').

PROTO CENTRAL POLYNESIAN. A reconstructed form of a sound or word occurring in Tahitian, Marquesan, Maori, or other East Polynesian languages as well as in Hawaiian, but not in the Easter Island language (2.2).

PROTO EAST POLYNESIAN. A reconstructed form of a sound or word occurring in the Easter Island language and in Hawaiian (2.8.2).

PROTO POLYNESIAN. A reconstructed form of a sound or word occurring in Tongan or Niue, as well as in Hawaiian (2.8.2).

RECONSTRUCTION. An ancestral form of a word or sound posited by comparisons with similar forms in related languages.

REDUPLICATION. The repetition of all or part of a base, commonly indicating repeated or continuing action or state (6.2).

SENTENCE. A sequence bordered by the longest type of juncture (3.1).

"SIGNIFICANT" SOUND. A sound that distinguishes meaning, as the glottal stop in Hawaiian (*kaʻi* 'to lead' contrasts with *kai* 'sea'); technically known as a phoneme (2.1).

SIMPLE SENTENCE. A sentence containing a single verb phrase with or without noun phrase(s) (3.1).

SOURCE. A grammatical form indicating the place of origin of a noun, as *i/ia* (9.3.1).

STATIVE. A type of verb that is rarely passivized and that generally marks condition or state (4.4).

STRESS. Loudness that accents a syllable of a word, phrase, or sentence (2.3).

STRESS GROUP. The smallest element in Hawaiian words receiving a single and predictable stress on long vowels marked with macrons or on the next to the last syllable; stress groups are separated by plus junctures (2.3).

SUBSTITUTE. A base that may replace nouns (pronouns, demonstratives, possessives, interrogatives) (3.3; 8).

SUFFIX. *See* AFFIX.

TRANSITIVIZER. A suffix that lends transitive emphasis to its base (6.6.4).

TRANSITIVE VERBS. A class of verbs that may take direct objects and passive/imperative markers. The two types in Hawaiian are deliberate (*'ai* 'to eat') and spontaneous (*aloha* 'to love') (4.3).

VELAR CONSONANT. A consonant pronounced with the base of the tongue touching the soft palate in the back of the mouth, as *k* in Hawaiian (2.1).

VERB. A base that may follow certain markers, especially the perfective *ua* (3.3).

VERBLESS SENTENCE. A sentence consisting of one or more noun phrases without a verb, sometimes called equational (3.1).

VOCATIVE PARTICLE. A preposition preceding and sometimes also following the names or titles of the addressee, serving to attract his attention; *ē* in Hawaiian (9.10).

VOWEL VALUES. Phonetic features of a vowel (2.2).

w-GLIDE. A glide separating *o* or *u* from a following vowel; these glides are not "significant" unless the element introduced by the *w*-glide is a recognizable base, as *wili* 'to twist' and the derivative *kūwili* 'to move restlessly' (2.1).

References

Abe, Isamu. "Hawaiian Accent and Intonation," *Bulletin of the Tokyo Institute of Technology* 100 (1970): 107–118.

Alexander, W. D. *A Short Synopsis of the Most Essential Points in Hawaiian Grammar.* Rutland, Vt.: Charles E. Tuttle Co., 1968. (First published in 1864.)

_____ "Introductory Remarks." In *A Dictionary of the Hawaiian Language* by Lorrin Andrews, pp. 7–14. *See* Andrews 1974.

Andrews, Lorrin. *A Vocabulary of Words in the Hawaiian Language.* Lahainaluna, 1836.

_____ "Peculiarities of the Hawaiian Language." *The Hawaiian Spectator* 1 (1838):392–420.

_____ *Grammar of the Hawaiian Language.* Honolulu: Mission Press, 1854.

_____ *A Dictionary of the Hawaiian Language, to which is Appended an English-Hawaiian Vocabulary and a Chronological Table of Remarkable Events.* Rutland, Vt.: Charles E. Tuttle Co., 1974. (First published in 1865.)

Apoliona, Haunani. "Hawaiian Neia." Unpublished manuscript, 1973. (In the office of the Department of Indo-Pacific Languages, University of Hawaii.)

Arago, J. *Narrative of a Voyage round the World, in the Uranie and Physicienne Corvettes, Commanded by Captain Freycinet, during the Years 1817, 1818, 1819, and 1820; on a Scientific Expedition Undertaken by Order of the French Government, in a Series of Letters to a Friend.* London, 1823. Pp. 291–294.

Ka Baibala Hemolele o ke Kauoha Kahiko a me ke Kauoha Hou; i Unuhiia Mailoko mai o na Olelo Kahiko, a Hooponopono Hou ia [The Holy Bible of the Old Testament and the New Testament; translated from ancient tongues and revised]. New York: American Bible Society, 1941.

Beckwith, Martha Warren. "The Hawaiian Romance of Laieikawai (by S. N. Haleole, 1863) with Introduction and Translation." *U.S.*

Bureau of American Ethnology, Thirty-third Annual Report, 1911–1912, pp. 285–677. Washington, D.C., 1919.

_____ *Kepelino's Traditions of Hawaii.* Bishop Museum Bulletin 95. Honolulu, 1932.

_____ *The Kumulipo, a Hawaiian Creation Chant.* Chicago: University of Chicago Press, 1951.

Biblia Sacra iuxta Vulgatam Clementinam [Sacred Bible in Accordance with the Vulgate of Clement]. Madrid: La Editorial Catolica S.A., 1965.

Biggs, Bruce. "The Structure of New Zealand Maaori." *Anthropological Linguistics* 3, no. 3 (1961).

_____ *Let's Learn Maori, A Guide to the Study of the Maori Language.* Wellington, N.Z.: A. H. and A. W. Reed, 1969.

Bloomfield, Leonard. *Language.* New York: Henry Holt and Co., 1933.

Buffet, Guy, and Pamela Buffet. *Na Hana Wiwo'ole o Kamapua'a* [The fearless deeds of Kamapua'a]. Honolulu: Island Heritage, 1972.

Buschmann, J. E. Eduard. *See* Humboldt, 1836, 1838, 1839.

Buse, J. E. "Problems of Morphology and Classification Illustrated from Rarotongan." *Lingua* 15 (1965): 32–47.

Campbell, Archibald. *A Voyage round the World from 1806 to 1812.* Facsimile reproduction of the third American edition of 1822. Honolulu: University of Hawaii Press, 1967. Pp. 165–187. (First published in 1816.)

Carr, Denzel. "Comparative Treatment of Epenthetic and Paragogic Vowels in English Loan Words in Japanese and Hawaiian." *Language Learning* 14 (1964): 21–36. (Reprint of a 1951 article.)

Chamisso, Adelbert von. "Remarks and Opinions of the Naturalist of the Expedition." In *A Voyage of Discovery into the South Seas and Beering's Straits,* by Otto von Kotzebue. *See* Kotzebue.

_____ *Über die Hawaiische Sprache, Vorgelegt der Königlichen Academie der Wissenschaften zu Berlin am 12, Januar, 1837.* Leipzig, 1837. (For a reprint, *see* Elbert 1969.)

Chapin, Paul G. "On the Hawaiian Language, by Adelbert von Chamisso. Translated from the German by Paul G. Chapin." *Working Papers in Linguistics* 5, no. 3 (March 1973). University of Hawaii.

_____ "Proto-Polynesian *ai." *Journal of the Polynesian Society* 83 (1974): 259–307.

Chen, Matthew Y., and William S.-Y. Wang. "Sound Changes: Actuation and Implementation." *Language* 51 (1975): 255–281.

Churchward, C. Maxwell. *Tongan Grammar.* London: Oxford University Press, 1953.

_____ *Tongan Dictionary (Tongan-English and English-Tongan).* London: Oxford University Press, 1959.

Dewey, Godfrey. *Relativ* [sic] *Frequency of English Speech Sounds.* Cambridge, Mass.: Harvard University Press, 1923. (Quoted by

Trnka, Bohumil, in A *Phonological Analysis of Present-day Standard English*. Revlned [sic] new edition. Alabama: University of Alabama Press, 1966.)

Dordillon, Msgr. I. R. *Grammaire et Dictionnaire de la Langue des Îles Marquises*. Paris: Imprimerie Belin Frères, 1904.

Dupont, John. "Linking *ai*." Unpublished manuscript, 1973. (In the office of the Department of Indo-Pacific Languages, University of Hawaii.)

Elbert, Samuel H. (ed.). *Selections from Fornander's Hawaiian Antiquities and Folk-lore*. Honolulu: University of Hawaii Press, 1959.

_____ "Introduction." In *Über die Hawaiische Sprache* by Adelbert von Chamisso. Facsimile edition, with a critical introduction and an annotated bibliography of literature relating to the Hawaiian language. Amsterdam: Halcyon Antiquariaat, Philo Press, 1969.

_____ *Spoken Hawaiian*. Honolulu: University of Hawaii Press, 1970.

_____ *Dictionary of the Language of Rennell and Bellona. Rennellese and Bellonese to English*. Copenhagen: National Museum of Denmark, 1975.

Elbert, Samuel H., and Noelani Mahoe. *Nā Mele o Hawai'i Nei: 101 Hawaiian Songs*. Honolulu: University of Hawaii Press, 1970.

Emerson, Nathaniel B. *Pele and Hiiaka, a Myth of Hawaii*. Honolulu: Honolulu Star-Bulletin, 1915.

_____ *Unwritten Literature of Hawaii: The Sacred Songs of the Hula, Collected and Translated, with Notes and an Account of the Hula*. Rutland, Vt.: Charles E. Tuttle Co., 1965. (First published in 1909 as Bureau of American Ethnology Bulletin 38, Washington, D.C.)

Fornander, Abraham. "Hawaiian Antiquities and Folk-lore." *Bernice P. Bishop Museum Memoirs*, vols. 4 and 5. Honolulu, 1917, 1918.

Gleason, Henry Allan, Jr. *Workbook in Descriptive Linguistics*. New York: Holt, Rinehart and Winston, 1955.

_____ *An Introduction to Descriptive Linguistics*. Revised edition. New York: Holt, Rinehart and Winston, 1967.

Green, Laura C. S., and Mary Kawena Pukui. *The Legend of Kawelo and other Hawaiian Folk Tales*. Honolulu: Territory of Hawaii, 1936.

Hale, Horatio. "Ethnography and Philology." In *United States Exploring Expedition during the Years 1838, 1839, 1840, 1841, 1842 under the command of Charles Wilkes, U.S.N.* Ridgewood, N.J.: The Gregg Press, 1968. (First published in 1846.)

Hall, Robert A., Jr. *Introductory Linguistics*. Philadelphia: Chilton Books, 1964.

Hawkins, Emily A. *Hawaiian Sentence Structure*. Ph.D. dissertation, University of Hawaii, 1975.

Hitchcock, H. R. *An English-Hawaiian Dictionary; with Various Useful Tables: Prepared for the Use of Hawaiian-English Schools*.

Rutland, Vt.: Charles E. Tuttle Co., 1967. (Reprint of the 1887 edition.)

Hockett, Charles F. *A Course in Modern Linguistics.* New York: The Macmillan Co., 1958.

Hohepa, P. W. "A Profile-Generative Grammar of Maori." *International Journal of American Linguistics* 33, no. 2. Memoir 20, 1967.

_____ "Not in English and *kore* and *eehara* in Maori." Unpublished manuscript, no date. (In the office of the Department of Linguistics, University of Hawaii.)

The Holy Bible, containing the Old and New Testaments: Translated out of the Original Tongues: and with the Former Translations Diligently Compared and Revised, by His Majesty's Special Command. New York: Thomas Nelson & Sons, no date. (Generally known as the King James Version, first published in 1611.)

The Holy Bible, Revised Standard Version containing the Old and New Testaments with the Apocrypha / Deuterocanonical Books, an Ecumenical Edition. New York, 1917.

Humboldt, Wilhelm von. *Über die Kawi-Sprache auf der Insel Java, nebst einer Einleitung über die Verschiedenheit des Menschlichen Sprachbaues und ihren Einfluss auf die Geistige Entwickelung des Menschengeschlechts.* Edited by J. E. Eduard Buschmann. 3 vols. Berlin, 1836, 1838, and 1839. (Buschmann added most of the third volume.)

Judd, Henry P., Mary Kawena Pukui, and John F. G. Stokes. *Introduction to the Hawaiian Language (an English-Hawaiian Vocabulary).* Honolulu: Tongg Publishing Co., 1943.

Kahananui, Dorothy M., and Alberta P. Anthony. *E Kamaʻilio Hawaiʻi Kakou, Let's Speak Hawaiian.* Honolulu: University of Hawaii Press, 1970.

Kelekona, Kahikina (John G. M. Sheldon). *Kaluaikoolau. Hoopaaia ke Kuleana Mana Hoolaha iloko o ke Keena Puuku o ka Teritore o Hawaii* [Copyright affirmed and published within the Treasury Department of the Territory of Hawaii]. Honolulu, 1906.

Kinney, Ruby Kawena. "A Non-purist View of Morphomorphemic Variations in Hawaiian Speech." *Journal of the Polynesian Society* 65 (1956): 283–286.

Knowlton, Edgar Colby, Jr. *Words of Chinese, Japanese, and Korean Origin in the Romance Languages.* Ph.D. dissertation, Stanford University, microfilm no. 59–02822, 1955.

Kotzebue, Otto von. *A Voyage of Discovery into the South Seas and Beering's Straits, for the Purpose of Exploring a North-east Passage, Undertaken in the Years 1815–1818.* Translated from the German by H. E. Lloyd. 3 vols. Amsterdam: N. Israel, 1967.

Krupa, Viktor. "The Phonemic Structure of Bi-vocalic Morphemic Forms in Oceanic Languages." *Journal of the Polynesian Society* 75 (1966): 458–497.

_____ "The Phonotactic Structure of the Morph in Polynesian Languages." *Language* 47 (1971): 668–684.

Lee, Kehau. "Distinctions between the *ko*-noun Locative and the *o*-noun Locative." Unpublished manuscript, 1973. (In the office of the Department of Indo-Pacific Languages, University of Hawaii.)

Lee, Makanani. "The Particle *la.*" Unpublished manuscript, 1973. (In the office of the Department of Indo-Pacific Languages, University of Hawaii.)

Lisiansky, Urey. *A Voyage Round the World in the Years 1803, 4, 5, and 6, Performed by Order of His Imperial Majesty, Alexander the First, Emperor of Russia, in the Ship "Neva."* London, 1814. Pp. 326–328.

Lyons, John. *Introduction to Theoretical Linguistics.* Cambridge: At the University Press, 1969.

Makanani, Russell. "The *ha'a*-type prefix." Unpublished manuscript, 1973. (In the office of the Department of Indo-Pacific Languages, University of Hawaii.)

Malo, David. *Hawaiian Antiquities (Moolelo Hawaii).* Translated from the Hawaiian by Nathaniel B. Emerson, 1898. Bernice P. Bishop Museum Special Publication 2, 2nd edition. Honolulu, 1971. (The Hawaiian original in Malo's own handwriting is in the Bishop Museum; a photostat copy is in the Hawaiian collection, Hamilton Library, University of Hawaii.)

Milner, George. *Samoan Dictionary, Samoan-English, English-Samoan.* London: Oxford University Press, 1966.

Nakuina, Moses. *Moolelo Hawaii o Pakaa a me Ku-a-Pakaa, na Kahu Iwikuamoo o Keawenuiaumi, ke Alii o Hawaii, a o na Moopuna hoi a Laamaomao* ["Hawaiian Story of Pāka'a and Kū-a-Pāka'a, the high-born attendants of Ke-awe-nui-a-'Umi, the chief of Hawai'i and also the grandchildren of Laamaomao"]. Honolulu, 1901. (In the Hawaiian collection, Hamilton Library, University of Hawaii.)

Newbrand, Helene Luise. *A Phonemic Analysis of Hawaiian.* Master's thesis, University of Hawaii, 1951.

Nida, Eugene A. *Morphology, the Descriptive Analysis of Words.* 2nd edition. Ann Arbor: University of Michigan Press, 1949.

Pawley, Andrew. "Samoan Phrase Structure: Morphology-Syntax of a Western Polynesian Language." *Anthropological Linguistics* 8, no. 6 (1966).

Pratt, George. *Pratt's Grammar and Dictionary of the Samoan Language.* Samoa: Malua Printing Press, 1960. (First published in 1862.)

Pukui, Mary Kawena, and Samuel H. Elbert. *Hawaiian-English Dictionary.* Honolulu: University of Hawaii Press, 1957.

_____ *Hawaiian Dictionary, Hawaiian-English, English-Hawaiian.* Honolulu: University of Hawaii Press, 1971.

Pukui, Mary Kawena, Samuel H. Elbert, and Esther T. Mookini. *Place*

Names of Hawaii. Revised and expanded edition. Honolulu: The University Press of Hawaii, 1974.

———— *The Pocket Hawaiian Dictionary, with a Concise Hawaiian Grammar*. Honolulu: The University Press of Hawaii, 1975.

Pukui, Mary Kawena, and Alfons L. Korn. *The Echo of Our Song, Chants and Poems of the Hawaiians*. Honolulu: The University Press of Hawaii, 1973.

Roberts, Helen H. *Ancient Hawaiian Music*. New York: Dover Publications, 1967. (First published in 1926 as Bernice P. Bishop Museum Bulletin 29.)

Schütz, Albert J. "Take My Word for It: Missionary Influence on Borrowings in Hawaiian." *Oceanic Linguistics* 15 (1976): 75–92.

———— "Accent Groups in Syllables in Fijian." Paper read at the Austronesian Symposium, University of Hawaii, 1977.

Schweizer, Niklaus R. *A Poet among Explorers: Chamisso in the South Seas*. Bern and Frankfurt: Herbert Lang, 1973.

The Septuagint Version [of the Old Testament]. Grand Rapids, Mich.: Zondervan (by special arrangement with Samuel Bagster & Son, Ltd., London), 1976.

Sheldon, John G. M. *See* Kelekona, 1906.

Topping, Donald M. "Review of *Tagalog Reference Grammar* by Paul Schachter and Fe T. Otanes." *Oceanic Linguistics* 11 (1972): 152–164.

Trnka. *See* Dewey, 1923.

Wilson, William H. "The *O* and *A* Possessive Markers in Hawaiian." Master's thesis, University of Hawaii, 1976.

190

Index

a, possessive, 136–145
ā, conjunction, 164–166
ā 'to', 136
Abe, Isamu, 14, 185
ablative, 145, 179
abstract words, 154
affixes, 44–45, 64–89, 179
agentive, 49–50, 107–108, 146
aha 'what', 55, 119, 120
aho 'better', 55
ai, anaphoric, 96–99
aka- 'carefully', 74–75
'akahi 'first time', 55
Andrews, Lorrin, 4–6, 7, 37, 62, 63, 89, 132, 159, 185
ala- 'quickly', 75
Alexander, W. D., 3, 4–6, 7, 89, 96, 132–133, 143, 159, 172, 185
aloha 'love, compassion', a greeting, 46, 51–52, 95, 111, table 8
ana, imperfective, 57–60, table 9
ana, ∅-demonstrative, 99–100, table 12
āna, ∅-possessive, 142
'ana, nominalizer, 79–81, table 11
anaphoric, 96, 179
'a'ohe, negative, 142, 157–158
'a'ole, negative, 5, 59, 142, table 2
Apoliona, Haunani, xiv, 114, 185
apposition, 150–152
articles, 154–158, 179
aspect, 57–60, 179

Biblical, 31–33, 37, 159
Bloomfield, Leonard, 88, 96, 114, 186
Buschmann, J. E. Eduard, 3–4, 186

Catholic, 32–33
causative/simulative, 68–74, table 10
Chamisso, Adelbert von, 1–3, 4, 7, 89, 186
Chapin, Paul G., 2, 3, 99, 186

Cheng, Robert L., xv, 33
Churchward, C. Maxwell, 63, 86, 186
Chinese, 33
comitative, 145, 180
comparative, 93
complex sentences, 40–41, 169–172
compounds, 37–38, 123–127, 180
conjunctions, 164–168, 180
consonants, 10–14

days of week, 158
definite articles, 154–158, 180
demonstratives, 99–100, 110–116, table 12
determiners, 153–158, 180
dialect, dialects, 7, 23–27
directionals, 79, 91–95, 180, table 12
drift, 35–36, 180, table 6
Dupont, John, xiv, 99, 187

e, agentive, 146
ē, vocative, 146–147
e (verb) *ana*, imperfective, 57–60, table 9
Emerson, Nathaniel B., 7–8, 187
English, 13, 27–30, tables 3, 4

fast speech, 22–23, table 2
French, 33
fronting, 98, 135, 143–145, 172–173, 180

Gleason, Henry Allan, Jr., 28, 88, 187
glottal stop, 5, 10–12, 32, 34, 35, 180
Greek, 32

ha'i, pronoun, 109
Hale, Horatio, 4, 96, 187
Hall, Robert A., Jr., 57, 187
Hana-/Hono- 'bay', 105–106
hau- 'unpleasant', 75, table 10
Hau- 'ruler', 75, table 10
Hawkins, Emily A., xiv, 9, 77, 134–135, 187

he, indefinite article, 152, 156–157
Hebrew, 32
Hockett, Charles F., 140, 188
horse, 30–31, table 5
Hsu, Robert, xv, 34
Humboldt, Wilhelm von, 3–4, 188

i, perfective, 59, table 9
i, purpose, 61, 62, table 9
i/iā, multifunctional preposition, 133–135
ia, demonstrative, 112, table 12
ia, pronoun, 107–109, 112, tables 12, 13
idioms, 54–56, 181
if, 166–167
imperative, 61–62, table 9
inā 'if', 166–167
indefinite article, 156–157, 181
interjections, 174–178, 181
interrogatives, 119–120
intransitives 48, 181

junctures, 18, 181

k, letter, 10, 24–26, 27, 34
k-, singular/definite, 153
ka/ke, definite article, 154–156
kā-, causative, 64, 68, 69
Kahananui, Dorothy M., xv, 58, 123, 188
kahi 'place', 121, 135
Kanahele, George, 9
kekahi 'some, other', 153, 157
Kelekona, Kahikina (John G. M. Sheldon), xiii–xiv, 124, 188
ke (verb) *nei*, present tense, 60–61, table 9
Kinney, Ruby Kawena, 22–23, 36, 188, table 2
kinship, 106, 137, 179
Knowlton, Edgar Colby, Jr., xv, 33, 188
Korn, Alfons L., xiv, 189
Krupa, Viktor, 35, 188–189
k-words, 153–154

l, letter, 12, 25–27, 35–36
lā, dubitative, 102
lā/-la, ∅-demonstrative, 60, 93, 99–100, table 12
laila, locative, 121, tables 2, 12
Latin, 6, 32
Lee, Kehau, xiv, 144–145, 189
Lee, Makanani, xiv, 99, 189
leveling, 50–51
lilo 'become, accrue', 53, 61, 62
loaʻa 'get', 22, 46, 52, 53, 95, tables 2, 8
loans, 27–34, 181
locatives, 120–123, 134–136, 142, 181, table 12

Lyons, John, 114, 189
Lyons, Lorenzo, 8

ma, locative/instrumental/manner, 135–136
mā 'and others', 129, table 7
mai, ablative, 145–146
mai, directional, 91–95, table 12
mai, imminence, 53, 63, table 9
mai, negative imperative, 61–63, table 9
Makanani, Russell, 68, 189
make 'dead', 53, 140
mau, plural marker, 162
me 'with', 145
Mexico, 33
Milner, George, 86, 96, 189
mood, 61–63
multiple-class verbs, 51–53

na, benefactive/agentive preposition, 147–150
-*na*, nominalizer, 80–82, table 11
nā, plural article, 156
nā, ∅-demonstrative, 111–112
Nakuina, Moses, xiii, 189
Newbrand, Helene, Luise, 8, 14, 23, 24, 189
Niʻihau, 23–25, 50
no, benefactive/causative/locative preposition, 147–150
nō, intensifier, 100–101
nominalizers, 79–83, 181
nouns, 43, 105–107, 181, tables 7, 15
n-prepositions, 147–150
numerals, 158–162

o, possessive, 136–145
ʻ*o*, apposition, 150–152
ʻ*o*, subject marker, 131–133
ʻ*ō*, locative, 121
orthography, 36–38

pā-, distributive, 159–160
paha 'perhaps', 103–104
particles, 44, 90–91, 100–104, 181–182
parts of speech, 43–44
passive/imperatives, 83–86
Pawley, Andrew, xv, 189
pe-demonstratives, 114–115
phrases, 41–43, 168–169, 182, table 7
pitch, 21–22
place names, 12, 155
plural articles, 156, 182
plural markers, 162–163
possessives, 115–119, 136–145, tables 12, 14
prefixes, 64, 158–160, table 10
prepositions, 131–152, 182
pronouns, 107–110, tables 12, 13

proper names, 12, 19, 32–33, 37, 123, 126, 155
Protestant, 32–33
Pukui, Mary Kawena, xiii, xv–xvi, 123, 189–190

qualifiers, 127–130

reduplications, 3, 64–67, 182

Samoan, 34, 86, 88
Schütz, Albert J., xiv–xv, 16, 30–31, 190
Schweizer, Niklaus R., xv, 190
sentences, 39–41, 169–172, 180, 182
sex, 130
simulative, 150
sound frequencies, 34
Spanish, 33
stative, 49–51, 182
stress, 16–21, 29, 182, 183
subject marker, 131–133

Tahitian, 34
tense, 60–61
thematic consonants, 80–89, table 11

transitives, 48–49, 182
transitivizers, 86–88, 183

u-, plural, 75
ua, demonstrative, 113–114
ua, perfective marker, 57–59

verb classification, 46–53, table 8
verbless sentences, 40, 152, 183
verb markers, 57–63, table 9
verbs, 43, 183, table 7
vocatives, 110, 146–147, 183
vowel length, 15
vowels, 14–16, 20–21

w, letter, 12–13, 155, 183, table 1
w-glide, 12–13, 180, 183
wahi 'a little', 162
wahi 'place', 155
wahi 'to say', 93, 106–107
Wilson, William H., xiv, xv, 9, 24–25, 81, 142, 145, 190
word order, 127–130
words, 43–44